# Model-Driven Design Using Business Patterns

T0254672

Pavel Hruby

# Model-Driven Design Using Business Patterns

with Contributions by
Jesper Kiehn and Christian Vibe Scheller

With 230 Figures and 3 Tables

 Springer

*Author*

Pavel Hruby
Microsoft Development Center Copenhagen
Frydenlunds Allé 6
2950 Vedbæk, Denmark
phruby@acm.org
http://reatechnology.com
http://phruby.com

ACM Computing Classification (1998): D.2.11, H.1, J.1

ISBN-13 978-3-642-06765-5       e-ISBN-13 978-3-540-30327-5

Springer is a part of Springer Science+Business Media

springer.com

© Springer-Verlag Berlin Heidelberg 2010
Printed in Germany

Cover design: KünkelLopka Werbeagentur, Heidelberg

*To Mom and Dad*

# Preface

This book describes the REA (resources, events, agents) model, which is going to revolutionize the way the software business applications are developed. REA specifies the fundamental laws of the business domain. Knowing these laws radically enhances the application designers' potential to configure business solutions without omissions, and ensures consistency of software applications from the business perspective:

- The application design based on REA is concise and easy to understand both for the users of software applications, for consultants, and for application developers. REA is a ubiquitous language ensuring unambiguous communication and understanding among all participants of the software development process.
- Software applications based on REA contain more business knowledge than applications developed merely from user requirements, and can therefore advise and guide the users during development and configuration, without restricting the end-users at runtime.
- The same modeling principles are used across all application areas in the business domain; the sales, procurement, production, marketing, human resources, finance, and other areas are described by a common set of patterns.
- As REA software applications store the primary data about economic resources, all reports and all accounting artifacts are always consistent, because they are derived from the same data; for example, the data describing the sale event is used in the warehouse management, payroll, distribution, finance and other application areas, without transformations or adjustments.
- The REA model provides for more complete, transparent, and up-to-date reporting for business decision makers than reporting based on the accounting artifacts, which dominates in current business applications.

REA can be extended using a number of patterns that comprise functionality necessary to build business applications that meet specific business needs. REA alone specifies domain rules assuring that the application model is sound from the business perspective, and forms the backbone of the application model. Knowing REA is useful but not sufficient to build a business application; similarly, knowing only Maxwell's laws is not sufficient to build a radio transmitter and receiver. We describe the patterns that extend REA in Part II of this book, Behavioral Patterns.

This book is primarily intended for

- Software architects, visionary managers, and anyone interested in understanding REA, and its strengths and limitations.
- Application developers designing business applications, and interested in the consistency that accrues from the REA model.
- Framework developers designing business frameworks, looking for general business domain concepts and for the principles that apply to these concepts.
- Students of university courses on enterprise information architectures.

We also include two implementation chapters illustrating how easy it is to build an REA-based software application, and how to implement the behavioral business patterns. A complete REA business application containing the code samples from this book can be downloaded from http://www.reatechnology.com.

## Structure of This Book

Part I, Structural Patterns, describes the REA model in detail. This part describes REA at the operational level (the level of actual business transactions), and at the policy level, specifying which transactions could or should happen. This part includes an implementation chapter that includes executable code of an REA business application.

Part II of this book, Behavioral Patterns, describes the patterns that extend REA with the functionality necessary to meet specific needs of the users of a business application. This part also includes an implementation chapter containing code for several behavioral patterns, as well as for the infrastructure necessary to run the implementation.

Part III of this book, Modeling Handbook, illustrates REA models in which the use of REA is less straightforward, such as insurance, guarantees and taxes.

Appendix A describes REA as an ontology for business systems; we recommend this to readers interested in the theoretical foundations of REA.

Appendix B, Notes on Modeling, describes the relationships between models, metamodels and the real world, describes how we use UML in this book, illustrates REA models at various levels of granularity, and explains modeling viewpoints in REA, the REA models in the trading partner view and the independent view.

Appendix C, Patterns and Pattern Form, describes the pattern form used for the patterns in this book.

The pattern map on the next page shows the patterns described in this book. The purpose of the model at the operational level, i.e., the *REA EXCHANGE PROCESS*, *REA CONVERSION PROCESS* and *REA VALUE CHAIN*, is to describe what happened or was just happening in the user's business. The entities in these patterns determine the skeleton of the application model.

This skeleton can be extended by adding the entities described in the patterns *TYPE*, *GROUP*, *COMMITMENT*, *CONTRACT*, *SCHEDULE*, *POLICY*, *LINKAGE*, *RESPONSIBILITY*, and *CUSTODY*. These patterns describe what could, should, or should not happen in the user's business. We call these REA models the policy level.

While all well-designed business applications more or less follow the structure described in the structural patterns, the behaviors of different business applications differ significantly, because specific requirements of the users of the business applications differ. Therefore, the REA structural skeleton at the operational and policy levels can be extended by patterns that model specific behaviors of the business application. We refer to these patterns as behavioral patterns. The patterns of general use are *IDENTIFICATION*, *DUE DATE*, *DESCRIPTION*, *NOTE*, *LOCATION*, *CLASSIFICATION*, *NOTIFICATION*, and *VALUE*; the patterns *POSTING*, *ACCOUNT*, *RECONCILIATION*, and *MATERIALIZED CLAIM* have their origins in financial applications. We will also describe a pattern for inventing new behavioral patterns called *INVENTOR'S PARADOX*.

# Pattern Map

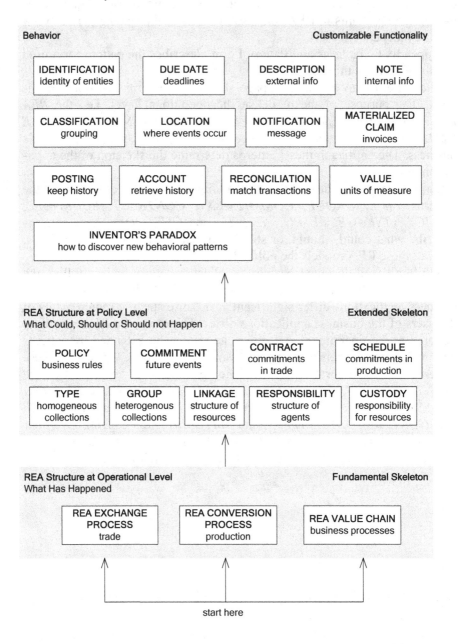

There are two natural starting points to using the patterns in this book. If an application designer is able to identify the economic resources the users want to plan, monitor, and control using the business application, then we can start with the *REA EXCHANGE PROCESS* or *REA CONVERSION PROCESS* patterns and integrate the processes into the *REA VALUE CHAIN*. If application designers are not able to identify the economic resources, we can start with the *REA VALUE CHAIN*, and, using functional decomposition of the processes, identify the level at which users want to plan, monitor and control the resources, and then, by applying the *REA EXCHANGE PROCESS* and *REA CONVERSION PROCESS* patterns, identify the economic events and agents.

## Internet Resources

The web site http://reatechnology.com contains executable code for the REA application Joe's Pizzeria, described in this book, as well as some non-trivial REA models, extending those included in Part III, Modeling Handbook. The mailing list at http://groups.yahoo.com/REATechnology is a forum for researchers interested in theoretical foundations of REA, as well as in solving specific modeling problems. The web site http://hillside.net/ is dedicated to patterns in software development in general. UML diagrams in this book have been produced using Microsoft Visio with a UML stencil available at http://phruby.com.

## Acknowledgements

This book would not have been possible without the help of two distinguished gentlemen, Jesper Kiehn and Christian Scheller.

First and foremost, Jesper Kiehn is one of few people who truly understand what REA ontology is all about. Thanks to Jesper's passion and enthusiasm, countless long discussions and arguments, during which we gradually began to understand REA, and the laws of the business domain. Jesper's many brilliant ideas helped me understand the full potential of REA, what modeling business software really means, ontologies, knowledge management, and their consequences in sometimes surprisingly different application domains.

Christian Scheller is the inventor of the architecture that utilizes orthogonal separation of concerns in business domain. Christian was probably the first person, back in 1999, who realized the potential of aspects for modeling and implementing business logic components and not just non-functional requirements; he is also a person who proved that business logic could be fully and completely described at the model level, as opposed to being described in a programming language. Christian wrote the implementation chapters in Part I and Part II of this book.

Many other people have helped and supported me along the way.

William E. McCarthy and Guido Geerts are the inventors of the REA ontology. Thanks to both for their patience in explaining the REA to me, for their visits to Copenhagen, for the many phone call meetings, and their valuable insight.

Thanks to Ralph Johnson for superb guidance; and for suggesting that I restructure Part I into its current form, with REA described as the exchange and conversion patterns.

Lars Hammer was the architect behind the Jamaica Project (1999-2002) at Navision, which proved that the architecture described in this book really does work, and has been a valuable in-house supporter.

This book can be seen as the result of NEXT, a shared project between the Microsoft Development Center Copenhagen and the IT University Copenhagen. A special thanks to Kasper Østerbye for keeping the project running, and Ph.D. students Mette Jaquet and Anders Hessellund whose thesis attempted to specify the semantics of REA, and significantly improved our understanding of this modeling framework.

I'd also like to express my thanks to the participants of the Software Architecture Group of University of Illinois at Urbana-Champaign, led by Ralph Johnson, for discussing the manuscript for several weeks and making their discussions available to me, the participants of the writers' workshops at the conferences Viking PLoP 2002, 2004 and 2005 for their feedback on the pattern style, and to Daniel May, Bob Hanmer, and Linda Rising for shepherding the patterns.

For the generous assistance in the technical aspects of this book, I would like to acknowledge the exceptional team at Springer, and especially my editor Ralf Gerstner.

I would be remiss if I did not mention my family for creating a friendly and enjoyable environment in which it was a pleasure to write this book and to think about REA.

Finally, thanks to the reviewers of this book, especially Paul Johannesson, Thomas Jensen, Krzysztof Czarnecki, Paul Adamczyk, Richard Kuo, Geert Poels, and Bob Haugen for their comments on the manuscript in its early stages, and to Allan Kelly, Janet Pehrson, and Keld Raaschou for valuable feedback on specific parts of the book.

# Table of Contents

# Part I  Structural Patterns

This part describes REA in detail, i.e. the patterns for a skeleton and fundamental structure of entities in a business software application. By using the patterns in Part I, an application designer should end up with a structure that is consistent, and without omissions from the business perspective.

This part consists of two sections: structural patterns at operational level, and structural patterns at policy level.

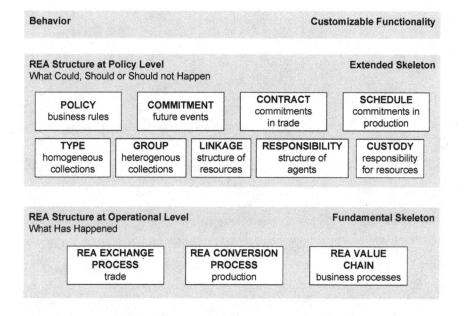

# 1 Structural Patterns at Operational Level

The first chapter in this section describes *What is REA,* and the chapter *Joe's Pizzeria* illustrates the fundamental interactions between the enterprise and its trading partners, that are examples of the *REA EXCHANGE PROCES* pattern. The chapter *Notes on Exchange Processes* describes the exchanges in more detail. The chapter *How Joe's Pizzeria Obtains Pizza* describes how the enterprise creates its products or services; these processes are examples of the *REA CONVERSION PROCESS PATTERN.* The section Notes on Exchange Processes describes the conversions in more detail. The pattern *REA VALUE CHAIN* explains how to combine the REA business processes into the chain of business processes of the enterprise.

| Behavior | Customizable Functionality |
|---|---|

| REA Structure at Policy Level<br>What Could, Should or Should not Happen | Extended Skeleton |
|---|---|

| REA Structure at Operational Level<br>What Has Happened | Fundamental Skeleton |
|---|---|

| REA EXCHANGE PROCESS<br>trade | REA CONVERSION PROCESS<br>production | REA VALUE CHAIN<br>business processes |
|---|---|---|

## 1.1   What Is REA?

There are several concepts that are present in almost all business software applications. Understanding these concepts makes it much easier to design business applications, to ensure that they do not violate the domain rules, and to adapt the applications to changing requirements without the need to change the overall architecture.

These concepts are known as REA (Resources, Events, Agents). Fig. 1 illustrates the most fundamental REA concepts, which are economic resource, economic agent, economic event, commitment, and contract.

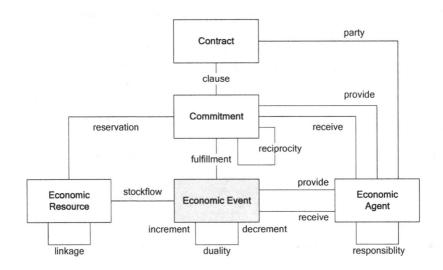

**Fig. 1.** Fundamental REA concepts

*Economic Resource* is a thing that is scarce, and has utility for economic agents, and is something users of business applications want to plan, monitor, and control. Examples of economic resources are products and services, money, raw materials, labor, tools, and services the enterprise uses.

*Economic Agent* is an individual or organization capable of having control over economic resources, and transferring or receiving the control to or from other individuals or organizations. Examples of economic agents are customers, vendors, employees, and enterprises. The *enterprise* is an economic agent from whose perspective we create the REA model.

*Economic Event* represents either an increment or a decrement in the value of economic resources that are under the control of the enterprise. Some economic events occur instantaneously, such as sales of goods; some occur over time, such as rentals, labor acquisition, and provision and use of services.

*Commitment* is a promise or obligation of economic agents to perform an economic event in the future. For example, line items on a sales order represent commitments to sell goods.

*Contract* is a collection of increment and decrement commitments and terms. Under the conditions specified by the terms, a contract can create additional commitments. Thus, the contract can specify what should happen if the commitments are not fulfilled. For example, a sales order is a contract containing commitments to sell goods and to receive payments. The terms of the sales order contract can specify penalties (additional commitments) if the goods or payments have not been received as promised.

REA also specifies the domain rules assuring soundness and consistency of business software applications from the business perspective. There are several other approaches attempting to describe the fundamental modeling entities, such as *archetypes* (Coad, Lefebvre, DeLuca. 1999) and *pleomorphs* (Arlow, Neustadt 2003), for the business domain, and many *business patterns* on more detailed levels; our favorite books include (Fowler 1996), (Hay 1996), (Silverstone 1997), (Marshall 2000), and (Evans 2003). The patterns and modeling entities described in these books can be expressed in terms of the REA concepts. These patterns are more specific, as they focus on certain subdomains within the business domain. They provide for further concepts, but do not change the concepts defined in the REA. Therefore, REA defines a ubiquitous language for business systems.

The fundamental idea of the REA model is

> If an enterprise wants to increase the total value of resources under its control, it usually has to decrease the value of some of its resources.

An enterprise can increase or decrease the value of its resources either by *exchanges* or by *conversions*.

- *Exchange* is a process in which an enterprise receives economic resources from other economic agents, and it gives resources to other economic agents in return.
- *Conversion* is a process in which an enterprise uses or consumes resources in order to produce new or modify existing resources.

The data associated with exchanges and conversions are the primary business data about the enterprise in REA software applications. Accounting artifacts such as debit, credit, journals, ledgers, receivables, and account balances are derived from the data describing the exchanges and conversions. For example, the quantity on hand for an inventory item can be calculated from the difference between the purchase and sale events, or between the production and consumption events, for that inventory item.

For comparison, in most current business software applications, whose paradigms are derived from double entry accounting, it is the opposite – they focus on the accounting artifacts, and economic data is derived from them. This, in some sense, puts the consequences before the cause and makes the models more complicated.

The fact that REA operates on primary and raw economic data explains why it offers a wider, more precise, and more up-to-date range of reports than models based on the traditional double entry accounting system that operates on derived accounting data.

REA was originally proposed as a generalized accounting model. It was first published by William E. McCarthy of Michigan State University (McCarthy 1982). McCarthy in his doctoral thesis at the University of Massachusetts analyzed a large number of accounting transactions, and identified their common features and formulated a general model describing and explaining the accounting transactions. Since then, the original REA model has been extended by McCarthy and Guido Geerts to a framework for enterprise information architectures and ontology for business systems (Geerts, McCarthy 2000a, 2002). REA became the foundation for several electronic interchange standards, such as ebXML and Open-edi (an ISO standard), which influenced the extensions of the original REA model into commitments and contracts.

Last but not least, an increasing number of business analysts have found that the models they develop become better when they have REA in mind.

## 1.2  Joe's Pizzeria

*We will create an REA model for Joe's Pizzeria*

Joe makes revenue by selling pizza to his customers. Joe's Pizzeria has employees whose task is to sell pizzas, as well as to produce pizzas from raw materials such as dough, tomatoes, cheese, pepperoni and other toppings. There are also other things necessary to produce pizza, such as the oven where the pizza is baked, electricity consumed to heat the oven, various kitchen equipment and many other things. Joe is interested in tracking information about some of them; in REA, the things that Joe is interested in planning, monitoring and controlling are called *economic resources*. Joe has decided that the economic resources that will be included in the business software application are the *Pizza, Cash, Labor* of the employees, and *Raw Materials and Ingredients* for producing pizza.

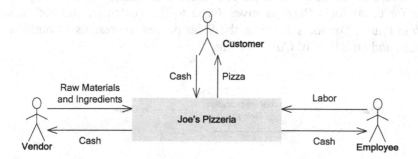

**Fig. 2.** Trading partners of Joe's Pizzeria

Trading partners of Joe's Pizzeria are customers, vendors and employees. They are capable of controlling economic resources; therefore, in the

REA application model the *Customer, Vendor, Employee,* and *Joe's Pizzeria* are economic agents, see Fig. 2.

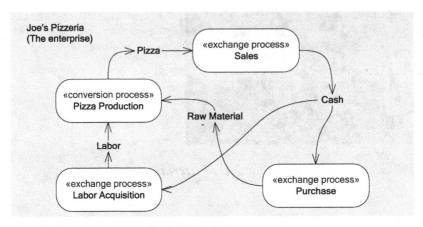

**Fig. 3.** Trading processes of Joe's Pizzeria

The main trading processes of Joe's Pizzeria, see Fig. 3, are selling pizza to the customers (the *Sales* process), purchasing raw materials from the vendors (the *Purchase* process), and purchasing labor from the employees (the *Labor Acquisition* process).  We will construct the REA model for each process.

### 1.2.1   Sales Process

The process of selling pizza to the customers is essentially an exchange of pizza for cash; Joe's Pizzeria gives *Pizza* to the customer, and receives *Cash* in return. For Joe's Pizzeria, the *Sales* process represents an outflow of *Pizza* and an inflow of *Cash*, see Fig. 4.

**Fig. 4.** Selling pizza is an exchange of pizza for cash

The REA model for the process of selling pizza is illustrated in Fig. 5. *Joe's Pizzeria* and the *Customer* are economic agents, and the *Pizza* and *Cash* are economic resources. One economic event is the transfer of ownership of the *Pizza* from *Joe's Pizzeria* to the *Customer* (we call this event *Sale*); in this transaction *Joe's Pizzeria* provides *Pizza*, and *Customer* receives it. Another economic event is the transfer of ownership of *Cash* from the *Customer* to *Joe's Pizzeria* (we call it *Cash Receipt*); in this transaction the *Customer* provides *Cash*, and *Joe's Pizzeria* receives it.

For *Joe's Pizzeria*, the *Sale* event (the transfer of ownership of the *Pizza* to the *Customer*) is a decrement event, because it decreases the value of the resources under the control of *Joe's Pizzeria*. The *Cash Receipt* is an increment event, because it increases the value of the resources under the control of *Joe's Pizzeria*. The terms decrement and increment are relative to the model viewpoint; they depend on the economic agent which is in the focus of the model. If we modeled the same process from the perspective of the *Customer*, the transfer of pizza would be an increment (would be called Purchase) and the transfer of cash would be a decrement event (would be called Payment or Cash Disbursement).

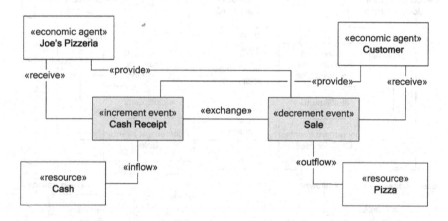

**Fig. 5.** The REA model for Joe's Pizzeria sales process

The REA model of the sales process in Fig. 5 focuses on the core economic phenomena, and therefore it covers many special cases. For example, most customers pay when they purchase pizza, but some customers may receive an invoice, and pay for all their purchases in a certain period at once. If the case of Internet sales, customers must provide their credit card information before the pizza is delivered, and Joe's Pizzeria receives money from the customer's bank later. When the sale occurs in the restaurant, the customers pay after they get pizza, either using cash or a credit card.

All these cases are covered by the model in Fig. 5; this is very useful if we would like to create a robust skeleton of a software application.

Customers may order pizza over the Internet. In this case, a software business application creates an electronic *Sales Order*, which specifies a commitment of *Joe's Pizzeria* to sell a specified *Pizza* to the *Customer*, and a commitment of a *Customer* to pay for the *Pizza* a specified amount of *Cash*.

The *Sales Order, see* Fig. 6, is an example of a contract between the economic agents *Joe's Pizzeria* and the *Customer*. The *Sales Line* and the *Payment Line* are not economic events; they are commitments to perform the economic events in well-defined future. The *Sales Line* is a commitment to perform the event *Sale*, and the *Payment Line* is a commitment to perform the event *Cash Receipt* in the future.

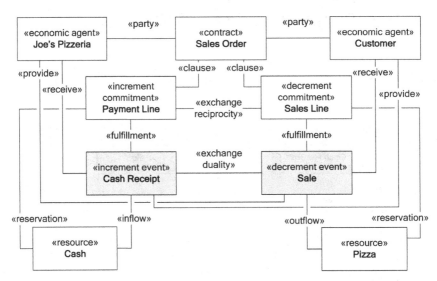

**Fig. 6.** The REA model for the sales process with sales order

The *Sales Order* often contains terms specifying what should happen if the commitments are not fulfilled, such as when the payment arrives late, or the customer is not satisfied with the pizza. The fact that a contract can be represented as a computer model is important for automatic tracking of the state of the contract at runtime, and also for computer-assisted evaluation of complicated financial contracts.

## 1.2.2 Purchase Process

When Joe's Pizzeria purchases tomatoes, cheese, pepperoni, flour and other raw materials, it essentially exchanges the raw material for cash. *Vendor* gives *Raw Material* to *Joe's Pizzeria*, which gives it *Cash* in return. For Joe's Pizzeria, the *Purchase* process represents an outflow of *Cash* and an inflow of *Raw Material*, see Fig. 7.

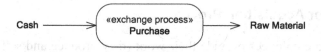

**Fig. 7.** Purchasing raw material is an exchange of raw material for cash

The REA model for the process of purchasing raw material is illustrated in Fig. 8.

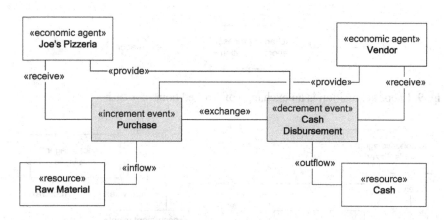

**Fig. 8.** The REA model for the purchase process

The *Vendor* and *Joe's Pizzeria* are economic agents, the *Raw Material* and *Cash* are economic resources. The transfer of ownership of the *Raw Material* from the *Vendor* to *Joe's Pizzeria* is an increment economic event (we call it *Purchase*), and the transfer of ownership of *Cash* from *Joe's Pizzeria* to the *Vendor* (we call it *Cash Disbursement*) is a decrement economic event; the increment and decrement are from *Joe's Pizzeria* perspective.

Similarly as for the REA model for sales, the REA model for purchases covers many special cases. Some raw materials can be paid by check or bank transfer; some can be made in different currencies. There can be several purchases paid using a single payment, and a single purchase can be paid in several installments. The model tracks the information about which purchases correspond to which cash disbursements, but abstracts from technical details and does not specify the order of these transactions. Again, this is useful if the skeleton of a software application is based on this model, because it does not have to be changed if some technical aspects of the purchase process change.

### 1.2.3  Labor Acquisition Process

Joe's Pizzeria employees provide their work (they produce and sell pizzas during specified periods of time) and receive their salary in return. Labor acquisition is essentially an exchange of *Labor* (the worked hours) for *Cash*. *Employee* sells his labor to *Joe's Pizzeria*, which gives him *Cash* in return. For Joe's Pizzeria, the *Labor Acquisition* process represents an outflow of *Cash* and an inflow of *Labor*, see Fig. 9.

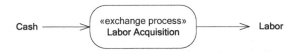

**Fig. 9.** Labor acquisition is an exchange of worked hours for cash

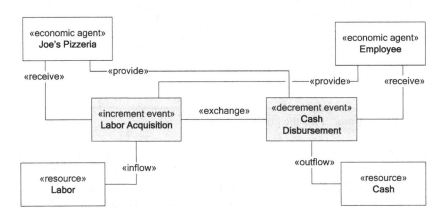

**Fig. 10.** The REA model for the labor acquisition process

The REA model for the labor acquisition process is illustrated in Fig. 10. The *Employee* and *Joe's Pizzeria* are economic agents; the *Employee* provides *Labor* and receives *Cash*, and *Joe's Pizzeria* provides

*Cash* and receives *Labor*. *Labor* (the worked hours) and *Cash* are economic resources. The *Labor Acquisition* is an economic event that occurs over periods of time (during the employee's working hours), while *Cash Disbursement* is an instantaneous event that occurs once a week or month when the *Employee* receives his paycheck.

The REA model in Fig. 10 can be applied to many forms of acquiring labor; it can be applied for full employment, temporary work, consulting, as well as for work acquired according to various other forms of contracts.

### 1.2.4  Summary

The REA model focuses on the core economic phenomena and abstracts from technical and implementation details. This has several advantages.

Firstly, the REA model abstracts from the technical aspects of the transfer of the resources. Cash can be transferred as bills and coins, as a check or as a credit card transaction. Customers can pick pizza themselves, or pizza can be delivered to their address. For all these cases we can apply the same REA model, which does not have to be modified even if the technical infrastructure supporting the business changes.

Secondly, the REA model abstracts from the order in which the economic events occur. Usually, pizza is paid at about the same time as it is given to the customer, but sometimes it is paid for beforehand, and sometimes it can be paid by credit card and there is a significant delay between the sale of pizza and the transfer of cash. If the business process was specified as a scenario consisting of a sequence of events, the business application would support only the scenarios identified at design time. The REA model allows the business application to flexibly record everything that actually happened. The actual order of events emerges at runtime, rather than being specified at design time.

Thirdly, for each REA model apply certain rules: each increment must be related to a decrement, each economic event must have a provider and recipient agent, and each resource must be related to both increment and decrement. Therefore, application designers can ask relevant questions leading to the discovery of missing information in the user requirements, and can construct the model even if the initial specification is incomplete.

### 1.2.5  The Illustrated Models Are Examples of a Pattern

The three illustrated models for the business processes *Sales*, *Purchase* and *Labor Acquisition* have many common features. They all model the transactions between Joe's Pizzeria and its trading partners as exchanges of economic resources.

These models can be generalized into a model at a higher level of abstraction, illustrated in the next chapter. The models for sale of pizza, purchase of raw materials and labor acquisition are examples of the *REA EXCHANGE PROCESS PATTERN*.

## 1.3   REA Exchange Process Pattern

*Trade is the voluntary exchange of goods, services, or money*

### Context

You are an application designer developing a business application. You are trying to create an object model of a business application and struggling to find the right structure for the model and the right relationships between entities in the model. You know the user requirements; they can be in a written document or non-written information obtained by an ongoing dialog with the users; but you know the requirements are incomplete. You want to know the right questions to ask to better understand the application domain. You also want the model to be consistent and robust enough for future changes in user requirements.

### Problem

How does one create a robust skeleton of an object-oriented model for interactions between the enterprise and it trading partners? User requirements are not a sufficient source of information, because they are known to be incomplete, often contradictory, and to change over time, and it is often impossible to find what requirements are missing. Shortly, you would like to create a business application that will satisfy even some of user requirements that have not been communicated to you.

## Forces[1]

The REA exchange process pattern resolves the following forces:

- The modeled software application should provide information about how the interactions between the enterprise and its trading partners change the value of the economic resources of the enterprise. The application should keep track of the increases and decreases of the value of the resources that are under the control of the enterprise, and should record which resources were exchanged for which others.
- Application designers want to concentrate on the fundamentals of the users' business, and separate those requirements which are likely to change. The fundamentals are often so obvious to the users of business applications that they do not communicate them, and they remain hidden until late stages of software development.
- The model should be consistent with the business domain rules. Application designers want to ensure that the model is consistent, complete, and correct, with respect to the domain rules.
- Application designers want to include business semantics into the entities in the application model. Semantics based only on the names of the entities is not good enough because it relies on common knowledge, and common knowledge is not available to software applications.

## Solution

Model the interactions between the enterprise and its trading partners as *exchanges* of economic resources.

Each exchange consists of at least one *increment economic event* that increases the value of a resource of the enterprise by transferring rights to the resource to or from other economic agents. Every increment event is related to at least one *decrement economic event* that decreases the value of a resource of the enterprise by transferring rights to the resource to or from other economic agents. We call the relationship between the increment and decrement economic events *exchange duality*, or in short, *exchange*. The *exchange duality* is a many-to-many relationship, indicating that in the application model there must be at least one decrement for each increment, and vice versa. Therefore, the exchange duality in the applica-

---

[1]   In the pattern literature the term *forces* is used for the constraints that restrict the solution of the problem, requirements, and properties that the solution should have. Appendix C describes the pattern form in detail.

tion model can be an n-ary relationship, that relates several increment and decrement entities.

In order for an exchange process to add value, the overall increase in value of the resources related to the increment events should be greater than the overall decrease in value of the resources related to the decrement events.

Each *economic event* is related to an *economic resource*, see Fig. 11. The relationship between an increment and a resource is called *inflow*, the relationship between a decrement and a resource *outflow*. In the application model there must be exactly one *economic resource* for each *economic event*, and at least one *increment* and one *decrement* for each *economic resource*.

Each economic event is related to two *economic agents*. The *economic event* in the exchange process transfers rights to the *economic resource* from one agent to another. When the event occurs, the *provider agent* loses rights to the resource, and the *recipient agent* receives the rights. In the application model for each economic event there must be at least one *provider* and at least one *recipient agent*. For each *agent*, there can be zero or more *economic events*.

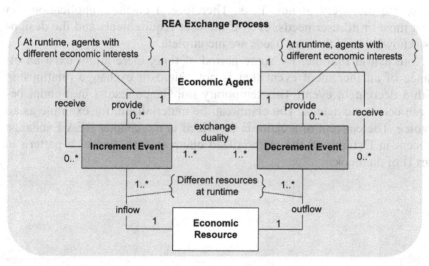

**Fig. 11.** The REA exchange process

Note that the model in Fig. 11 determines the rules for constructing the application model. The application model determines the structure of the runtime instances.

The following domain rules apply for any application model describing the REA exchange process.

Every increment economic event must be related by exchange duality to a decrement economic event, and vice versa.

Every increment economic event must be related by inflow relationship to an economic resource.

Every decrement economic event must be related by outflow relationship to an economic resource.

Every economic event must be related by a provide relationship to an economic agent, and by a receive relationships an economic agent. At runtime, these two agents must represent entities with different economic interests.

## Resulting Context

The domain rules in this pattern allow application designers to derive new facts from the facts provided by the users, and to formulate questions leading to the discovery of new facts. Therefore, a business application can meet most or all user needs, even if the user requirements and the designers' knowledge of the user needs are incomplete.

Note that at runtime, for some period of time, there might exist an instance of an increment event that is not paired in exchange relationship with a decrement event. This temporary imbalance results in a claim between economic agents. The claim can be materialized, for example as an invoice. The concept of a claim is described in the chapter REA Exchange Process in Detail, and the materialized claim is described as a pattern in Part II of the book.

## 1.4 REA Exchange Process In Detail

In this section we explain semantics of the resources, events, agents, inflow, outflow, exchange, provide, and receive, in the REA exchange process.

> The purpose of the REA exchange process is to receive or give up rights associated with economic resources by receiving or giving up rights to other resources.

### 1.4.1 Economic Resources

Economic resources are things that are scarce, and have utility for economic agents, and users of business applications want to plan, monitor, and control. This definition of a resource is common to both an exchange and a conversion process[2]; however, the resources expose a different interface to the exchange and conversion processes.

> In the REA exchange process, a resource can be seen as a collection of certain *rights* associated with it: ownership rights, usage rights, copy rights.

Rights contribute to the resource value for an economic agent.

#### 1.4.1.1 Rights Associated with the Resources

REA does not explicitly specify how to model the rights associated with the resource. In this book, we follow the approach in which the inflow and outflow relationships at the application model level determine the rights transferred from one economic agent to another.

For example, Fig. 12 illustrates an REA application model for a *Reader* of a *Book* (Fig. 15 models the same process from the perspective of *Library*). Economic resource *Book* is borrowed from *Library*. A reader can identify what rights it has to the book by traversing the inflow and outflow relationships related to the *Book*. In the model in Fig. 12 the *Reader* has the right to read the *Book*, i.e., the *Reader* has the right to attach the *Read* economic event to it. Precise specification of the "right to read" in the REA framework, for example, whether it includes the right to borrow the

---

[2] Please see the section REA Value Chain in Detail for discussion on economic resources in general.

book for another reader, requires the concept of types, and can be explained using the *POLICY* pattern.

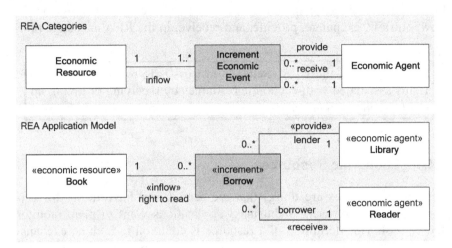

**Fig. 12.** Features and rights of the economic resource[3]

Note that there are alternative approaches to modeling the transfer of rights than as instances of inflow and outflow. These approaches are outlined in the following section.

### 1.4.1.2  *Alternative Approaches of Modeling the Rights*

Researchers involved in modeling business systems using REA still discuss appropriate ways of modeling the rights. The other possible approaches to modeling rights are (Haugen 2005):

- Rights are properties of economic resources.
- Rights are components of economic resources, attached to the main resource to which they give rights.
- Rights are properties of inflow and outflow relationships.
- Rights are types of commitments (see the *COMMITMENT PATTERN*).
- Rights are refinements of the custody relationship between economic agents and economic resources.
- Rights are defining characteristics of economic events.

---

[3] Modeling conventions, and the correspondence between the model and metamodel are outlined in Appendix B.

All approaches have their advantages and disadvantages, and combinations of these approaches may also be possible.

## 1.4.2  Inflow and Outflow

In the previous section we described resource as a portfolio of rights, and economic events in exchange processes transfer some of them.

> *Inflow* is a relationship that relates economic resource with an increment economic event. The enterprise receives some rights to the resource as a result of the related increment event.

For example, as a result of a purchase economic event, the enterprise will receive ownership rights, and during a rental economic event, the enterprise will receive rights to use the premises for the period of the rental.

> *Outflow* is a relationship that relates economic resource with a decrement economic event. The enterprise loses some rights to the resource as a result of the related decrement event.

For example, after payment (an economic event), the enterprise will lose ownership rights to money, and during rental, the owner will lose the rights to use his premises for the period of the rental.

The inflow and outflow relationships and their cardinalities are illustrated in Fig. 13. The model illustrates an *Apartment* that can be purchased, rented or sold.

At the level of the REA categories (which describes how application models are constructed), the inflow and outflow are one-to-many (1 to 1..*) relationships; one economic event is related to one resource, and a resource can be related to one or more economic events. For example, as illustrated in Fig. 13, an *Apartment* is related to one increment and two decrement events. The enterprise receives ownership of *Apartment* (the *Purchase* event), rents it (the *Rental* event) and terminates the ownership (the *Sale* event). *Rental* is an economic event that lasts over an interval of time; rights to use the apartment are transferred to the renter at the beginning of the rental and returned at the end of the rental.

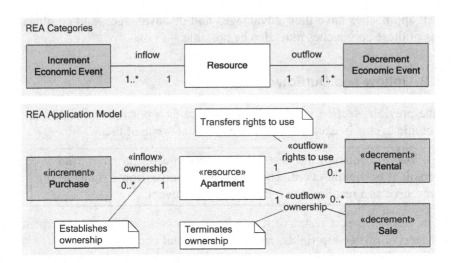

**Fig. 13.** Inflow and outflow relationships

In the REA application model (which describes the construction of run-time entities), the inflow and outflow are one-to-many (1 to 0..*) relationships; one economic event is related to one resource, and a resource can be related to zero or more economic events. An actual *Apartment* can over time be rented, purchased, and sold zero or more times by the same economic agent. Each *Rental*, *Purchase*, and *Sale* event is related to exactly one *Apartment*. If several *Apartments* are rented to the same renter at the same time for the same period, this would be modeled as several economic events that occur simultaneously.

### 1.4.2.1  *Inflow and Outflow are Linked to Actual Resources*

An economic event is always related to the (actual) resource, which reflects the fact that a real thing is purchased or sold; an economic event[4] is never related to the resource type or group (see the discussion on *TYPE* and *GROUP* patterns for definitions of type and group). A car dealer always sells a physical car, and guest always occupies a physical room in a hotel. If an engineering company sells know-how and blueprints of a car to a car manufacturer, we would model these artifacts as resources (not resource types) in this transaction. If a person buys a season ticket, e.g. all Barcelona games in 2005-2006, the economic resources are the actual seats when the Barcelona games are played, and the economic events are the

---

[4]  A commitment for an economic event can be related to a type. See the discussion on *COMMITMENT* pattern.

person's actual attendances. For objects that consist of elements without identity, such as water, gasoline, electricity, or money, the resources (resource instances) are the volumes limited by the scope of the economic events. The section on resource types gives examples of instances of these kinds of resources.

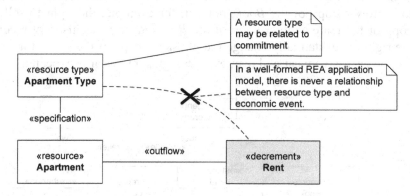

**Fig. 14.** Economic event is always related to the actual resource

Nevertheless, software applications sometimes contain a relationship between economic event and resource type. For example, if an electricity consumer is interested only in the total amount of delivered electricity, and not in voltage, frequency and current at each moment in time, it is useful to omit the electricity instance from the model, and relate the electricity sale event and electricity resource type. Such a decision is a *modeling compromise*, and the missing information is a trade-off for simplicity.

### 1.4.3  Economic Events

Economic events in the exchange processes represent the permanent or temporary transfer of rights to an economic resource from one economic agent to another. The transfer of the rights represents increment or decrement of the value of the resources.

> The purpose of an economic event in the REA exchange process is to transfer some of the rights associated with the resource from one economic agent to another.

An increment event increases the value of the related resource, and the decrement event decreases the value. An increment event does not always mean that the enterprise should receive rights; for example, waste is a resource with negative value, therefore, by transferring ownership of waste to the recycle station the enterprise increases overall value of its resources.

In the process illustrated in Fig. 15 the *Lend* economic event represents a time-limited transfer of rights to the economic resource *Book* from *Library* to the *Reader* and back. The economic agent *Library* provides some rights related to a copy of a book to the *Reader*. *Reader* receives the right to borrow a copy of the *Book*, but not, for example, the right to sell this copy or to create another copy of the *Book*. *Reader* has also not received the right to substantially change the physical shape of the book, for example, by excessive wear and tear, even though some wear is expected.

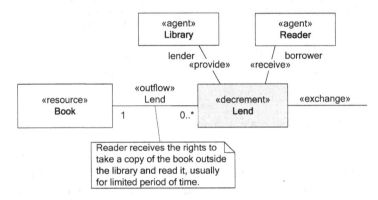

**Fig. 15.** The event in the exchange process transfers rights associated with the resource

*Lend* is a decrement economic event in Library's REA model, because it restricts the Library's rights to the *Book* during the *Lend* event. For example, *Library* cannot lend the book to another *Reader*.

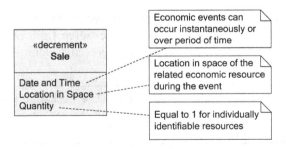

**Fig. 16.** Economic event in an exchange process

The economic events address *when* economic agents had the rights to the resources, and consequently *when* economic resources changed value. If the economic resources can be located in space, the economic event also determines *where* the economic resources changed their value.

The economic events in REA application models usually encapsulate properties for *Date and Time* and *Location in Space*. As these properties usually have specific behavior that differs from one application to another, we describe them as behavioral patterns *POSTING* and *LOCATION* in the Part II of this book. The *Quantity* property determines the quantity or amount of the resources for which the rights are transferred. The *Quantity* property of the events related to the resources that are individually identifiable is always one, as there is one economic event for every resource unit. Note that whether a resource is individually identifiable is often a decision of the users of a business application. This topic is discussed in the chapter REA Value Chain in Detail.

*Date and Time* and *Location in Space* are related; if we specify one of them, we might often determine the other, and vice versa. As a result, although many economic events are determined by the time at which they occurred, (for example, an employment event is often specified by its start and end), many are also often determined by the resource's location in space. For example, economic agents can agree that the sale event (transfer of ownership rights) occurs when goods are delivered to the customer; the payment event occurs upon cash transfer between the bank accounts. Typically, a contract between economic agents specifies when ownership or other rights to a resource are transferred between them and how is it related to change of location.

### 1.4.3.1 Economic Events are Moments or Time Intervals

The economic events in exchange processes might occur instantaneously or over an interval of time. For example, the sale of an apartment and its payment occur instantaneously. The *Sale* event in Fig. 17 is a transfer of ownership rights of the *Apartment* from the *Seller* to the *Buyer*. The *Apartment* is owned by the *Seller* before the economic event *Sale*, and after *Sale* the *Apartment* is owned by the *Buyer*.

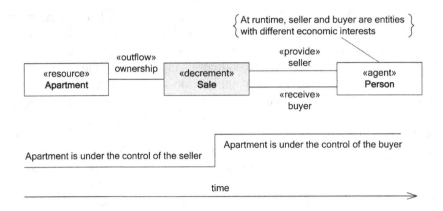

**Fig. 17.** Transfer of ownership can be an instantaneous event

The economic events that transfer rights other than ownership can occur over a period of time, such as rental, loan, or lease; see Fig. 18. The *Rental* event in this figure is a transfer of the right to use the *Apartment* from *Owner* to *Renter* at the beginning of the *Rental* economic event. The *Renter* has the right to use the premises for the duration of the *Rental* event, and this right is returned to the *Owner* at the end of the *Rental*.

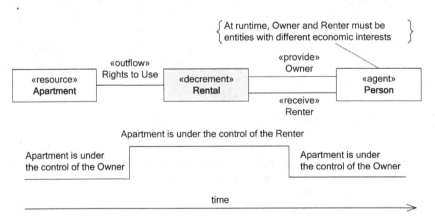

**Fig. 18.** Transfer of rights other than ownership is often a time interval

The sale of resources that cannot be individually identified, such as electricity, water, or other fluid materials, as well as most services occur over a period of time. The graph in Fig. 19 illustrates that the amount of electricity changed ownership from seller to buyer over a period of time.

The rate at which resources change rights is not constant. For example, in the middle of the graph in Fig. 19, there is a flat period in which no electricity has been sold. Likewise, labor acquisition is an economic event that occurs over the period of employment, but labor is acquired only during working hours and not, for example, during weekends.

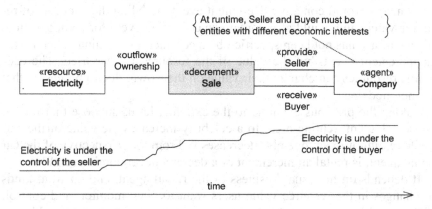

**Fig. 19.** Transfer of ownership can be a time interval

If an economic event in an exchange process occurs instantaneously, we can deduce that this economic event transfers ownership between economic agents. The opposite rule does not apply; transfer of ownership can be instantaneous, as illustrated in Fig. 17, or occur over an interval of time, as illustrated in Fig. 19.

### 1.4.3.2  Economic Events Occur in the Past or Present

A business application can register only economic events that have already occurred or are occurring in the present. Economic events can certainly be planned or expected to occur in the future; the REA concept of *commitment* describes the events that have not yet occurred. A business application can also register commitments for future economic events, and the fulfillment relationship between commitment and economic event specifies how good the prediction is. Commitments are described in the *COMMITMENT PATTERN*.

### 1.4.3.3  Increment Does Not Always Increase Value, and Decrement Does not Always Decrease It

If the enterprise acquires the maintenance of equipment from a service center, the acquisition is an *increment* economic event, because the value of the equipment for the enterprise is usually higher after the maintenance than before.

What if maintenance sometimes does not succeed, and the service center damages the object to be maintained, and its value after the maintenance is *lower* than before? If such a case has been specified by a contract (see the *CONTRACT PATTERN*) between a service centre and the enterprise, the REA model would contain a decrement event modeling the decrease of resource value, and would also contain an economic event for compensation. If such a case has not been specified by a contract, then maintenance is still an increment event, but the value of the resource is decreased. The economic resources can change their value on their own, due to processes that are not modeled.

Taking the previous example to the extreme, let us suppose that for the car rental agent, renting a car to a celebrity increases the value of the car, while renting it to anyone else decreases it. From the perspective of the car rental agent, is rental an increment or a decrement economic event?

It depends on the usual business of the rental agent, and on what kinds of changes in the resource value users want to plan, monitor, and control. If the usual business is to rent cars to ordinary people, rental would be a decrement economic event. If the car occasionally increases its value during rental, the application model will be the same, but this particular instance of the decrement event will increase the value of the car. If the rental agent's usual business is to rent cars to both celebrities and others, the model must contain two economic events: "ordinary rental" and "celebrity rental." As "celebrity rental" is an increment, it must be paired via a duality relationship to some decrement event. Therefore, the model must also specify what resources are used or consumed in relation with this "celebrity rental" event.

### 1.4.4  Exchange Duality

The exchange duality binds increment and decrement economic events together into an REA exchange process.

> The purpose of the exchange duality is to keep track of which resources were exchanged for which others.

Exchange dualities  represents in the model *why* economic events occur. For example, the pizzeria receives cash from the customer *because* the customer gets his pizza. Conversely, the pizzeria gives the pizza to the customer *because* the customer gives him cash. By asking (and answering) "why do the economic events happen," the REA domain rules help create a complete and consistent business model. However, answers to some questions, such as "why do we pay taxes," is not always obvious. Examples of such models, and how they are answered by the exchange dualities, are illustrated in the Modeling Handbook.

> In the REA application model of an exchange process, every increment economic event must be related by an exchange duality to a decrement economic event, and vice versa.

An example of an exchange duality is illustrated in Fig. 20.

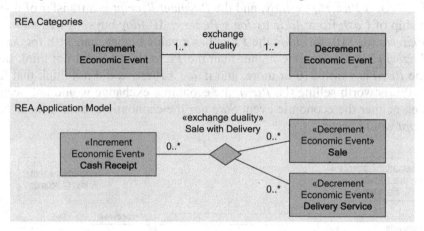

**Fig. 20.** The exchange duality

The exchange duality at the REA category level (which describes how to construct the application model) is a many-to-many (1..* to 1..*) relationship, see Fig. 20. For example, a customer can pay (a *Cash Receipt* event) for the *Sale* of an item and for receiving *Delivery Service*. The exchange duality must relate at least one increment event entity and one decrement event entity.

The exchange duality in the REA application model (which describes constraints of the runtime entities) is a many-to-many (0..* to 0..*) relationship. At runtime, several *Sale* events can be paid for by one check (an actual *Cash Receipt* event), and one *Sale* can be paid in several installments (several actual *Cash Receipt* events). However, there is no "must" here; actual *Sale* can remain unpaid, usually for a period of time. Sometimes, the *Sale* is never paid.

An application developer can restrict the cardinalities in the application model; for example, if there is *always* a single payment for a single sale, the cardinalities can be restricted to 0..1. If it then happens that the customer pays for a sale with two payments, the software application will not support it. Sometimes this might be a reasonable trade-off for simplicity.

### 1.4.4.1  The Value of Exchanged Resources

Each resource that is subject to exchange has a different value for the economic agents participating in the exchange. For rational economic agents, an economic exchange can occur only if both economic agents perceive the value of the received economic resources higher than the value of the given resources; otherwise, they will not exchange them.

For example, see Fig. 21; the *Sale* is a transfer of ownership of *Pizza* from *Joe's Pizzeria* to *Addy*, and the *Payment Receipt* is a transfer of ownership of *Cash* from *Addy* to *Joe's Pizzeria*. If *Addy* buys a *Pizza* at *Joe's Pizzeria* for $10, for *Addy* the *Pizza* has a value higher than $10; for *Joe's Pizzeria* $10 has a value higher than the *Pizza*. If *Addy* did not think that the *Pizza* is worth $10 or more, and if *Joe's Pizzeria* did not think that for $10 it is worth selling the *Pizza*, the economic exchange would not occur. I.e., neither the economic event *Sale* nor the economic event *Payment Receipt* would occur.

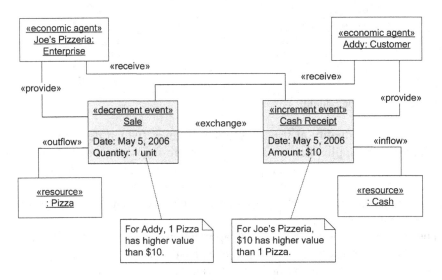

**Fig. 21.** Resource has different value for each agent.

How does *Joe's Pizzeria* evaluate how much *Pizza* is worth selling for? *Joe's Pizzeria* usually wants to sell the *Pizza* for a price higher than its cost price. If *Addy* is an end customer (the one that consumes *Pizza*), his evaluation of how much the *Pizza* is worth is often much less objective. *Addy's* immediate needs, the prices of *Joe's Pizzeria* competitors, and a discount of $3 from original price $13 to the new price of $10 may make *Addy* believe that the *Pizza* is worth more than $10. It is also likely that the first pizza *Addy* buys has for him a higher value than a second pizza of the same type, which explains why *Addy* in this hypothetical example buys only one unit.

The purpose of the exchange duality is not to determine whether the values of the related increments and decrements match (this is the purpose of behavioral patterns). The only thing we can deduce from an exchange duality in the REA model is that, for each participating agent, the overall value of all increments is higher than the overall value of all decrements.

Users of business applications usually require more sophisticated functionality of the exchange duality. The *RECONCILIATION PATTERN* described in Part II, Behavioral Patterns, can be used to identify which instances of increment events correspond to which instances of decrement events, and vice versa, for example to identify which sale events correspond to specific cash receipt events. The *MATERIALIZED CLAIM PATTERN* can be used to determine the unbalanced value between the increment and decrement events.

### 1.4.4.2  Time Order of Increments and Decrements

There is no logical constraint on the order of time in which the resources will be exchanged. There can also be a significant delay between the occurrence of the increment and decrement economic events.

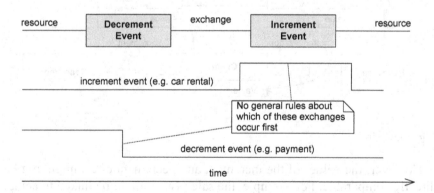

**Fig. 22.** Increment and decrement events occur independently of each other

For example, a customer can pay before he can rent a car (see Fig. 22), and vice versa. It is also quite common that one economic event occurs during another one, for example, in the case of renting an apartment against monthly payments. In such a case, one rental economic event would be related through an exchange duality to several payment economic events, some of which might occur before, some during, and some after the rental.

If the economic agents would like to specify the desired time order of the future economic events, they can specify it by commitments that are part of the contract; see the discussion on *CONTRACT PATTERN* for details.

### 1.4.4.3   Claim

Increment and decrement economic events in exchange processes usually do not occur simultaneously. Whenever an economic event occurs without the occurrence of all corresponding dual economic events, there exists a claim between economic agents related to these economic events. A claim is illustrated in Fig. 23.

If the values of the increment and decrement economic events are comparable, the V*alue* of the claim can be obtained as the difference between the values of the increment and decrement economic events. For example, if the sale event specifies the price of the sold product, and cash is received in the same currency, the value of the claim is simply the difference between these two monetary values. This example is illustrated in Fig. 23.

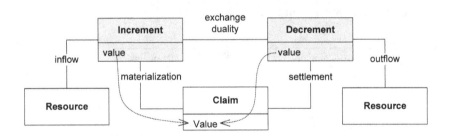

**Fig. 23.** Claim

However, the values of the increment and decrement event might not be directly comparable. For example, the sale events might be linked to actual products (there is one event per product unit), and the cash receipt event represent the amount in a specific currency. If such a sale is partially paid for, the claim between the sale and cash receipt events contains two kinds of values: the quantities of the sold products and the value of the partial payment.

In cases where the value of the increment cannot automatically be compared with the value of the decrement, additional information can be received from commitments (see the discussion on *COMMITMENT PATTERN*). This example is illustrated in Fig. 24.

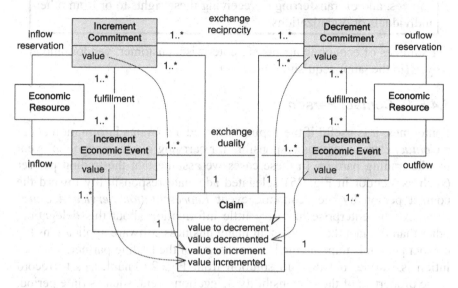

**Fig. 24.** Claim in a model with commitments

For example, the economic agents agree to sell 4 units of Pizza for $10; the value of the decrement commitment is 4 units, and the value of the increment commitment is $10. If the enterprise sells 3 units of Pizza and receives $8, the values of the claim are 1 unit of Pizza and $2.

A claim is often materialized; i.e., users of business applications print a document that states the value of the claim to a given date, and that often contains additional information. Invoice is an example of a materialized claim. As the methods to materialize the claim differ from one business application to another (due to legislation in various countries and company standards), we describe the *MATERIALIZED CLAIM* as a behavioral pattern.

## 1.4.5 Economic Agents

Economic agents are the providers and recipients of the rights associated with economic resources.

> Economic agents in exchange processes are individuals or organizations capable of holding the rights associated with economic resources, and of transferring or receiving these rights to or from other individuals or organizations.

Examples of economic agents are enterprise, customer, vendor, and employee (in the labor acquisition process).

### 1.4.5.1  Contact Person

Sometimes, it is useful if the application model contains information about a *Contact Person*, who is responsible for carrying out the economic event for the trading partner. In these cases we assume that the trading partner (such as Vendor in Fig. 25) delegated adequate responsibility toward the contact person by the economic event *Representation Service Acquirement*. As the enterprise has very little information about this delegation, other than the fact that it exists, in many business software applications the contact person is implemented as a property of the trading partner. This solution is simple, but the full solution from Fig. 25 enables us to record some properties of the responsibility delegation event, such as time period, as well as to associate several contact persons with a particular trading partner and economic event type.

The model Fig. 25 also illustrates, that sometimes it is useful to include a part of business partner's REA model in a solution, although the enterprise has limited information about it.

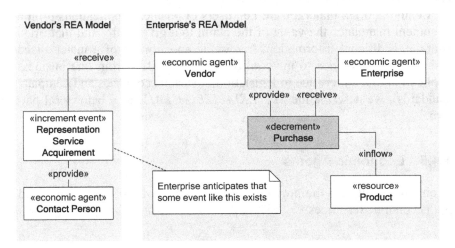

**Fig. 25.** Vendor's contact person

### 1.4.6  Provide and Receive

Provide and receive are relationships between economic agents and economic events. Provide and receive relationships answer the question about between *whom* rights are transferred, and, consequently, *who* has rights to a resource at a given time.

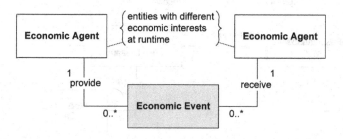

**Fig. 26.** Provide and receive relationships

> A provide relationship in an exchange process determines the economic agent who loses rights to the economic resource as a result of the economic event.

> A receive relationship in an exchange process determines the economic agent who receives rights to the economic resource as a result of the economic event.

During an economic event, rights to an economic resource are transferred from one economic agent to another. Therefore, there are exactly two economic agents related to each economic event. In order to create a complete model for the enterprise, we must specify for each economic event which agent receives and which agent loses rights to the resource. The following REA axiom specifies what the REA application models should support.

> In the REA application model, each economic event must be related by a provide relationship to an economic agent, and by a receive relationship an economic agent. At runtime, these two agents must represent people or organizations with different economic interests.

In the trading partner view (see Appendix B), one of the agents is always the enterprise, and the other agent is the economic agent to whom the enterprise transfers or from whom it receives some rights to economic resources.

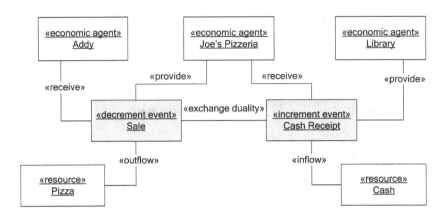

**Fig. 27.** Joe's Pizzeria sells pizza to Addy and receives payment from Library

In most cases we illustrate so far, the increment economic event has the same providing and receiving agents as the decrement economic events related to it by the exchange duality. In the *Sales* process of Joe's Pizzeria, the *Customer* and *Joe's Pizzeria* are related to both the increment and decrement economic events. However, actual agent participating in the increment and decrement events can be different. In the example illustrated in Fig. 27; *Joe's Pizzeria* sells *Pizza* to *Addy*, and receives payment from *Library*; the *Sale* event has different participating agents than the *Cash Receipt* event.

This exchange process must still add value for all participating agents. Is it worth it for *Addy* to get *Pizza* paid by *Library*? Well, if it would not be the case, the *Addy* would not receive *Pizza*, *Joe's Pizzeria* would not sell it, or *Library* would not pay for it.

## 1.5  How Joe's Pizzeria Obtains Pizza

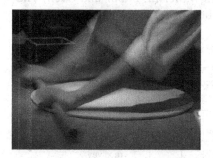

*The REA EXCHANGE PROCESS pattern does not apply, because Joe's Pizzeria does not obtain pizzas from its trading partners*

### 1.5.1  Producing Pizza

Joe's Pizzeria produces pizza from *Raw Materials* such as dough, pepperoni, tomatoes and cheese, by using an *Oven* and by consuming *Labor*. The process of producing pizza is essentially a conversion (transformation) of the *Raw Material*, *Labor* (the worked hours) and the *Oven* (the time when the oven has been used) into a *Pizza*, see Fig. 28. The *Raw Materials* become part of *Pizza*, they are consumed during production. Employee's *Labor* is also consumed; the time when the employee has worked on pizzas is gone when the pizza is finished, and is not available anymore. On the other hand, the *Oven* can be used again, although it might need some cleaning and maintenance after a *Pizza* has been baked.

In principle, there are also other resources required to produce pizza, such as the kitchen in the building in which Joe's Pizzeria is located, heating of the building, and maintenance of the oven. Joe has decided he is not interested in tracking how they are transformed into each *Pizza*. Therefore we do not model them as economic resources in this process.

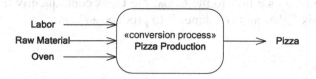

**Fig. 28.** The pizza production process

The REA model for pizza production is illustrated in Fig. 29. The *Material Issue, Labor Consumption*, and *Oven Use* are decrements of resources, because they decrease the value of the *Raw Material, Labor* and *Oven*. The *Pizza Production* is an increment event, because it creates a new resource with a positive value.

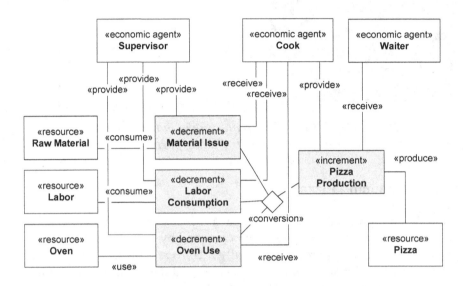

**Fig. 29.** The REA model for the pizza production

The economic resources *Raw Material, Employee Labor* and *Oven* are under the control of the employees *Supervisor, Cook* and *Waiter*. The employees physically control the resources on behalf of Joe's Pizzeria, but they do not own them, neither do they have any legal rights to these resources; the model in Fig. 29 illustrates that the economic agent *Supervisor* issues the *Raw Material* to the agent *Cook*, who bakes a *Pizza* and passes it to the *Waiter*. The *Supervisor* also provides *Oven* to the *Cook* to bake a *Pizza*. To explain who controls *Labor* requires deeper analysis (see the section on Labor in the Modeling Handbook): the *Supervisor* controls *Cook's Labor*, he assigns a task to the *Cook*; the *Cook* consequently takes of the control of his *Labor* and consumes it to produce a *Pizza*.

## 1.5.2  Summary

The REA model focuses on the core economic phenomena and abstracts from technical aspects of the conversion. This has several advantages.

The model answers the question as to which economic resources have been used, consumed and produced during the process. The economic events provide the information on when, where and how the changes of the resources occurred, and the economic agents provide the information on who controlled the economic resources during these changes. This is the information the business decision makers need in order to plan, monitor and control the economic resources.

The REA model does not imply any restrictions on the time order in which the economic events occur. If the users of a business application wish to specify the desired order of events, the model can be extended using commitments (described in the *SCHEDULE PATTERN*) to specify when the events should occur. However, the model can still record what actually happened, and thus determine the difference between the schedule and the actual production.

### 1.5.3  The Pizza Production Process is an Example of a Pattern

In addition to producing pizza, Joe's Pizzeria performs additional activities in order to keep the company running. Cleaning of the restaurant and maintenance of the equipment are the examples. If Joe schedules the pizza production in order to purchase the right amount of raw materials, or if he has an accountant who keeps his financial books, the planner's and accountant's labor are transformed into the services that, as their end result, make Joe's Pizzeria a better company. The cleaning, maintenance, planning, accounting are essentially conversions of labor and tools into other economic resources.

The pizza production, and the abovementioned processes are examples of a pattern, the *REA CONVERSION PROCESS*.

## 1.6   REA Conversion Process Pattern

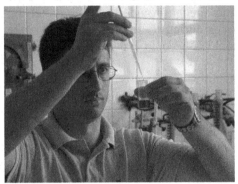

Photo by Ulrik de Wachter

*Conversion is a physical, structural, or design change or transformation from one state or condition to another*

### Context

You are an application designer developing a business application. Among the business processes of the enterprise, there usually are one or more processes that create new products or services, or add value to the existing ones. These processes might be specified by the users of a business application, but you know the user requirements are incomplete. You want to know the right questions to ask to better understand the application domain. You also want the model to be consistent, and robust against future changes in user requirements.

### Problem

How does one create a robust skeleton of an object-oriented model for a business process that creates new products or services, or adds value to the existing ones? User requirements are not a sufficient source of information, because they are known to be incomplete, often contradictory, and to change over time, and it is often impossible to find out what requirements are missing. In short, you would like to create a business application that will satisfy even some of the user requirements that have not been communicated to you.

## Forces

The solution to this problem is influenced by four forces.

- The model should provide information about how the process of creating and modifying resources influences their value, and when the value has been changed.
- The model should provide information about who was responsible for the resources and when.
- The model should capture the fundamentals of the users' business, and filter out those user requirements that are likely to change.
- The model should be consistent, complete, and correct with respect to the business domain rules.

## Solution

Model the process that creates new products or services or adds value to the existing ones as a *conversion* of some economic resources to others. During the conversion, the enterprise uses or consumes economic resources in order to produce the resources of the same or another kind.

Each conversion consists of at least one *increment economic event* that increases the value of the resource by modifying its features, and at least one *decrement economic event* that decreases the value of a resource by modifying its features. The *increments* and *decrements* in the conversion processes typically occur over a period of time.

Each *increment event* is related to exactly one *economic resource* by a relationship called *produce*. The *produce* relationship means that the economic event creates a new *economic resource* or modifies some features of an existing *resource*. Each *decrement event* is related to exactly one *economic resource* either by a *use* or by a *consume* relationship. The *consume* relationship means that the economic resource does not exist after the decrement event (the resource is consumed). The *use* relationship means that the economic resource still exists after the decrement event, but some of its features have been modified.

In order to keep track of which *resources* have been used or consumed in order to produce others, the *increment* and *decrement* economic events are related by the *conversion duality* relationship, or in short, *conversion*. The *conversion duality* is an n-ary relationship; in the application model there can be many increment and many decrement events related by a single conversion duality.

Each *economic event* is related to two *economic agents*. The *economic event* in the *conversion process* transfers the control over the *economic resource* from one *agent* to another. Each *event* is related to exactly one *economic agent* by a *provide* relationship, and to exactly one *economic agent* by a *receive* relationship, see Fig. 30. The transfer of control can occur at the beginning, at the end or during the *economic event*. Each *agent* can be related to zero or more *economic events*.

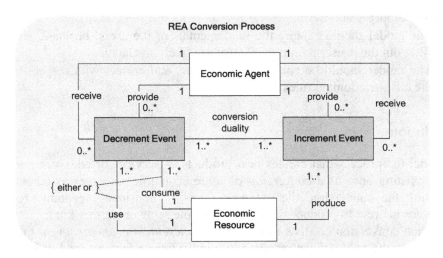

**Fig. 30.** REA conversion process

In order for a conversion process to add value, the overall increase in value of the resources related to the increment events should be greater than the overall decrease of value related to the decrement events, over the period reflecting the entrepreneurial goals of the enterprise.

The following domain rules apply for any REA application model describing the conversion process.

> Each increment economic event must be related by a conversion duality relationship to a decrement economic event and vice versa.
>
> Each increment event must be related by a produce relationship to an economic resource.
>
> Each decrement event must be related either by a use or by a consume relationship to an economic resource.

> Each economic event must be related by both provide and receive relationships to an economic agent.

## Resulting Context

The domain rules in this pattern allow application designers to derive and discover new facts from the facts provided by the users of a business application. Therefore, a business application can meet most or all fundamental user needs, even if the user requirements and the designer's knowledge of users' needs are incomplete.

Note that at runtime, for some period of time, there might exist a decrement event that is not paired in conversion duality with an increment event. For example, the oven must be turned on good time before the baking of pizza can start.

## 1.7    REA Conversion Processes in Detail

In this chapter we explain the semantics of the resources, events, agents, use, consume, produce, conversion duality, provide, and receive, in the REA conversion process.

> The purpose of the REA conversion process is to create new economic resources or to change features of existing resources by using or consuming resources of the same or another kind. Economic events in the conversion processes can change the values of the features, as well as add and remove features to and from the resources.

### 1.7.1    Economic Resources

Economic resources are things that are scarce, and have utility for economic agents, and users of business applications want to plan, monitor, and control. This definition of a resource is common to both an exchange and a conversion process[5]; however, the resources expose a different interface to the exchange and conversion processes.

> In the REA conversion process, a resource can be seen as a collection of certain features associated with it.

Features are properties, characteristics, capabilities or states of a resource that establish the utility of the resource for an economic agent: pizza has a certain weight, size, packaging, taste, vitamins and minerals content, is delivered on time, is freshly baked, and is known from TV. These features contribute to the resource value.

REA does not explicitly specify how to model the features of the resource. Some features can be modeled as properties of the resource, such as the weight of a pizza, some as relationships to other REA entities, such as the freshness of a pizza determined by the end of the Pizza Production event. In Part II of this book we model the features of the resources as modules of functionality called aspects. In the REA application models, the names of the produce and use relationships can indicate the features of the resource expected to be modified by the related economic event.

Fig. 31 illustrates an example of the resource *Pizza*, created during economic event *Baking* (i.e. this event changes the *Existence* feature of the

---

[5]  Please see the section REA Value Chain in Detail for discussion on economic resources in general.

*Pizza*). The increment event *Packing* changes the *Packaging* feature of the *Pizza*. The decrement event *Issue for Packing* temporarily (i.e. during the duration of this event) changes the *Availability* feature, e.g. when issued for packing, a Pizza cannot be used for other purposes. The decrement economic events for usage and consumption of the resources needed to bake the pizza are omitted in the diagram for simplicity.

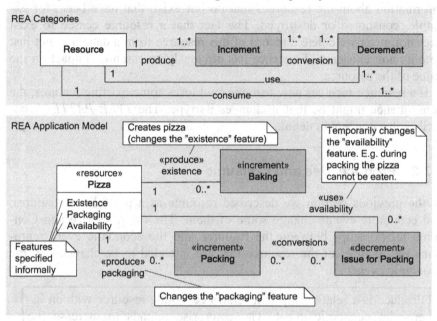

**Fig. 31.** The conversion process changes features of the resource

In the REA software application, it is necessary to store the features on the resource entity, while the rights an economic agent has to the resource are determined by relationships to the economic events. The main reason is that while rights can be transferred only by economic events, resource features can change on their own, as a result of the processes that are not part of the application model.

Features can change on their own, not only as a result of economic events in the application model. The reason of this fact is that the application model does not need to contain all conversion processes that might affect the features of the resource. If the features of the resource change on their own, it usually means they have been changed by some conversion process, which the application designers have not modeled. This is natural; model is not an exact copy of the world, but contains only the information relevant for the model. Therefore, features, and consequently also *values* of resources can change as a result of the processes that are not part of the application model.

Existence is one of the features of the resource; the only feature that the resource must have. This seems obvious for real-world objects. However, software applications do not contain real-world objects; they contain information about real-world objects, therefore, there is often need to keep information about the resources that do not exist, that have been, for example, consumed or destroyed. The fact that a resource ceased to exist does not mean we delete a record of this resource from a database, but just note its non existence. Existence has obviously an essential impact on the value of the resource.

If a resource receives new features, and loses some existing features, the consequence might be that it changes its type. The *TYPE PATTERN* describes this concept in detail.

### 1.7.2  Produce, Use and Consume

In the previous section we described resource as a portfolio of features, and economic events change some of them. The Produce, Use and Consume relationships between the resource and the economic event represents the features of the resource that are intended to be changed by the economic event.

> Produce is a relationship that relates economic resource with an increment economic event. The enterprise intends to increase the value of the resource as a result of the related increment event.

Produce means both creation of the resource, such as baking a pizza from raw materials, and improvements to the resource, such as packing a pizza. Maintenance and transport are other examples of the inflow economic event with a produce relationship.

> Consume is a relationship between an economic resource and a decrement economic event. After a decrement economic event, the resource is entirely used up and does not exist after the event ends.

For example, the flour and water are consumed during the pizza production process; see Fig. 32.

> Use is a relationship between an economic resource and a decrement economic event. After the decrement economic event, the resource still exists, and its value may be unaffected.

For example, an oven still exists after the pizza production process in Fig. 32.

The use relationship does not specify anything about the value or the economic resource *after* the related decrement event. The economic event is a *decrement* because the value of the resource for the enterprise becomes smaller *during* the event. For example, the economic event might somehow restrict the utilization of the resource: the oven used for a pizza production in Fig. 32 may not at the same time be used for other purposes. However, after the event, the value can be the same as before; other typical example is playing a CD in a CD player. In other cases, the value of the resource is smaller after the decrement event, and after a certain number of decrement events the value of the resource can become zero or even negative; after many uses, the enterprise might decide to transfer the oven ownership to the recycle station.

The *Pizza Production* process illustrated in Fig. 32 is an example of a conversion process with produce, use and consume relationships.

At the REA category level (which describes how application models are constructed), the produce, use and consume are one-to-many (1 to 1..*) relationships. For example, as illustrated in Fig. 32, the enterprise consumes the resources *Flour* and *Water*, uses the resource *Oven*, and produces the resource *Pizza*, which is then transported to the *Customer* using the resource *Vehicle*. All economic events last over an interval of time.

In the REA application model (which describes the construction of runtime entities), the *consume* is a one-to-one (1 to 0..1) relationship; one decrement event is related to one resource, and a resource can be related to zero or one decrement event. An actual volume of *Flour* and *Water* can be added at most once (then they do not exist), each *Flour Addition* and *Water and Flour Mixing* is related to a specific volume of *Flour* and *Water*.

The *use* is a one-to-many (1 to 0..*) relationship; one decrement is related to one resource, and a resource can be related to zero or more decrements. An actual *Oven* can over time be used zero or more times, and each *Oven Use* is related to exactly one *Oven*.

The *produce relationship which creates a resource* is a one-to-one (1 to 0..1) relationship; one increment event is related to one resource, and a resource can be related to zero or one increment event. An actual Pizza can be created at most once, and each Pizza production produces exactly one Pizza.

The *produce relationship which modifies an existing resource* is a many-to-many (1..* to 0..*) relationship; one increment event is related to one or more resources, and a resource can be related to zero or more increments. For example, an actual *Pizza* can be *Transported* zero or more times, and each *Transport* economic event is related to one or more *Pizzas*.

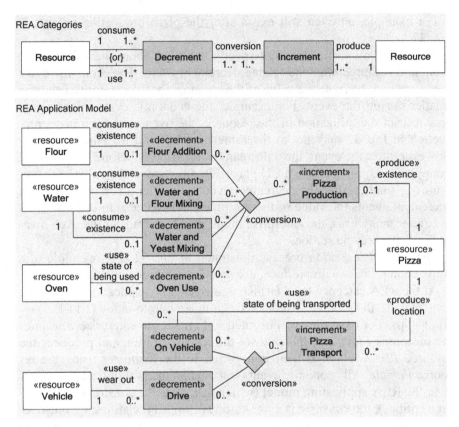

**Fig. 32.** Produce, use and consume relationships

This example also illustrates that the users' viewpoint determines what the economic resources are. If users are also interested in how making *Pizza* affects resources such as ingredients, tools, and kitchen, these resources must be included in the model. This process also produces waste; if the users are interested in modeling the produced waste, the waste should also be included in the model.

## 1.7.3  Economic Events

Economic events in the conversion processes represent changes to the features of the resources, and the transfer of control of an economic resource from one economic agent to another. The changes to the features represent increments or decrements of the value of the resources.

> The purpose of an economic event in the conversion process is to create or consume a resource, or to change some of the features of an existing resource.

An increment event increases value of the related resource, but it does not mean that every actual event must increase the value; the increment events increase the overall value of the resources over the period reflecting the entrepreneurial goals of the enterprise. The same applies for the decrement events.

The economic events address *when* the resource features have been changed, *when* economic resources changed value, and *when* economic agents had the resources under their control. If the economic resources can be located in space, the economic event also determines *where* the economic resources changed their value.

The economic events in the conversion processes do not transfer rights to the resources between economic agents. If a resource has been created in the conversion process, the enterprise has ownership rights to this resource by default. If a resource has been consumed, enterprise loses the ownership and no other agent can receive rights to the resource that does not exist.

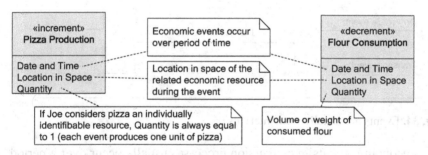

**Fig. 33.** Economic event in a conversion process

The economic events in REA conversion processes usually occur over a period of time. The properties for *Date and Time* and *Location in Space* typically have behavior that differs from one application to another, we describe them as behavioral patterns *POSTING* and *LOCATION* in the Part II of this book. The *Quantity* property determines the quantity or amount of the used, consumed or produced resources. The *Quantity* property of the events related to the resources that are individually identifiable is always one, as there is one economic event for every used, produced or consumed resource unit. Whether the resources are individually identifiable is often a decision of the users of a business application. For example, if Joe does not want to keep track of each individual *Pizza*, the *Quantity* property of the *Pizza Production* event in Fig. 33 would be a natural number different than 1, and the resource related to this event would represent an identifiable (by Joe) set of pizzas, such as the pizzas produced during a period of time. Please see also the discussion in the chapter REA Value Chain in Detail.

### 1.7.3.1  Economic Events are Time Intervals

The economic events in conversion processes usually occur over an interval of time. For example, in Fig. 34, the *On Vehicle* is a decrement event representing the time interval when an *Item* is on a truck, and the *Transport* event the time interval when the *Item* is actually changing its location.

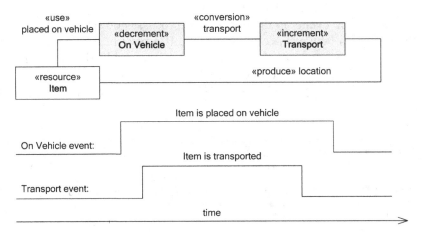

**Fig. 34.** Events are usually time intervals

As economic events in conversion processes usually occur over a period of time, it is useful to specify when exactly the participating economic agents transfer control over the resource. The answer is different for resources that can be individually identified (such as cars) and resources that cannot (such as fuel).

Transfer of control over resources with individually unidentifiable elements, but whose identity is determined by their quantities, such as fluid resources and some services, occurs continuously during their use, produce and consume economic events; see Fig. 35. For example, production or consumption of electricity occurs continuously, and the transfer of control over electricity from the distributor to the customer is continuous.

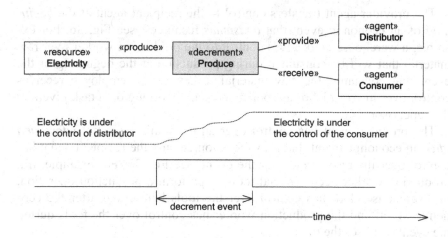

**Fig. 35.** Transfer of control over resources that cannot be individually identified

From the model in Fig. 35 we can determine that the provider economic agent controls the resource *before* the economic event, and that the recipient agent controls the resources *after* the economic event. *During* the economic events, the provider agents control some amount of the resource and the recipient agent some other amount.

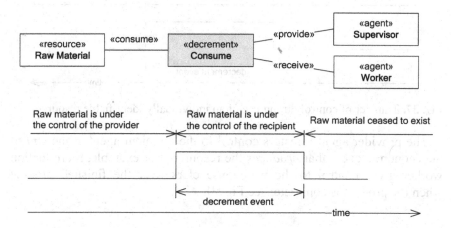

**Fig. 36.** Transfer of control occurs at the beginning of the consumption of an individually identifiable resource

For individually identifiable resources the answer is more specific, and depends on whether the relationship is use, consume, or produce.

The provider agent transfers control to the recipient agent at the *beginning* of an economic event that *consumes* resources; see Fig. 36. For example, a warehouse clerk gives control to the production worker over raw material that will be consumed during production at the beginning of the event that consumes the raw material. Likewise, an employee receives control over his own labor as soon as he starts working on a task given by the supervisor.

The provider agent has control over an economic resource *before and after* an economic event that *uses* the resource, and the recipient agent has control over the resource *during* the event; see Fig. 37. For example, if a production worker needs special tools to perform a production operation, the warehouse clerk has control over the tools before and after the economic event, and the production worker has control over the tools during the event that uses the tools.

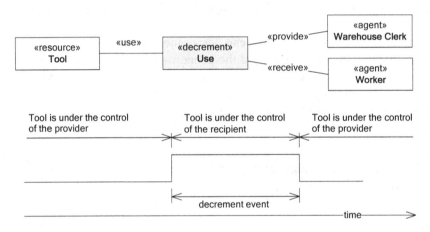

**Fig. 37.** Transfer of control during use of an individually identifiable resource

The provider agent transfers control to the recipient agent at the *end* of the economic event that *produces* the resource. For example, a production worker gives control to the warehouse clerk over the finished product when the product is complete; see Fig. 38.

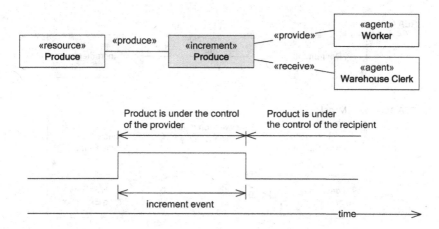

**Fig. 38.** Transfer of control at the end of production of an individually identifiable resource

## 1.7.4  Conversion Duality

The conversion duality binds increment and decrement economic events together into an REA conversion process.

> The purpose of the conversion duality is to keep track of which resources were used or consumed in order to produce others.

Conversion duality represents in the model *why* some resources are used or consumed. For example, the pizzeria uses oven and consumes raw materials and labor *because* it produces pizza.

The following REA axiom specifies what the REA application models should support.

> In the REA application model of a conversion process, every increment economic event must be related by a conversion duality to a decrement economic event, and vice versa.

An example of a conversion duality in the process of disassembling a bicycle is illustrated in Fig. 39.

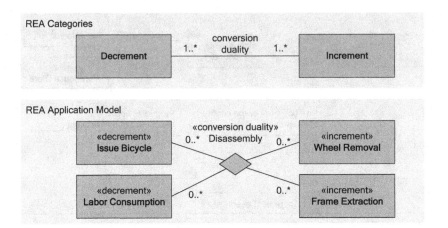

**Fig. 39.** The conversion duality

The conversion duality at the REA category level (which describes constraints of the application model) is a many-to-many (1..* to 1..*) relationship, see Fig. 39. For example, a mechanic can consume his labor (the *Labor Consumption* event) and a bicycle (the *Issue Bicycle* event) for the *Wheel Removal* and for the *Frame Extraction* events. The conversion duality must relate at least one increment event entity and one decrement event entity.

The conversion duality in the REA application model (which describes constraints of the runtime entities) is a many-to-many (0..* to 0..*) relationship. At runtime, typically two *Wheel Removal* events occur for one *Frame Extraction* event.

### 1.7.4.1   The Value of Produced, Used and Consumed Resources

In the conversion process, the enterprise use or consume resources in order to produce other resources. The increment economic event either creates a new resource unit, or increases the value of an existing resource by changing some of the resource's features. In return, the decrement economic events use or consume the enterprise's resources.

The overall incremented value of the produced resources (considering the enterprise's entrepreneurial goals) should be higher than the overall decremented value of the consumed or used resources. This statement is true only on average. A specific production run can be unsuccessful and the overall value of the resources is decreased. However, on average the process must add value; otherwise, a rational enterprise would not perform this process.

### 1.7.4.2 Time Order of Increments and Decrements

There is a logical constraint on the order of time in which the resources are used, consumed, and produced in the conversion process. Usually the increment event starts *after or at the same time* as some decrement event starts, and ends *before or at the same time* as some decrement event ends (resources cannot be produced from nothing); see Fig. 40.

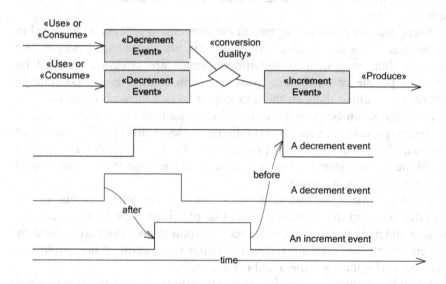

**Fig. 40.** Time constraints on conversion processes

### 1.7.5 Economic Agents

Have you ever witnessed a situation in which an administrative assistant of a department is running around asking colleagues, "Who ordered this package?" This situation can occur when the enterprise receives an item, and probably also holds the legal rights to this item, but the physical control of this item is held by an employee, and the business application of the enterprise or vendor, or both, is missing information about which person should physically control the item.

> Economic agents in conversion processes are individuals (not organizations) capable of controlling economic resources, and of transferring or receiving the control to or from other individuals.

Examples of economic agents in conversion processes are employees (in the labor consumption process), and people providing services for the enterprise.

In the conversion processes, the agents related to economic events can transfer to each other control of the resources, but cannot usually have ownership or other legal rights to these resources. These agents bear the responsibility for the resources on behalf of the enterprise or of other agents.

Therefore, the economic agents in the conversion process do not need to be entities in the legal sense; the agents are always physical people. We can say that, in general, economic resources are always controlled by physical people or machines. However, sometimes it is not possible or relevant to include them in the application model. In such cases the economic agents can be an organizational unit, such as team, department, or even enterprise (as organizational unit, not as legal entity). The meaning of this *modeling compromise* must be specified by the application designer; it could mean, for example, that "someone from the department" has control over the economic resource.

The economic agent that holds the rights to the economic resources can be different from the economic agent that physically has the economic resource under its control. For example, equipment and tools are owned by the enterprise, but they are physically under the control of the employees that work with the equipment and use the tools.

Likewise, a single economic agent can participate in both exchange and conversion processes. For example, an employee has rights to his labor, which he exchanges with the enterprise for financial compensation. Simultaneously, the employee physically controls some of the resources of the enterprise, because he participates in the enterprise's conversion processes.

### 1.7.6  Provide and Receive

Provide and receive are relationships between economic agents and economic events. Provide and receive relationships answers the question about between *whom* control is transferred, and, consequently, *who* controls a resource at a given time.

> A receive relationship in a conversion process determines the economic agent who receives control over the economic resource as a result of the economic event, but has no legal rights to the resource.

> A provide relationship in a conversion process determines the economic agent who loses control over the economic resource as a result of the economic event, but has no legal rights to the resource.

During an economic event, the control over an economic resource is transferred from one economic agent to another. Therefore, there are exactly two economic agents related to each economic event. In order to create a complete model for the enterprise, we must specify for each economic event which agent receives and which agent loses control over the resource.

> In the REA application model of a conversion process, each economic event must be related by a provide relationship to an economic agent, and by a receive relationships an economic agent.

In conversion processes, the provider and the recipient can be the same agent, for example, in cases where the same economic agent is responsible for consecutive business processes. For example, if an economic agent *Cook* is the only employee in Joe's Pizzeria, he would be both provider and recipient in the economic events *Material Issue* and *Pizza Production*.

### 1.7.6.1  Rights to the Resources in Conversion Processes

The purpose of conversion processes is to change the features of the resources, not to exchange the rights to the resources. The enterprise holds the rights to the created, used, and consumed resources. In a liberal legal system, the enterprise owns the resources it creates. Likewise, if resources are consumed, the enterprise loses its rights to these resources.

> In the REA application model, the enterprise holds the rights to the resources the enterprise produces, uses and consumes.

An enterprise can by contract with other economic agents commit itself to transfer to them ownership or other rights to the resources at the moment they are created or acquired by exchange. For example, employees might during employment produce intellectual property, which we model as an economic resource. Employees that create intellectual property own it, but many companies have a clause in their employment contracts according to which employees transfer to the company their intellectual property, for example, protected by patents, that they produce during the employment period. Such a transfer would be modeled as an economic event in the scope of the labor acquisition process, see Fig. 41. For the *Enterprise*, the increment events are the receiving rights of employee's *Labor* and the receiving rights to employee's *Intellectual Property* from the *Employee*, and the decrement event is the *Salary Payment*.

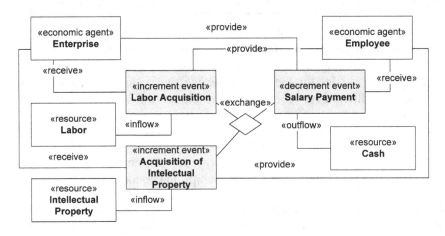

**Fig. 41.** Acquiring intellectual property

### 1.7.6.2  The Enterprise Does Not Always Controls Its Resources

The enterprise does *not always* control the resources it has rights to; the economic agents that control the resources of the enterprise do not necessarily act on behalf of the enterprise. Typical examples are services that are provided by other agents to the enterprise's resources, such as transport, maintenance, and outsourced manufacturing operations.

The model in Fig. 42 illustrates an example of maintenance of an enterprise's *Equipment*. The *enterprise* acquires a maintenance service from a service provider by economic event *Maintenance Acquisition*. During economic event *Maintenance Consumption*, the enterprise, which "owns" the service when it is acquired, passes control over this service to the *Service Provider* agent, who consumes it in order to perform the *Maintenance* economic event. The *Service Provider* is the economic agent who controls the enterprise's *Equipment* during the *Maintenance* economic event. At the end of the *Maintenance* event, the *Equipment* is again under the control of the *Enterprise*.

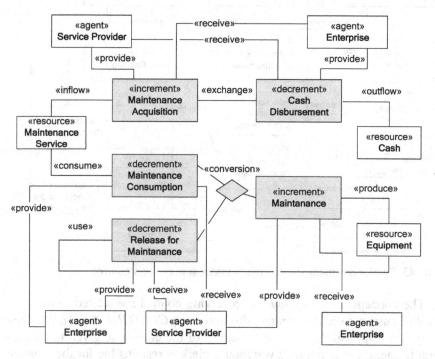

**Fig. 42.** Equipment is not under the control of the enterprise during maintenance

### 1.7.6.3  Who Has Changed The Features Of The Resource?

The economic agents participating in the economic events during conversion processes are not necessarily the same as the agents that changed the features of the resources. The agents that changed the features of the resource are those whose labor has been consumed during the process.

For example, in the model in Fig. 43, the economic event *Painting* changes a feature of a *Product*. The economic agent *Supervisor* has control over the *Product* before, during, and after the *Painting* event. The economic agent that changed the feature of the product was *Painter*, because his *Labor* has been consumed in the *Painting*.

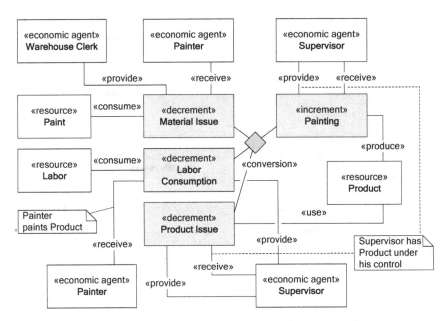

**Fig. 43.** Painter has painted the product under supervisor's control

The concepts of providing and receiving control are related to the concept of custody; see the separate discussion on *CUSTODY PATTERN*. Custody is a responsibility for the resources of the enterprise given to an economic agent; for example, a warehouse clerk is responsible for the items in the warehouse. The difference between custody and responsibility is that custody can be established, transferred, and cancelled independently of the economic events in conversion processes. Economic agents who have custody for the enterprise's resources can be different of the agents whose services are consumed in conversion processes that affect these resources. For example, a manager of gas station has custody over the fuel in the underground tanks, but the process of disposing of the fuel is provided by other agents, often the customers in self-service gas stations.

## 1.8 Value Chain of Joe's Pizzeria

*Each business process utilizes resources generated by other processes*

So far, we identified several exchange and conversion processes of Joe's Pizzeria, the *Sales, Purchase, Labor Acquisition,* and *Pizza Production.* At the output of each process there is an economic resource that is an input of another process, see Fig. 44.

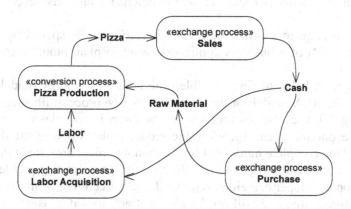

**Fig. 44.** Value chain of Joe's Pizzeria

The *Pizza Production* process produces *Pizza,* which is exchanged in the *Sales* process for *Cash.* Joe's Pizzeria uses *Cash* to purchase *Raw Materials* and *Labor* in the *Purchase* and the *Labor Acquisition* processes. The *Raw Materials* and *Labor* are consumed to produce *Pizza* in the *Pizza Production* process.

Each business process in Fig. 44 can be modeled using the economic resources, events, agents, and, if needed, also the commitments, contracts, and other entities that we introduce later in this book. This expansion is symbolically illustrated in Fig. 45.

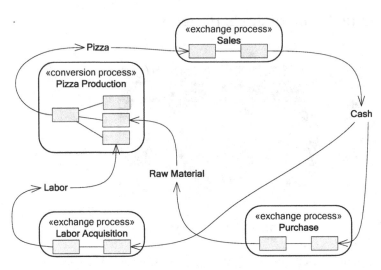

**Fig. 45.** Value chain with expanded processes

Modeling the value chain helps the application designer to get an overview over the business processes of the enterprise and has several other advantages.

Firstly, it helps to identify the economic resources, by specifying which things the users of a business application want to plan, monitor and control.

Secondly, it helps to find possible omissions in the REA models. For example, the REA model for the *Pizza Production* process, illustrated earlier in Fig. 29, uses the resource *Oven*. The *Oven* is not related to any increment economic event, therefore the model violates one of the domain rules, and the complete model in Fig. 45 cannot explain how Joe's Pizzeria receives and loses the rights to use the *Oven*. To resolve this problem, an application developer can either remove the resource *Oven* from the model (and, consequently, Joe will not be able to track its value using the software application), or add a process with an increment event related to the *Oven*. Joe can also decide to leave the model inconsistent (we call it a modeling compromise), but it will be a rational and qualified decision (not an omission) and Joe will be aware of its consequences.

The model in Fig. 45 is created from Joe's Pizzeria's point of view. For every exchange process in Joe's Pizzeria's REA model, there must be a corresponding exchange process in the REA model of Joe's Pizzeria's trading partner. For example, in the REA model of the *Customer*, there must be a *Purchase* process with the events *Purchase* and *Cash Disbursement,* corresponding to the *Sales* process of Joe's Pizzeria. Likewise, in the

REA model for the *Employee*, there must be a *Labor Provision* process with the events *Labor Sale* and *Cash Receipt*, corresponding to the *Labor Acquisition* process of Joe's Pizzeria, see Fig. 46.

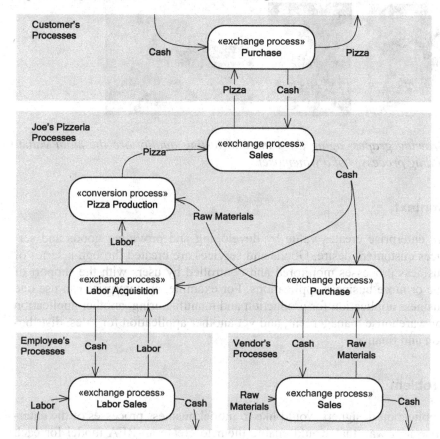

**Fig. 46.** Semantics of exchange processes

We can generalize Joe's Pizzeria's chain of business processes into a pattern, *REA VALUE CHAIN*.

## 1.9   REA Value Chain Pattern

*Growing grapes, aging the wine and testing quality are the main value-adding processes of a winemaker*

### Context

An enterprise creates value by developing and providing goods and services customers desire. Goods and services are created through a series of business processes monitored and controlled by users with the support of one or more business applications. For example, an enterprise can use one business application for production and manufacturing, another application for warehouse management, and yet another application for sales, distribution and finance.

### Problem

Application designers would like to model business processes of the enterprise in a way that would enable them to create an REA model for each process, with an option to implement each REA model as an independent software component. However,

- They are not able to identify all the resources that users of business applications would like to manage, monitor, and control. At what level of granularity should the resources, and, consequently, the REA models, be?
- Application designers have already created REA models for several processes, but would like to relate them together, get an overview of the whole model and eventually identify missing processes.

## Forces

The solution to this problem is influenced by four forces.

- The business process model should be independent of the technology the customer uses, and should rather describe fundamentals of the users' business. As the implementation technology often changes the sequential order of processes and events, the relationships between processes and events should be expressed as logical constraints rather than as sequential order. The software solution should cover any sequence physically allowable, and only restrict the order by business rules configurable at runtime.
- On the other hand, the business process model should be precise enough to be compatible with the REA model, i.e., it should be possible to refine this model to an object-oriented application model expressed by resources, events, and agents, from which a software application can be generated.
- If each business process will be implemented as an independent software component or an application, the components and applications must have well defined interfaces that enable them to communicate.
- There are several methods for modeling business processes, such as IDEF0, Porter's value chain, flow charts, organization charts, and workflows, but none of them is sufficiently compatible with REA.

## Solution

Model an enterprise as a chain of value-adding business processes that influence the value of the resources, which users of business application want to plan, monitor and control. Inputs to each business process are the resources used or consumed by the business process or given away to other economic agents; outputs of each business process are the resources produced by the business process or obtained from other economic agents. Both the exchange and conversion processes accomplish the business objective of adding value to the resources that are under the control of the enterprise, over the period reflecting the entrepreneurial goals of the enterprise.

**Fig. 47.** The REA value chain

The resources that are inputs and outputs to business processes should be the resources that users of business applications want to plan, monitor, and control. This determines the level of detail of the model.

The REA value chain consists of three modeling elements: *REA Conversion Process*, *REA Exchange Process* and *Resource Value Flow*.

> An REA conversion process is a process that uses or consumes the resources that are under the control of the enterprise, and produces new resources or changes some of the features of existing resources.

Examples of a conversion process are a manufacturing operation and a service operation such as transportation.

> An REA exchange process is a process that transfers some rights to the enterprise's resources to other economic agents, and receives some rights to other resources in return.

Examples of an exchange business process that transfers ownership rights are the sales and purchase processes; examples of processes that transfer other rights, such as usage rights, are financing, labor acquisition, and insurance.

> A resource value flow is a relationship between REA processes. This relationship represents the resource input and output of a process. The *direction* indicates that of the value flow; the process at the beginning of the flow (the end without an arrow) adds value to the resource; the process at the end of the flow (the end with an arrow) takes away value from the resource.

Each resource value flow must start and end in some business process; no "loose ends" are allowed for resource value flows in well-formed models. This does not mean that at runtime the resource cannot just appear and disappear due to unexpected events that are not part of the model; but this is not the usual way in which an enterprise creates value. The value chain describes the usual (not exceptional) way in which how enterprise creates value; more precisely, it describes the processes that users of a business application want to plan, monitor, and control.

> Each resource value flow must start and end in some business process. Each business process must have an incoming and an outgoing resource value flow.

The resources that come from outside the enterprise or leave the enterprise are modeled as inputs and outputs of the exchange business processes.

A single resource can be both input and output of a single business process. For example, cash is both the input and the output of the financing business process; an item is both the input and the output of the quality assurance process.

> An REA business process is either an exchange process or a conversion process.

The statement above specifies that there are no "mixed" business processes whose responsibility would be both to change features of the resource and transfer rights between economic agents. In such a configuration, a business application would leave out some information about economic resources.

## Process for Creating a REA Value Chain

As the first step in creating the value chain of the enterprise, it is helpful to think about the context of the enterprise. To whom does the enterprise give resources and from whom does it receive resources? The result can be something similar to that diagrammed in Fig. 48.

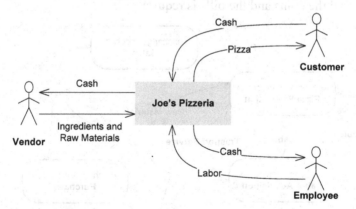

**Fig. 48.** Business context of the enterprise

*Customer* buys *Pizza* that the *Enterprise* produces, which is an exchange of *Pizza* for *Cash*. *Vendor* gives the *Enterprise Ingredients* and *Raw Materials* in exchange for *Cash*. *Employees* provide the *Enterprise* their labor in exchange for *Cash*. A context diagram for the enterprise similar to the one in Fig. 48 is useful as a starting point in identifying the company's resources.

The second step in creating an REA value chain is to identify the business processes of the enterprise; an example is in Fig. 44.

The exchange business processes of a pizzeria would be the *Sales* process that exchanges *Pizza* for *Cash* with the *Customers*, the *Purchase* process that exchanges *Raw Material* for Cash with the *Vendors*, and the *Labor Acquisition* process that exchanges *Labor* for *Cash* with the *Employees*.

The enterprise typically also has one or more conversion processes, in which it produces or adds value to the product or service that it sells to the customers, and in which it consumes or uses the resources obtained from the vendors and employees. The conversion process of the pizzeria is the *Pizza Production* process that produces *Pizza* from *Raw Material* and labor.

The third step in creating a value chain is to hierarchically decompose the business processes to find the resources which the users of a business application would like to plan, monitor, and control. The level of detail at which to stop the decomposition is determined by the needs of the users of a business application. The REA value chain should be decomposed to the level at which the users of a business application need information to plan, monitor and control the resources of the enterprise. This level varies from one company to another. For example, for most companies it is sufficient to know the total amount of cash in the treasury, but in some cases keeping track of all the coins and the bills is required.

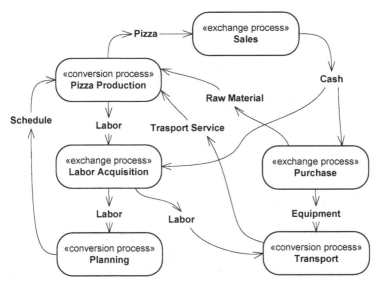

**Fig. 49.** Value chain with supporting processes

The fourth step in creating the value chain is to identify the rest of the business processes, such as planning, marketing, accounting, human resources, and legal services, and to add them to the enterprise's value chain. These processes consume the resources of the enterprise, but using traditional modeling techniques it is not always a trivial task to determine what value they add. The REA framework helps analyze the purpose of these processes, and how they add value to the enterprise's resources.

Fig. 49 illustrates the value chain with two more processes: *Planning*, which consumes *Labor* to assure that all resources needed to produce *Pizza* are available, and *Transport*, which consumes *Labor* and *Equipment* to deliver *Pizza* to the *Customers*. The Part III of this book is devoted to these modeling issues.

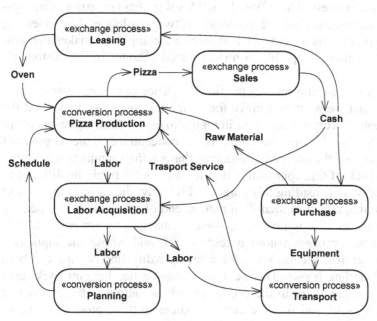

**Fig. 50.** Value chain after the consistency check

The fifth step in creating the value chain is to consolidate the model with the REA models for each process, and to assure that the model does not violate the domain rules. For example, a model for Pizza Production in Fig. 29 contains a resource *Oven* related by a use relationship to a decrement event *Oven Use*. As every economic resource must be related to both an increment and a decrement event, an application designer might decide either to remove the resource *Oven* from the model, or to add an increment event related to the *Oven*. Joe told the application designer that Joe's Pizzeria has a leasing contract for the *Oven*. Leasing is essentially an exchange of the *Oven* for *Cash*, and Fig. 50 illustrates the value chain with the *Leasing* process.

## Resulting Context

An application designer is focused on processes that add value to the final products and services directly, as well as on supporting processes. A software solution may need to support some of these processes, others may be manual.

Due to well-defined resource interfaces between business processes, application designers can design a different business software application for each business process. Therefore, the REA value chain determines the system level architecture of the business software solution. Implementing each REA process as an independent software component makes the software solution more adaptable to unanticipated changes in the customer's business.

The REA value chain ignores the time sequence of the processes, which is exactly what we want to achieve for design purposes. We know that the time sequence is very volatile, and in reality many of these processes occur concurrently. At this point we would like to concentrate on the purposes of the processes and the economic resources that are their inputs and outputs.

A drawback of this approach is that for a reader it might be difficult to find a place to start reading this diagram. Probably, the easiest way to start reading the diagram is to identify a natural end of the value chain, i.e., the sales process, or if it is not there, some exchange process equivalent to sales, usually a process whose output is cash and whose the input is a product or service; for example, for a municipality library, this can be a process of lending books. Then, continue reading the diagram backwards through the value chain to the processes, whose output is the product or service being sold, and find the input resources to these processes; and so on.

## 1.10 REA Value Chain in Detail

In this section we explain semantics of the economic resources, and REA exchange and conversion processes.

> The purpose of the REA value chain is to link together REA models into a chain of value-adding processes, and define the interfaces between them.

The REA Value Chain is a network of business processes whose purpose is to directly or indirectly contribute to the creation of the desired features of the final product or service, and to exchange it with other economic agents for a resource that has a greater value for the enterprise in its perception of its entrepreneurial goals.

The REA value chain model does not describe sequences, steps, and tasks of the business processes. Time sequences of activities vary often with technology changes, but the changes in sequence typically do not change the fundamental way in which the process adds value. Therefore, the value chain model focuses on the core phenomena of the business, and abstracts the time sequences that change often.

The time sequence is given indirectly in the form of logical constraints. For example, the conversion process *Pizza Production* cannot start unless the resources *Labor* and *Raw Materials* are available.

### 1.10.1 Resource Value Flows

Economic resources are the inputs and outputs of the REA exchange and conversion processes.

In order to create a complete model for the enterprise, we must specify for each resource how the enterprise obtains rights to it, for example, how is it received, or produced, and how the enterprise loses rights to it, i.e., how it is consumed, or given away.

An enterprise can receive rights to a resource by producing it in a conversion process, or by receiving it in an exchange process. In the REA model, it is indicated by a produce or an inflow relationships between the resource and an increment economic event, respectively.

An enterprise can lose rights to a resource by consuming it in a conversion process, or by giving it away in an exchange process. In the REA model, it is indicated by consume or outflow relationships between the resource and a decrement economic event. The enterprise does not lose rights to a resource by using it in a conversion process, as the resource exists after the economic event related to the resource by a use relationship.

> In the REA application model, every economic resource must be related to at least one increment event by an inflow or produce relationship, and to at least one decrement event by an outflow, use, or consume relationship.

### 1.10.2 Economic Resources

Economic resources represent the values that users of a business application seek to control.

> Economic resources are things that are scarce and have utility, that are under the control of an economic agent, and that users of business applications want to plan, monitor, and control.

Examples of economic resources are products and services the enterprise provides, money, and raw materials, tools, and services the enterprise uses and consumes.

Things we call economic resources must be *scarce*, not readily available at no cost, such as air, or sea water by the seashore. Antarctica ice is an economic resource in Europe, but not in Antarctica.

The *users of business applications* are important in the definition of economic resource: the perspective of the users of a business application determines which economic resources are modeled. As different users are interested in different resources, the REA application model must contain economic resources for all intended users of the application.

Value of an economic resource for an economic agent is determined by the rights the agent has to the resource, and by the features of the resource. An agent can change its rights to the resource by an exchange process; and the features by a conversion process

### 1.10.2.1 Quantity of the Resource

Economic resources typically have a property *Quantity* that indicates whether and how much of the resource is under the control of the enterprise. For example, the quantity of the economic resource cash indicates the amount of cash that the enterprise has under its control. This amount can consist of owned and borrowed cash. If we would like to know how much is owned and how much is borrowed, we need to examine the economic events that are related to the economic resource cash.

Quantity for discrete items that can be identified as individual units, such as cars and buildings, is always measured in pieces and may have values 1 and 0, indicating whether the item is, or is not, under the control of the enterprise. Quantity for resources that cannot be individually identified, such as screws, gasoline, electricity, and work, is measured with an appropriate unit such as kilogram, liter, joule, or hour. Occasionally, we might come across discrete items that can be split into smaller parts, such as pizza. We model a process of cutting pizza into slices as a conversion process, which produces several units of a new resource "a slice of pizza," each with quantity 1.

Setting the value of quantity to 0 means that the resource is not under the control of the enterprise, and that the enterprise wants to keep information about this resource in its software system. For example, the resource has been sold and the enterprise is bound by guarantee or service agreement to the new owner of this resource, or the resource has been consumed or destroyed, and the enterprise has to keep record of this resource for reporting or statistical purposes.

The property *quantity* is different than property *quantity on hand*. Quantity on hand is usually a property of a resource group, see the *GROUPING PATTERN*, and is a non-negative integer for discrete items, and a real number for the resources that cannot be individually identified.

### 1.10.2.2 Value of the Resource

The value of the resource indicates how much the resource is worth to the economic agents that are related to it via economic events or commitments. The value of the resource depends on four factors:

- On the features of the resource, we discussed the features in the Conversion Processes in Detail chapter.
- On the rights an economic agent has to the resource; we discussed the rights in the Exchange Processes in Detail chapter
- On the economic agent related to this resource via economic events and commitments. As the resource can be related, via economic events and commitments, to different economic agents simultaneously, it might have (and typically has) a different value for each economic agent. For example, goods in trade have different values for the seller and the buyer.
- On how the resource is used or potentially can be used by the economic agents. The actual use is specified by related economic events, and po-

tential use by commitments (see the *COMMITMENT* pattern for details). As the resource can be related to several economic events and commitments simultaneously, a resource might have different values for a single economic agent at the same time. For example, a car has a different value (and consequently a different price) for the agent, in the case he intends to rent it, than in the case he intends to sell it.

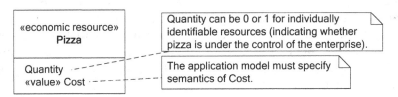

**Fig. 51.** Value and quantity of the economic resource

Although for the reasons mentioned above the resource can have several values simultaneously, it is useful to model the resource value as an property on an economic resource, as illustrated in Fig. 51; but since such a value is a derived (calculated) property, the model must specify how the value is obtained, or it might otherwise be interpreted incorrectly. For example, the value can reflect the cost of the resource for the enterprise, or the price in the case of sale of the resource, or the price in the case of rental of the resource.

The value of the resource is variable in time and can change on its own, not only as a result of economic events in the application model. For example, the value of food or medicine rapidly decreases after expiry date. However, the enterprise does not know the exact value of such expired food or medicine, until they dispose of or consume it, perhaps for other purposes than originally intended. Therefore, the full explanation of this phenomenon requires a notion of economic contract or schedule, and its evaluation; we intend to return to the evaluation of contracts in the addendum to this book on the Internet.

The value of some resources can be negative, for example, the value of toxic waste: to dispose of toxic waste decrements the company's resources.

The value of the economic resources is often affected by economic events that are unknown at the time users of business applications want to estimate the value. For example, the precise value of goods on stock (the sale price) is unknown until the goods are sold. Therefore, the value of the economic resources must often be estimated, considering the entrepreneurial goals of the enterprise. Estimation of the value of the resources therefore encompasses considering the resources' transformation in the enterprise's value chain, and then estimating the price of a contract with a potential customer. As this is difficult to do in the real-world, most resources use two value attributes: cost and unit price, both substituting the real resource value.

### 1.10.2.3 Cost and Unit Price

The cost indicates the aggregated value of the decrement events from exchange processes directly or indirectly related to the resource. For example, maintenance (an economic event) increases the cost of equipment; more precisely, the cost of equipment is increased by the aggregated value of the economic resources that have been used and consumed during maintenance.

The cost of a resource is often affected by economic events that occur continuously and will be registered in the future (such as the heating of buildings). Therefore, various estimation methods are used to determine the approximate cost of the resource.

In some business applications, resources have attributes unit price or list price. They hold the suggested price of the resource in the sales process; more precisely, they determine the default price of the resource in sales contracts to unknown customers. Resource can have these attributes for convenience, but they are not an intrinsic part of the REA application model.

### 1.10.2.4 Modeling Ad Hoc Resources

A company might sometimes sell ad hoc resources or services that are not registered in their business applications. Some business applications allow for typing free text on an invoice, such as "miscellaneous," with a price. In this case the economic event has not been related to any resource, and, furthermore, the "miscellaneous" resource instance has not been created in the business application. This is an example of *modeling compromise*. This might be convenient in some software applications, but an application designer must be aware of its consequences. It would not possible to create reports on the "miscellaneous" resources, and the reports on "standard" products might be incorrect. A better solution would be to create a "miscellaneous" or "unspecified" resource group and relate it using the outflow to an economic event, see Fig. 52. This is also a *modeling compromise*, but the application will be more consistent, and allow for better reporting than by omitting the outflow relationship from the model.

Fig. 52. Miscellaneous or unspecified resource (modeling compromise)

### 1.10.2.5 Individually Identifiable Resources

Economic resource in the REA model is an actual unit, which reflects the fact that a real thing is produced, used, consumed, purchased or sold. The resources whose units are individually identifiable, have, or in principle may have, a serial number or its equivalent, see Fig. 53. The *IDENTIFICATION* behavioral pattern discusses this concept in detail.

Fig. 53. Individually identifiable resources

Whether the resources are individually identifiable is often a decision of the users of a business application. For example, Joe might decide that he does not want to keep track of each individual *Pizza*. In this case, the *Pizza* entity in Fig. 53 would represent a set of pizzas, such as the pizzas produced in a period of time, or other identifiable set, which Joe is interested in planning, monitoring and controlling. Screws and nails are other examples of the resources, which, in principle, are individually identifiable, but which users of business applications often do not want to plan, monitor and control individually. Such resources are modeled as resources with individually unidentifiable elements, described in the following section.

### 1.10.2.6 Resources with Individually Unidentifiable Elements

Resources such as money, bulk or fluid material, consist of individually unidentifiable elements; for example, molecules in gasoline or grains in pizza flour are not individually identifiable. Such resources are identified by the volumes of material in the scope of the economic events, such the volumes of material related to sales, production, and transportation. For example, the volume of gasoline produced during a certain time interval is identifiable, and flour is delivered in bags, which are identifiable. Packages of screws can be assigned unique numbers. There might be legal reasons to identify and register them – in the food and chemical industries it is usual to keep samples of raw materials from the delivered bags.

### Heating Oil as a Resource

Fig. 54 illustrates two REA models for supplying heating oil from a truck to a house tank. The upper part illustrates the heating oil supplier viewpoint; the bottom part illustrates the household (customer) viewpoint. The conversion processes in Fig. 54 model the movement of heating oil is from a truck into a house oil tank. The exchange processes model the sale (change of ownership) of the *Supplied Heating Oil*.

There are three identifiable instances of heating oil: *Heating Oil in Truck Tank*, *Supplied Heating Oil*, and *Heating Oil in House Tank*. *Supplied Heating Oil* is the oil that actually flows through the pipe from the truck to the house tank. It is a transient resource, consumed at the same time as it is created: the supplied heating oil is created by removing it from the truck's pipe, and it is consumed by mixing it with the oil already present in the house tank. After the supplied oil is in the house tank, it is not possible to distinguish the supplied oil that came from the truck from the oil that was already in the house tank.

### Money as a Resource

Coins and bills are identifiable entities; therefore, they are (actual) resources. Money in a bank account is also an (actual) resource, but it does not have individually identifiable elements. Therefore, coins and bills on one side, and money in a bank account on the other side must be modeled as different kinds of resources. Fig. 55 illustrates withdrawal of *Cash*, an exchange process between *Bank* and *Customer*; the *Customer* gives to the *Bank* an amount of *Money* from his bank account, and receives *Coins* and *Bills* in return. Some banks charge a fee for this transaction, which is also illustrated in Fig. 55. The increments and decrements are from customer's perspective.

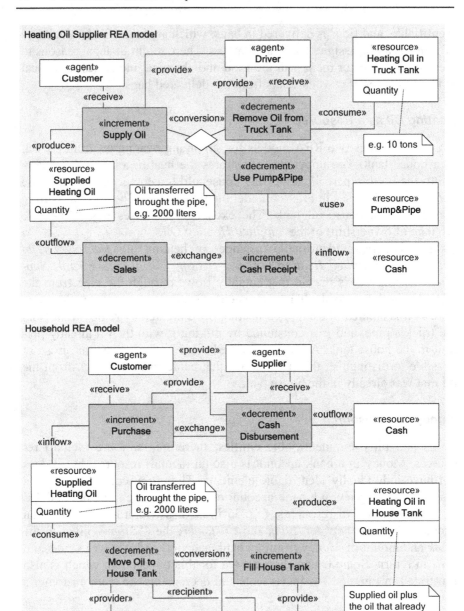

**Fig. 54.** Fluid materials as resources

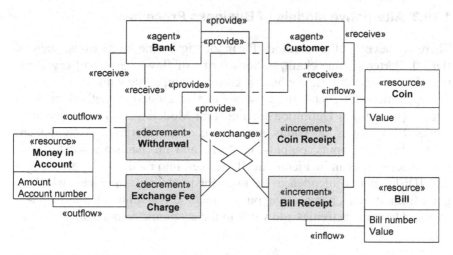

**Fig. 55.** Coins, bills, and money in an account as resources

### Labor as a Resource

We can think of labor instance as having a specific identity, which consists of the identity of the person providing the labor, and the time and place the labor is provided. A labor also has a length (acquired amount in hours or days) specified by the *Acquire Labor* event; this is similar to the volume of resources with individually unidentifiable elements.

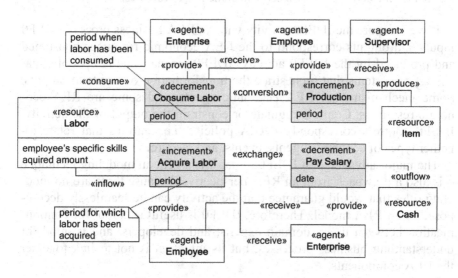

**Fig. 56.** Labor as a resource

### 1.10.3 Alternative Models of Business Processes

There are several other methods for modeling business processes, such as IDEF0, Porter's value chain, various forms of flow charts, and organization charts. Any of these methods is entirely compatible with REA.

Application designers could use a function modeling method, such as *IDEF0* (Integration Definition for Function Modeling, 1993), designed to model the activities, decisions, and actions of an enterprise. Activities are related by their inputs, outputs, controls, and mechanisms; see Fig. 57. IDEF0 activities can be hierarchically refined into models with greater detail. IDEF0 is not intended to be used for modeling sequences, which is good from an REA perspective; but the method is not intended to help understand how the activities add value to the economic resources.

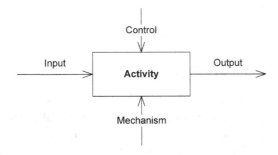

**Fig. 57.** IDEF0 activity is less specific than the REA Processes.

If we compare the IDEF0 activity with an REA business process, IDEF0 inputs and outputs correspond to the REA economic resources consumed and produced by the IDEF0 activity. IDEF0 mechanisms are people, machines, or systems that orchestrate the transformation of inputs to outputs. Some mechanisms are REA economic agents, and some are REA economic resources. Controls regulate or constrain the output of the activity. IDEF0 controls correspond to REA policies, i.e., entities that relate together types of economic agents, events, and resources.

The major advantage of IDEF0 – that it is a general modeling technique – is also a drawback from an REA perspective, because there are no modeling rules that would guarantee that the activity can be seamlessly decomposed to an REA model. Therefore, IDEF0 is useful as a tool for communication between users, domain experts, and developers, and is good for understanding business processes, but its intention is not to link together the REA components.

An application designer could use *flow charts* for modeling all business processes of the company. Flow charts, or its UML version called activity diagrams (UML 2.0 Superstructure Specification, 2005), focus on the order and sequencing of the activities. Creating such model is good for understanding the processes of the enterprise, but it is not at all suitable for designing a software application that should support many variants of sequences. If we could describe the purpose of each process instead of actual sequences of activities, the software application would increase its ability to adapt to changes. This way of modeling becomes increasingly important when the essence of the customer's business remains the same, but the technology the customer uses changes. You would like the application model to be robust against and easily adapt to new patterns of commerce, such as outsourcing, sub contracting, direct sales, and also patterns unknown today.

An application designer could use *organization charts*. Organization charts are good for expressing what resources managers and workers will control, execute, and monitor, but the model should focus rather on the flow of value in the transition of raw materials to a finished product.

An application designer could use *Porter's value chain* (Porter 1980). Porter's value chain is a tool and conceptual framework for examining and diagnosing the competitive advantage of a company. Although very useful as a modeling technique for business systems, the original purpose of Porter's value chain was not to design software business applications. Porter's value chain divides processes of a company into core business processes that add value to the end products of the enterprise, and support processes that enable the core processes and add value indirectly. In fact, *every* process adds value (otherwise a rational company would not have it), and the result of analysis should be a complete model expressing how every process contributes to the complete chain. Sometimes it makes sense to exclude a process from the value-adding chain, but you should make such decision as a modeling compromise *after* the analysis has been performed, rather than at the beginning of the analysis. Overall, Porter's value chain, by considering all known processes of the enterprise, is a good starting point in creating the REA model.

# 2 Structural Patterns at Policy Level

The previous section, Structural Patterns at Operational Level, described how to create REA-based application models that model economic exchanges that actually occurred.

This section focuses on REA application models that describe the general rules that govern what events should, could, or should not occur under certain conditions. The *COMMITMENT* pattern specifies which events economic agents agreed upon to occur in the future. The central patterns in this section are the *CONTRACT PATTERN* and the *SCHEDULE PATTERN*, that bind together commitments and terms, which instantiate additional commitments in case the agreed commitments have not been fulfilled. The *POLICY PATTERN* describes certain kinds of business rules, the rules or restrictions that the enterprise wants to apply to the economic events and commitments in which it participates. The *GROUP PATTERN* and the *TYPE PATTERN* introduce the essential infrastructure at the policy level, as the commitments are often related to types of resources instead of actual resources, and policies are typically applied to groups of entities instead of actual entities.

The patterns *LINKAGE*, *RESPONSIBILITY* and *CUSTODY* are not the essential part of the modeling infrastructure, but they are often needed by business logic as structural elements of the REA application model.

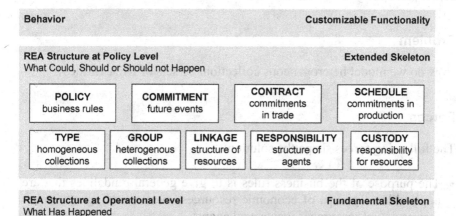

## 2.1  Group Pattern

*Often it does not make sense to talk about just actual instances such as "a copy of Lewis Carroll's Alice's Adventures in Wonderland," or "a copy of Linda Rising, and Mary Lynn Manns' Patterns for Introducing New Ideas"; we would like to talk about "items on the shelf"*

### Context

Business rules seldom refer to a specific instance, such as an actual customer or an actual item. For example, Joe's Pizzeria gives a 20% discount to the customers living in a specific geographic area. In principle, Joe can create an individual discount rule for every customer from this area. However, if Joe's Pizzeria has 100 customers from this area, then the business application would contain 100 rules, and they would all be the same. This is possible, but impractical. A better solution is to have one rule, and apply it to the entire set of these customers. However, the REA entities at operational level represent actual resources, events and agents; there is no concept representing sets or collections.

### Problem

How do we model heterogeneous collections or sets of REA entities?

### Forces

The following forces shape the solution:

- The purpose of the business rules is to give general guidelines that are applicable to groups of economic resources, events, and agents, rather than to actual resources, events, and agents.

- The REA model at operational level does not contain any entity that could naturally represent groups of things that share something in common.
- There are no restrictions on who the members of the group could be. Members of the same group do not need to have anything in common, except the fact that they belong to the same group. For example, there can be a group containing both economic events and resources. In other words, groups are heterogeneous collections.

## Solution

Introduce a *group* as a structural element of the REA application model. An REA entity *group* represents a set of REA entities that have something in common. The *group* entity is related to its members by a *grouping* relationship. Members of the group can be any entity in the REA model: resources, events, agents, commitments, claims, contracts, types, or other groups.

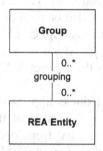

**Fig. 58.** Group and grouping

Grouping is a many-to-many relationship. An REA object can be a member of several groups simultaneously, and a group can have (and usually has) several members. There can be REA objects that do not belong to any group, and there can be a group that does not have any members (for example, there can be no books on the shelf).

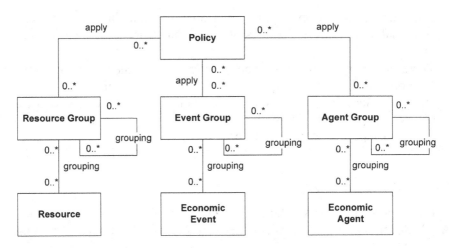

**Fig. 59.** Groups and their relationships to other REA entities

Fig. 59 illustrates some relationships between the *group* entity and other REA entities. *Policy* (see the *POLICY PATTERN*) can be related by an *apply* relationship to groups of events, agents, and resources. *Groups* can also be related to other groups; and they can also be members of other groups.

In the simplest cases, users of business applications maintain links between members and groups. For example, if a user creates a new catalogue item, he will also assign this item to the correct VAT (value added tax) group.

More sophisticated solutions let business applications determine what groups a member belongs to based on the value of the properties of the member entity. This functionality can vary from one application to another, and from one grouping to another. One possible implementation is *CLASSIFICATION PATTERN*, described in Part II, Behavioral Patterns. Another possible implementation is *BUDGET (not described in this book)*; a budget is a group of economic events or commitments that are expected to occur in the future.

## Examples

The group is an important element in specifying business rules. Groups can be used to classify resources into tax groups; trading partner groups can reflect their value to the enterprise; and employees can be grouped according to their skills. A budget is a group of events or commitments expected to occur in a well-defined time interval in the future. Customers can be high-volume and low-volume.

**Fig. 60.** Groups of products in MSN shopping

Fig. 60 illustrates examples of groups at http://shopping.msn.com. A product can belong to the groups *Home, Beauty, Books, Clothing, Computers, Deals, Electronics, Flowers* and others. The *Home* group has subgroup *Books & Magazines*, which has a subgroup *Children & Teen Books*, which has a subgroup *Juvenile Fiction*. A specific product can belong to several groups; for example, *Harry Potter and the Half-Blood Prince* by Rowling, J. K. is both a *Science Fiction, Fantasy, & Magic* and an *Action & Adventure* book.

## 2.2   Type Pattern

*Types are homogeneous groups; all their members conform to certain definitions, descriptions or blueprints*

### Context

Product catalogues often contain a description of the resources that a customer can buy, rather than actual resources. When customers place an order, they specify the parameters of the product; when a vendor successfully fulfills the order, he delivers an actual product that conforms to the parameters of the customer's order.

A similar story can be told for production. A recipe or blueprint contains the parameters, description, or definition of a product that is produced or a raw material that is consumed. When the production is successfully completed, products that match the blueprints are produced.

If you design a business application, you often need to create a model that contains catalogue-like descriptions of resources, events, and agents.

### Problem

In the REA application models, there is often need for an entity that holds the description or definition of a resource, an event, an agent, or another REA entity. However, the REA model at operational level does not have an entity that can naturally represent the catalogue-like description, definition, and blueprints.

### Forces

The following forces need consideration:

- Catalogue items describe economic resources, but they often do not refer to actual, unique items. It is also common that sales order lines refer to catalogue items specifying features of the resources, rather than specifying actual instances of goods.
- Business rules seldom refer to an actual instance, such as a physical customer or a physical item. The purpose of the rules is to give general guidelines that are applicable to certain types of economic resources, events, and agents, rather than actual resources, events, and agents.
- As similar entities share their features and properties, the model can be simplified by extracting the shared features and properties and moving them to another entity, which will be related to the entities that share the features or properties.

### Solution

Introduce an *Economic Resource Type, Economic Agent Type, Economic Event Type, Commitment Type,* and *Contract Type* as structural elements of the REA application model. They hold the definition or description of an economic resource, event, agent, commitment and contract, see Fig. 61.

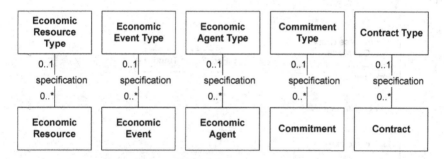

**Fig. 61.** REA types and REA entities

Conceptually, every REA entity has an REA type, but an REA application model does not need to contain the REA types if there is no need for it. Conversely, for a given REA type, there is no requirement for there to be an instance of this type. An REA entity and its type are related by a *specification* relationship. Resource types can be related by a *reservation* relationship to the commitments. Fig. 62 illustrates typical use of *Economic Resource Type.*

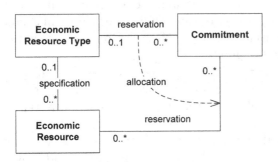

**Fig. 62.** Relationships between REA types

## Examples

A seat on a train with the following description "business class, non-smoking, window" is a resource type. The seat with "number 11 in car number 22 of train IC 129 from Copenhagen to Aarhus on   25 April 2005, departing at 9:00 hours from Copenhagen" is an implementation of this type.

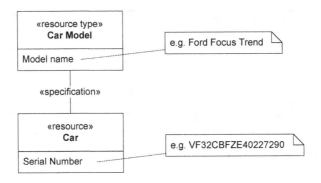

**Fig. 63.** Car model as a resource type

A specific car with serial number e.g. VF32CBFZE40227290 is an economic resource; its resource type is a definition or specification of this resource, such as Ford Focus Trend, see Fig. 63.

A labor type (see Fig. 64) is a qualification or set of standard skills required for a specific job. A labor instance is the qualification and the set of skills of a physical person. A work of a certified public accountant is a labor type. The work of accountant "Jette Friisdahl on 8 May 2005 from 8:30 a.m. to 11:30 a.m." is an implementation of this type.

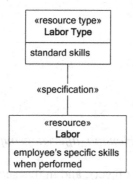

**Fig. 64.** Labor type and actual labor

## Resulting Context

In many business applications, the list of resource types should not be encoded into a business application; that is, the users of a business application should be able to add and remove resource types at runtime. For example, Navision Financials has an entity *Item*, representing all tangible resource types, and an entity *Work*, representing resource types similar to services.

Types enable users to add more business knowledge into a business application, something that has both benefits and drawbacks. The drawback is that the business knowledge in the software system needs maintenance. The benefit is that a software application that is aware of the business knowledge can more efficiently guide and help its users.

Sometimes we come across a situation in which a resource changes its type during its lifetime. The change of type is usually the result of a conversion process; therefore, we suggest modeling the type change as the consumption the resource of the old type and the production of a resource of the new type.

## 2.3  Difference Between Types and Groups

*All tomatoes are of the same type, but belong to different groups*

Types and groups both represent sets of objects, and in this sense types and groups are similar. However, information captured by a group and a type is different.

Groups are heterogeneous collections; they can contain members of different types, although their members might share some characteristics, for example, we might have a group of tomatoes that are all red.

Types are homogeneous collections; all members have the same characteristics defined by the type. A type is a special kind of group. It is a group that defines concepts and characteristics that apply to all current and future embodiments of the type.

The decision whether a specific collection should be modeled as a type or group often depends on its intended use in the REA model. In REA, groups are typically used to specify *policies*; policies are typically applied to groups. Types are typically used to specify *reserved resources* (in the cases the actual resources cannot be specified at the reservation time); commitments via reservation relationships are typically related to types.

An REA entity can be a member of several groups simultaneously, and can change its group and be removed from a group, usually as a result of the changing of values of its attributes, properties, methods or other characteristics. When an object changes its group, it does not change its definition, because it is defined by its type.

Groups, but seldom types, often contain properties for aggregated or statistical values derived from the properties of their members. For example, the group of tomatoes in a basket might contain a property for the total number, total weight, and average weight of the tomatoes in the basket.

## 2.4  Commitment Pattern

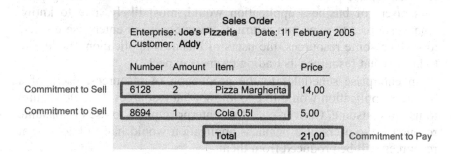

*Sales order lines are not economic events; they are promises of economic events*

### Context

Most economic events do not occur unexpectedly. Economic events are usually scheduled or agreed upon beforehand by economic agents. For example, a sales order line is a promise to sell goods to a customer; the total price is a customers' promise to pay for the goods, and the seller's promise to accept the payment.

### Problem

How do we model promises of future economic events?

### Forces

Solving this problem requires the resolution of the following forces:

- Application designers would like to have a mechanism in the application model specifying details about the promises of economic events. Economic events cannot be used for this, because economic events specify actual increments and decrements of resources, while promises result only in reservations of resources.
- There might be (and usually is) a difference between plans and what actually happens. The users of a business application would like to know

whether the economic events occurred as they were promised, and informed about eventual differences.

- If an enterprise promises to give its own resources to its trading partners, users of business application would, most likely, like to know, what resources to expect in return. Conversely, if an enterprise expects to receive some resources, the users of business application would like to know what resources its trading partners expect.
- If an enterprise schedules to the production of resources, users of a business application would like to know what resources it would require to use or consume. Conversely, if an enterprise plans to use or consume resources, the users of a business application would like to know what resources will be produced from them.
- The users of a business application would like to know who should be responsible for the received or produced resources, and who should be responsible for the resources used or consumed during the production or given to other economic agents.
- For each promised exchange, the users of a business application would like to know the trading partners to whom the resources should be transferred, and from whom they should be received.

## Solution

Model the promise of the economic event as a *commitment* entity. A *commitment in exchange processes* represents obligations of economic agents to provide or receive rights to economic resources. A *commitment in conversion processes* represents scheduled usage, consumption, or production of economic resources.

Each *commitment* is related to an *economic event* by a *fulfillment* relationship, representing the fact that commitments are fulfilled in the future by one or more economic events executed by the participating economic agents, see Fig. 65. Commitments have usually properties for the *Scheduled Date* or period of the economic event, and the *Scheduled Value* of the event.

The *Scheduled Value* does not need to be expressed as an actual number, but, for example, as a rule. For example, the price of a service can be determined according to actual costs.

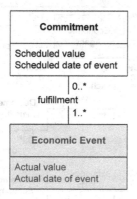

**Fig. 65.** Commitment and economic event

Each promised exchange and conversion consists of at least two commitments: *increment commitments*, which are expected to increase the value of economic resources, and are fulfilled by increment economic events, and their related *decrement commitments*, which are expected to decrease the value of economic resources, and are fulfilled by decrement economic events. The relationship between increment and decrement commitments identifies which resources are promised to be exchanged or converted to which others, and is called *exchange reciprocity* or *conversion reciprocity*.

Fig. 66 illustrates relationships between commitments, economic events, economic agents, and economic resources in exchange processes. Fig. 67 illustrates the same relationships in conversion processes.

### Provide and Receive

Commitments are related by the *provide* and *receive* relationships to the economic agents that are scheduled to participate in economic events, and they consequently determine *who* should have rights to or the control over economic resources. The *provide* and *receive* are one-to-many relationships. One economic agent can participate in zero or more commitments; an economic commitment must have exactly one committed provider and exactly one committed recipient economic agent.

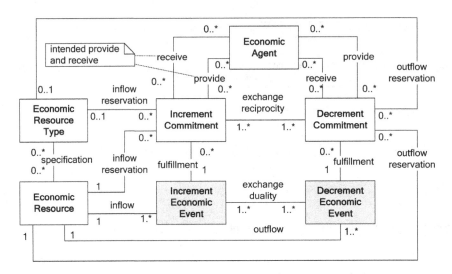

**Fig. 66.** Relationships of commitments in exchange process

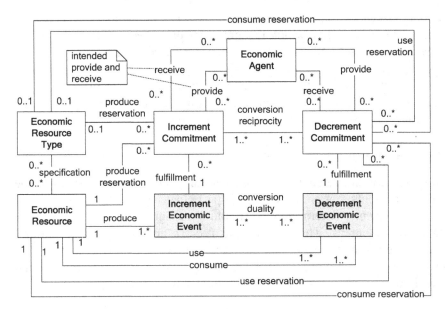

**Fig. 67.** Relationships of commitments in conversion processes

### Exchange and Conversion Reciprocity

The exchange reciprocity relationship between the increment and decrement commitments identifies in the model which resources are promised to be exchanged for which others. Likewise, the conversion reciprocity identifies which resources are promised to be used or consumed in order to produce others.

The commitments paired by the reciprocity relationship do not need to be instantiated (created at runtime) at the same time. For example, the insurance process illustrated in the Modeling Handbook contains an example of an increment commitment (insurance payment) that is instantiated only under certain conditions specified by the insurance contract. Another example is a commitment to buy shares of a company, paired with a reciprocal commitment of dividend payments. The two commitments are instantiated at different times.

### Fulfillment

The purpose of the fulfillment relationship is to validate whether the economic events fulfill their commitments.

This can often be done automatically. For example, the *RECONCILIATION PATTERN* (see Behavioral Patterns) can validate that quantity on the sales order line (i.e., the value of the commitment) is the same as the sum of the shipped quantities (values of the economic events).

Sometimes, a human decision is needed to determine whether the economic events fulfill their commitments. For example, if a payment commitment was fulfilled by payment in different currency, due to variable exchange rates the monetary value of the commitment can differ from the monetary value of the economic event. In such cases, a human decision might be needed to judge whether the difference is sufficiently small to consider the commitment fulfilled.

The fulfillment relationship is a many-to-many relationship between the economic commitment and the economic event. One economic commitment can be fulfilled by several economic events, just as one shipment commitment can be fulfilled by partial shipments, and one economic event can fulfill several economic commitments, just as several installments can be paid once.

### Reservation

In order to specify what resources will be needed or are expected by future economic events, each economic commitment is related to an economic resource or a resource type by a *reservation* relationship. For example, a sales order line is a decrement commitment to ship goods; the sales order line is related by the *outflow reservation* relationship to the goods or the goods type.

When sales persons accept customer orders, they want a business software application to check whether there are products available when the order is due, and to make sure that these products will be available to the customers during the economic event related to the economic commitment.

The reservation relationship between the resource and commitment represents the features of the resource and rights associated with the resource that will be changed or transferred by a future economic event, see Fig. 68.

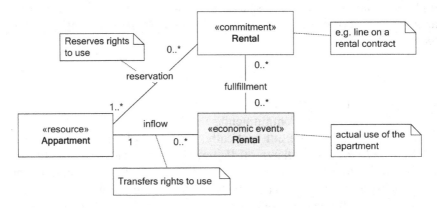

**Fig. 68.** Reservation

The commitment can be related to either a *resource type* or a *resource*. For example, a sales order for a new car contains a commitment to deliver a car of a certain model, (i.e., resource type); a sales order for a used car contains a commitment to deliver a physical car (i.e., resource). The reservation of a hotel room contains a commitment to provide a hotel room with certain characteristics, such as of a certain size and with certain number of beds (i.e., resource type); but sometimes a guest might require a specific room, in which case the commitment is related to an (actual) resource.

If economic commitment is related to resource type, at some point in the future, but always before the economic events starts, the commitment must also be related to an actual resource that conforms to the reserved resource type, see Fig. 69.

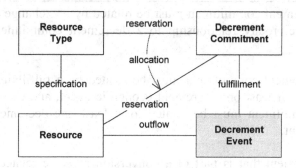

**Fig. 69.** A commitment must eventually be related to an actual resource

The time of allocation varies. For example, in the hospitality business, the reservation is related to a room specification until the day of the guest's arrival. The morning of the day of arrival, the receptionist assigns (a human assisted, and not an automated task) a room numbers for each reservation that starts that day. In the airline business, physical seats are assigned at the time of reservation, with the possibility of replanning. In theatres and cinemas, the tickets are assigned at the time of reservation. The algorithm first reserves the best seats within a certain price group, such as those in the middle of the theatre, and later reserves the seats closest to the best places.

We call the commitment fully specified if it is related by the reservation relationship to an (actual) resource.

## Domain Rules

The following domain rules apply to any REA application model. As commitments are a mirror image of the economic events at the policy level, the domain rules are similar to the rules for the REA model at operational level, with one addition: commitments must be fulfilled by economic events. These rules can be used to ensure consistency of REA application models.

> Each commitment must be related to a resource, and might (but does not have to) also be related to a resource type.
>
> Each commitment must be related by provide and receive relationships to economic agents.

> Each increment commitment must be related by a exchange or conversion reciprocity relationship to a decrement commitment, and vice versa.
>
> Each increment commitment must be related by a fulfillment relationship to at least one increment economic event, and each decrement commitment must be related to at least one decrement economic event.
>
> A commitment that is part of a conversion must be related to the economic event of a conversion process; likewise, a commitment that is part of an exchange must be related to an economic event of an exchange process.

## Resulting Context

The reciprocity relationship often has additional functionality that relates together the values of the increment and decrement commitments. For example, in economic exchanges, the reciprocity can calculate the total price (value of the outflow commitments) based on the line item prices (value of the inflow commitments). The reciprocity might also validate that the cost (value of the outflow commitments) is lower than the price (value of the inflow commitments). The functionality of the reciprocity relationship can vary in different implementations; but the fundamental point is that the increment and decrement commitments are related.

## 2.5 Contract Pattern

*Contracts are statements of intent that regulate the behavior among organizations and individuals. Clauses of a good contract define what should happen in the cases of cancellation and violation of the commitments*

### Context

Commitments represent the optimistic path of an exchange. For example, a sales order contains commitments to deliver goods and commitments to pay. However, sometimes goods are not delivered as expected and payments arrive late. Partners usually also agree upon what should happen if the initial commitments are unfulfilled.

### Problem

How do we specify in the REA model what should happen if the commitments are unfulfilled?

### Forces

We need to balance the following forces:

- Commitments specify what economic events should occur. However, in the case in which they do not occur as they should, economic agents usually agree upon what should happen next. The rules specifying what should happen next can be very complex, and keeping track of what should happen, and when, can be cumbersome. Therefore, application developers would like this information present in the business application, so that these rules and actions can be monitored and triggered automatically.

- There are usually several inflow commitments paired through exchange reciprocity with several outflow commitments. These commitments are often considered a unit. Sometimes, it does not make sense to fulfill only some commitments and not to fulfill others, but sometimes this is acceptable. Application designers would like some entity to contain such rules.
- Intended recipients or providers of the resources might be different economic agents than the agents that agree about the exchange.

## Solution

If a commitment is unfulfilled, the *terms* of a contract specify additional commitments.

A *Contract* is an entity in the REA application model containing *increment* and *decrement commitments* that promise an exchange of economic resources between economic agents, and *terms*. *Commitments* were discussed in the previous pattern. *Terms* are potential commitments that are instantiated if certain conditions are met. These conditions can be various, such as a commitment not being fulfilled, or a resource being at a certain location. For example, economic agents can agree upon penalties if the commitments are unfulfilled. If the commitments are unfulfilled, the contract will instantiate a new commitment to pay a penalty. The *terms* and *commitments* are the *clauses* of the contract

Every contract must be related to two or more economic agents by a *party* relationship. These agents do not necessarily have to be the provider and recipient of economic resources. The economic agents that are parties in a contract can be different from the economic agents related to the commitments within the same contract, and different from the agents participating in the economic events which fulfill these commitments. For example, a flower shop can deliver flowers to a different person than the one who placed the order, and the flowers will be paid for by a third person, different from the persons who placed the order and received the flowers.

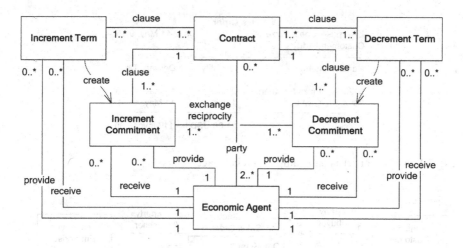

**Fig. 70.** Contract, commitments and terms

*Offer* and *Quote* have the same structure as contracts that have not been accepted by all parties in a contract. Economic agents negotiate the content of the commitments and terms, and when they agree upon commitments and terms, the quote or offer becomes a contract that binds the agents that are parties in the contract. There is usually certain period of negotiations and draft versions from when the offers and quotes are created and until the contracts are accepted by both contracting parties.

## Examples

Examples of contracts are sales orders, purchase orders, contracts for providing various services, and employment contracts. We illustrate several examples of contracts in the Part Four of this book, Modeling Handbook.

Fig. 71 illustrates a business document for a simple sales order without delivery and payment terms. The REA application model for this sales order is illustrated in Fig. 72. The *Sales Order* contains two *Sales Lines* specifying the goods; the sales line entity corresponds to the line item in Fig. 72. The *Payment Line* specifies the price (i.e. expected amount of received cash); the entity *Payment Line* corresponds to the *Total* line in Fig. 72.

| Sales Order | | | |
|---|---|---|---|
| Enterprise: **Joe's Pizzeria** | | | Date: 11 May, 9:15 |
| Customer: **Addy** | | | |
| Number | Item | Quantity | Delivery Time |
| 6128 | Pizza Margherita | 2 units | 11 May, 18:00 |
| 8694 | Cola 0.5l | 1 unit | 11 May, 18:00 |
| | **Total** | **21,00 USD** | 11 May, 18:30 |

**Fig. 71.** A sales order is an example of a contract

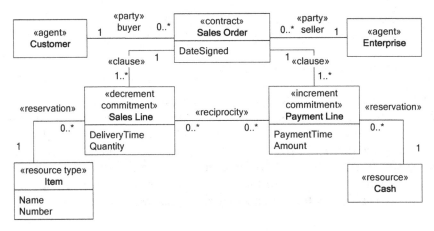

**Fig. 72.** The REA application model of a sales order

Fig. 73 illustrates an instance of this Sales Order (an actual sales order that conforms to the application model from Fig. 72; the data of this sales order corresponds to that in the example in Fig. 71.

Note that the REA model does not specify how to calculate *Total*, e.g. how the amount of 21 USD is related to two units of pizza and 0,5l of Cola. The calculation rules may range from a simple sum of the unit prices of the pizza and cola, to the complex rules taking into the account the identity of the customer, date, time, and volume of the sale. The fact that price calculation vary from one software application to another, is the reason why the price calculation is not part of REA. REA formulates the fundamental principles common to all business applications. Part II of this book, Behavioral Patterns, shows how to extend the REA skeleton by application specific functionality.

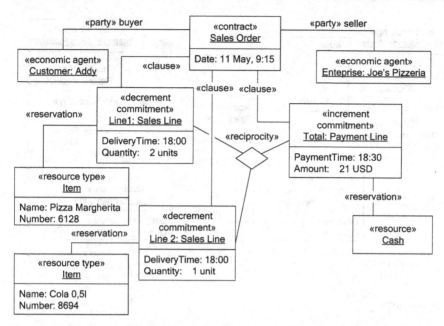

**Fig. 73.** An instance of the REA application model of a sales order

Fig. 74 illustrates a more complicated example of a sales order with shipment and payment terms. For example, Joe' Pizzeria and Addy agree that Joe's Pizzeria will sell five units of Pizza Margherita to Addy on Tuesday, and Addy will pay for them on Friday. If Joe's Pizzeria does not ship on Tuesday, Joe's Pizzeria pays a 20 USD penalty to Addy on Friday. If Addy does not pay on Friday, he pays a 30 USD penalty to Joe's Pizzeria the following Monday. The informally sketched properties of the terms and commitments can be implemented as *DUE DATE PATTERN* and *VALUE PATTERN*; see Part II, Behavioral Patterns.

If Joe's Pizzeria does not deliver 5 units of Pizza Margherita on Tuesday, the contract instantiates the penalty, and the model between Thursday and Friday looks as in Fig. 75.

After the Penalty Payment commitment has been instantiated, all commitments still need to be fulfilled by economic events. According to this contract, the Joe's Pizzeria still has to ship and the agent Addy has to pay, even in the case in which Joe's Pizzeria does not ship at all. A better contract might specify that the payment should occur within a certain time period from the shipment.

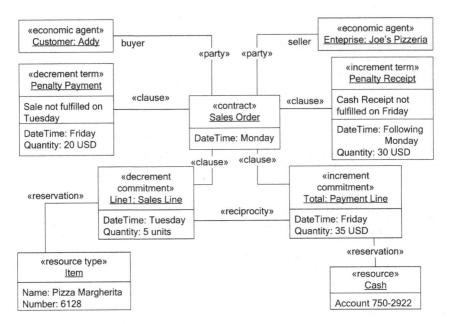

**Fig. 74.** Simple contract with shipment and payment terms

## Resulting Context

The precise specification of commercial contracts is a subject of intensive research. Simon Peyton-Jones, Jean-Marc Eber, and Julian Seward have developed a functional language for financial contracts; this language does not have an REA concept of reciprocity (Peyton-Jones, Eber 2003). A language for REA-compatible contracts is being developed by Fritz Henglein and his students (Henglein 2005).

There are also higher level *agreements* between economic agents that regulate the behavior of the individual contracts. *Agreements* differ from contracts in that they do not contain commitments, but only conditional clauses, and they are hierarchical in nature. Agreements are sketched in Fig. 76.

An example of an agreement is a service level agreement for maintenance of equipment, which specifies, for example, that the enterprise may place maintenance orders (i.e. contracts) under specific conditions, and receive discounts for specific services.

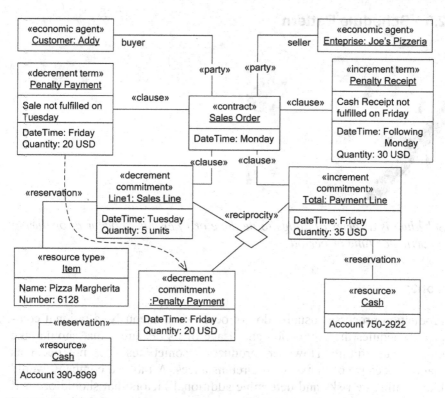

**Fig. 75.** Simple contract after one of the terms' conditions has been met

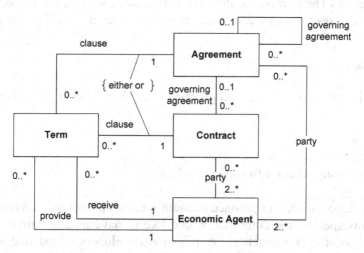

**Fig. 76.** Agreement and contract

## 2.6  Schedule Pattern

*Schedule is a series of things to be done or of events to occur at or during a particular time or period*

### Context

Production processes usually do not occur spontaneously; a rational company schedules the production and usage of its resources that should take place in the future. However, production sometimes does not occur as planned because of unexpected circumstances. A rational company would like to mitigate risks and determine additional factors that should occur if the originally planned operation does not occur as expected. Making a plan is a way to minimize the risks of missing some resources in the middle of a production. The purpose of the plan is to make sure that for all processes the needed resources are identified, as well as when they will be needed.

### Problem

How do we specify conversion processes that should occur in the future?

### Forces

The following forces influence the solution:

- If use, consume, and produce economic events do not occur as commitments specify, the enterprise would like to have an alternative plan to mitigate the consequences. Application developers would like this information present in the business application.

- A conversion process usually consists of several use, consume, and produce economic events that have various, often complex dependencies on each other. If some of these events do not occur as committed, the mitigation plan depends on a combination of the values of the economic events. The application model should contain an entity containing such dependencies.
- The economic agents that are responsible for the overall conversion process can be different from the agents that control the economic resources.

## Solution

A *schedule* is a collection of *increment* and *decrement commitments* in conversion processes and *mitigation plans*. Mitigation plans instantiate additional commitments under certain conditions, typically if some of the original commitments are unfulfilled, see Fig. 77. Unlike invoking penalties in the contracts, instantiating commitments from mitigation plans is usually not an automated task, and it requires the assistance of the users of business applications.

A schedule is related by a *party* relationship to the economic agents that are responsible for the schedule. The agents that are related to the schedule can be different from the agents that are related to the commitments. There are usually two agents related to the schedule. One of the agents sets the requirements of what should be done (representing a client in the planning process), and another agent is responsible for the actual conversion, (representing the supplier in the planning process).

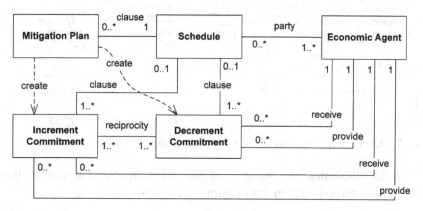

**Fig. 77.** Schedule

## Example

The example in Fig. 78 illustrates a simple schedule of a project *Produce Pizza*, assigned to Tom, Susie, and Mike. Project *Produce Pizza* is an increment commitment, and the consumption of the labor of *Tom*, *Susie*, and *Mike* are decrement commitments.

| ID | Task | Resources | Duration | 11 February 2005 | | | | | | | | | | | | |
|----|------|-----------|----------|---|---|---|----|----|----|----|----|----|----|----|----|
| | | | | 7 | 8 | 9 | 10 | 11 | 12 | 13 | 14 | 15 | 16 | 17 | 18 |
| 1 | Produce Pizza | | 10h | ██████████████████████ | | | | | | | | | | | |
| 2 | Dough | Tom | 1h | ██ | | | | | | | | | | | |
| 3 | Toppings | Susie | 3h | ██████ | | | | | | | | | | | |
| 4 | Baking | Mike | 4h | | | | | | | | ████████ | | | | |

**Fig. 78.** A simple schedule

The REA application model corresponding to the diagram in Fig. 78 is illustrated in Fig. 79. The schedule *Project Schedule* has an increment commitment *Project*, which reserves (expects) the economic resource *Pizza*. The decrement commitment *Task* reserves consumption of the economic resource *Labor*. The properties start, finish, and duration can be implemented as *DUE DATE PATTERN*; see Part II, Behavioral Patterns.

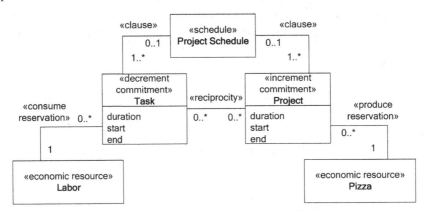

**Fig. 79.** REA application model for simple schedule

Fig. 80 illustrates an instance of the REA application model from Fig. 80 that corresponds to the example in Fig. 78.

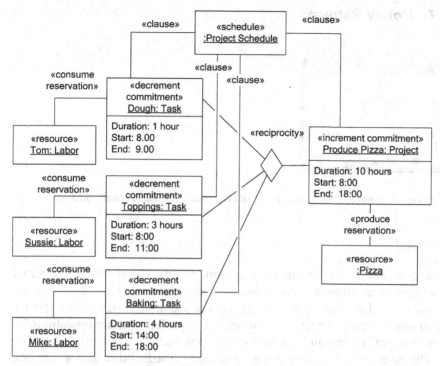

**Fig. 80.** An instance of the REA application model of a schedule

There are many examples where the detailed schedule means success or failure for the whole company. In just-in-time production, the resources are delivered exactly when they are needed. Delivery too early would mean a need for storage and late delivery can stall the production.

## 2.7   Policy Pattern

*A policy is a rule of practice or procedure to guide decisions and actions*

### Context

Not everything is allowed; law, system, tradition, culture, and internal company rules constrain the economic exchanges or conversions that are possible or desirable in any situation. For example, rules might specify what qualification of employees is needed to perform certain operations, or what kind of equipment is needed to transport hazardous materials.

The rules and constraints can be specified in media other than a software application, for example, in a policy handbook that users of business applications have to study. However, it would be more efficient and useful if a software application could be aware of the rules and constraints, and help users act upon them. For example, if a user tries to register or orchestrate an event that does not conform to the rules, the business application could inform the user of the rule violation, advise him on what to do instead, and prohibit him from committing or executing an illegal exchange or conversion.

The REA application model specifies the economic events, agents, and resources applicable to a certain line of business. Using the core REA application model, users of business applications can plan and register any kind of economic event that is part of the application model. The core REA model alone does not have a placeholder for rules governing what types of economic events are allowed or not allowed in certain situations.

### Problem

How do you make the business application aware of the fact that some economic events are not allowable or desirable in certain circumstances, and even prevent users from doing something illegal?

## Forces

We need to balance the following forces when modeling such rules:

- The users of business applications, without the help of an application designer, should themselves be able to create and modify the rules about the allowability of economic events.
- Business rules are not localizable into a single entity because they represent constraints that affect several entities. However, these rules must be part of some entity in the model.
- Although constraints are not localizable into a single entity, their implementation should not be scattered across entities in the application. There should be a single place in the model to hold the rules. It should be easy to find and document the rules in the system. Likewise, if an entity is affected by some rule, it would be nice to easily identify all rules that affect this entity. For example, it should be easy to determine what rules apply to a given customer group.
- As the software application needs to interpret the rules, they should be represented in the language at the same level of abstraction as the software application. If the application model is an object-oriented model, then rules should also be represented in terms of objects and relationships, and not, for example, as free text. If the model is represented in a domain-specific language determined by a framework, the rules should also be represented in the domain specific language, and not, for example, as code in a general purpose language.
- The software application with rules should be open to extensions. For example, existing rules on customers should not be affected by adding a new customer group.
- If the rules change, the software application should be able to keep the old version of the rules, and also to execute the business logic according to the old rules. For example, there is sometimes a need to register economic events that occurred before the rules changed; such a registration should be processed according to the previous version of the rules.

## Solution

The *policy* entity encapsulates constraints on the economic exchanges and conversions. The policy is related to (can be applied to) a *group*; see Fig. 81.

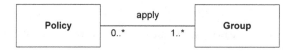

**Fig. 81.** Policy

An example of the REA application model with a Sale Policy is Fig. 82. The *Sale Policy* can be applied to *Item Group*, *Event Group*, and *Customer Group*. This policy can specify that, for all *Events* related to specific *Items* and to specific *Customers*, certain rules apply. An instance of this policy is given in Fig. 83.

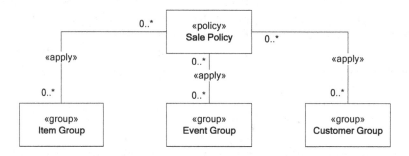

**Fig. 82.** Policy in the REA application model

Policies should be related to the entities at the policy level, i.e., to the groups or types, rather than to the entities at the operational level. Policies related to the groups or types have more explanation power than policies related to the actual entities, and allow for reasoning about the policy. For example, if *Addy* is a customer of *Joe's Pizzeria*, which introduces a policy *We do not sell to Addy,* this policy includes no explanation. However, if the enterprise introduces a policy *We do not sell to people who have mis-behaved several times*, and *Addy* belongs to this group, this policy explains the reason.

Sometimes it might seem that there is a specific policy affecting only a specific resource, event, or agent. In these cases, the solution in Fig. 81 leads to creating a group with only one member. Although this might be considered an unnecessary complication, this model forces an application developer to generalize the policies, and other entities that belong to this group are typically discovered later.

## Examples

Consider the policy specifying that an enterprise is not allowed to supply tobacco products to minors. The *Supply Policy* "Tobacco to Minors" is applied to the *groups* "Tobacco Products," "Supply," and "Minors." Fig. 84 illustrates that if a user of the business system attempts to register an instance of the *Sale* economic event with "*PM Box*" as an *Item* and "*Addy*" as a *Customer* (illustrated by dashed lines), the policy would be enforced; thus, the sale would not be allowed.

What would really happen in the business application depends on the implementation of the policy. The system response could range from notifying the user of the business system about the violation of the policy (by raising an information event) to preventing him from registering the event.

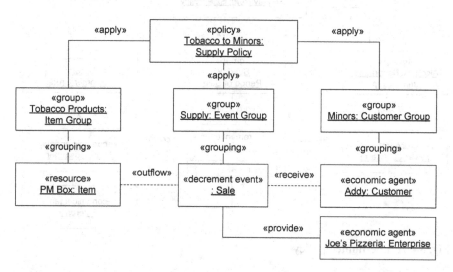

**Fig. 83.** A policy

There are policies applicable only during certain time intervals. For example, the *Sunday Rule* policy specifies that the *Joe's Pizzeria* does not sell alcoholic beverages on Sundays. The REA application model in Fig. 84 contains a group *Period of Sale*, representing a group of moments in time. The *Period of Sale* has the value "Sunday," and *Item Group*, has the value "Alcoholic Beverages," and they are related to the *Sale Policy* entity. If Joe's Pizzeria attempts to sell an item that belongs to the group "Alcoholic Beverages" and the time of sale belongs to "Sunday," the policy would be enforced. Please notice that the *Sunday Rule* policy is not related to the *Customer Group*, which means that it applies to all customers.

This example also illustrates that if a policy becomes obsolete, the users of the business application can easily restrict its validity in time, rather than deleting the policy. As the economic events are always registered after they have occurred, this practice enables the users to enforce the policy on the events that occurred when the policy was still in force, although the events have been registered after the policy became obsolete. Of course, in such cases it is not practical for the business application to prevent users from registering the events that violate the policy, as they already occurred, but the business application might notify the users that the policy has been violated.

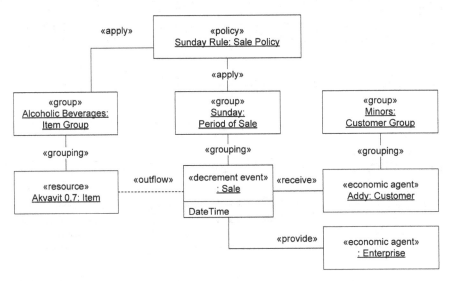

**Fig. 84.** A time-limited policy

Another example of a policy is "A junior bookkeeper cannot approve a payment over $50,000." This policy would be related to the groups "Junior Bookkeeper," "Payment," and "Over $50.000".

The functionality of the policy entity can be implemented in various ways. One possible implementation is a behavioral pattern called *MATRIX RULE* (not included in this book, but sketched below), which can be used to implement policies. The name "matrix rule" comes from a representation of this rule in the form of matrix, in which the columns represent the groups and the rows represent the different policies that apply to these groups. The matrix representation of the policy is illustrated in Table 1.

**Table 1.** A matrix representation of the matrix rule

| Period of Sale Value | Resource Group Value | Event Group Value | Event Group Value | Agent Group Value | Result |
|---|---|---|---|---|---|
| All | Tobacco | All | Supply | Minor | Not allowed |
| All | All | Over $50.000 | Payment | Junior Book-keeper | Not allowed |
| Sunday | Alcoholic beverages | All | All | All | Not allowed |

## Resulting Context

This pattern expresses rules in the form of relations, instead of code. Therefore, users of business applications can add more rules, and modify and remove existing ones without modifying code.

It is easy to determine which policies apply to a specific entity by identifying the groups of which this entity is member, and traversing the relationships between the groups and policies.

The architecture of the business application must support adding new groups and policies and relating them at run time. If the actual implementation of a business application does not support it, or if the business application has only one or very few policies, and they are not going to be changed and no new ones added, then this pattern does not apply. The models described in this book allow for adding new groups and policies, but not new group types and policy types. For example, if the application model contains a policy called Sale Policy, users of the business application can add, modify, and remove various Sale Policies. However, the users of business applications cannot add a policy of type Purchase Policy because it would require modifying the application model. We made that choice because the model with the entities Customers, Vendors, etc. is easier to explain than a more general model that would allow for dynamic modifications.

Users of a business application need to identify the right groups; otherwise, they cannot specify the policies. The information necessary to evaluate the policy must be in the system. For example, if there is a policy not to supply alcoholic beverages to people under a certain age, the age of the buyer must be in the system.

We need to consider the intended results of the individual policies, and to establish the infrastructure that supports these results. The results of policies always prohibit some events, but they can be implemented with varying levels of enforcement, from notifying the user of the application to preventing him from executing the prohibited action.

A policy entity does not have to be related to groups of commitments, as information about whether the commitments conform to the policy can be derived from the policies applied to groups of economic events.

## 2.8 Linkage Pattern

*If you build a house, what are you going to build it out of?*

### Context

Some economic resources, such as gasoline, are homogeneous units, but some consist of parts. Parts of the economic resources are also often economic resources. A bicycle consists of a frame and wheels, and a wheel consists of a tire, hub, a rim, and spokes. For scheduling a conversion process, it is useful to specify the parts of an economic resource consists.

### Problem

How do we capture in the REA model information about the structure of the economic resources?

### Forces

Three forces drive the solution to this problem:

- Many resources can be considered as consisting of parts. However, including a new "part" entity in the REA modeling framework is not a good solution, because parts are economic resources as well.
- There can be multiple levels of decomposition. A part can consist of parts, which again can consist of parts.
- Hierarchical structure between parts exists at both the operational and the policy level. Users of business applications would like to specify the parts an actual economic resource consists of, as well as the parts a re-

source type should consist of. A resource type can consist of multiple instances of the same type, just as bicycle consists of two wheels (and other parts).

## Solution

The structure of a resource can be captured by the *linkage* relationship; see Fig. 85. Linkage exists at two levels of abstraction. The *linkage* relationship between economic resources specifies their actual structure. The *linkage type* between economic resource types specifies the bill of material, a compositional structure that characterizes all resources of the type.

An economic resource that contains other resources is called *parent*, and economic resources contained in the other resources are called *components*. This terminology (inconsistent with the terminology used in object-oriented software) has been standardized by the American Production and Inventory Control Society (APICS) (Arnold 1998).

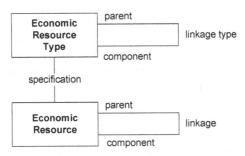

**Fig. 85.** Linkage

Linkage and linkage type are many-to-many relationships. A resource can be used as a component in zero or more other resources, and a resource can consist of zero or more other resources.

Like many other REA relationships, the linkage and linkage types relationships also have properties. The *Quantity Required* property of linkage type specifies how many components a parent should consist of, and the *Quantity Used* property of linkage specifies how many components the parent actually consists of.

Linkage type can be seen as a recipe to perform the transformation of resources. A linkage type contains information about the structure of materials and the tasks necessary to perform a transformation. A schedule adds actual time intervals to this structure, and links it to actual resources and economic agents that would be responsible for the transformation.

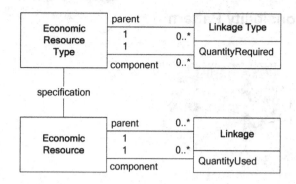

**Fig. 86.** Linkage in detail

There might exist several linkage types for an economic resource, which basically means that we might have several recipes to produce the resource. For a given schedule, we must specify both the resource and the linkage type we are planning to use for the transformation.

## Examples

*Bill of Material.* A bill of material states precisely how much of each resource must be used or consumed to produce a given amount of another resource, and perhaps even in what order.

*Work Breakdown Structure.* A work breakdown structure is similar to bill of material, but specifies activities or tasks necessary to perform a larger task or project.

## Resulting Context

Business applications with linkage relationships can report on the variations between the recipes and described procedures and the actual production runs.

Users of business applications are expected to modify the linkage type relationships over time to improve the transformation processes. This might lead to the requirement in business applications for recording the history of the changes of the linkage type relationship.

Sometimes it is not worth standardizing all the tasks in a work breakdown structures. In some business situations it is easier to specify the expected result (an economic resource type), and to rely on humans to do what they know best.

## 2.9   Responsibility Pattern

*Responsibility is a capacity for decisions, thoughts or actions*

### Context

In many cases, an economic agent is responsible for other economic agents. For example, a manager is responsible for the employees in his organization, and the enterprise is responsible for the actions of its subsidiaries.

### Problem

How can we represent responsibility between economic agents in the REA application model?

### Forces

The solution needs to balance the following forces:

- An economic agent can change its responsibility to other economic agents independently of the exchange or conversion processes with which it is involved. For example, employees can change their reporting relationships during their employment.
- Responsibility often determines the organizational structure of a company. Employees report to their managers, who report to *their* managers, and so on. However, there can be multiple organizational hierarchies. In some organizations, employees reporting to their department manager (this is often called "solid line reporting"), are simultaneously members of a team and report also to a team leader (this is often called "dashed line reporting").

- Organizational structures significantly vary from one company to another. Many organizations consist of divisions, departments, and teams, but there are a number of different organizational structures. The reasons for an the organizational structure are practical, such as a certain limit of how many direct reports a manager is able to coordinate, rather than things that can be derived from domain rules.
- The organizational structures as departments and teams can be independent of the reporting relationships. A manager can establish several teams from his direct subordinates, and there can be members of a single team that report to different managers.

## Solution

The *responsibility* relationship between economic agents describes a dependency between two economic agents, in which the superordinate agents are responsible for the economic events in which the subordinate agents participate, see Fig. 87.

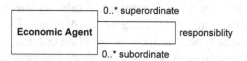

**Fig. 87.** Responsibility

Responsibility can be used to model the *reporting* relationship that forms the organizational structure of the enterprise.

Organizational units such as departments and teams are more or less arbitrary sets of economic agents, and we can model them in the REA application model as groups. The fact that an economic agent is a member of an organizational unit is modeled as a *grouping* relationship. The grouping relationship can also be applied between groups and models the hierarchical structure of the organizational units; see Fig. 88.

Responsibility can also be used to model *assignment*, a relationship describing, for example, that a salesperson is assigned to specific customers, or a purchaser is assigned to specific vendors.

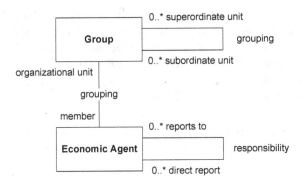

**Fig. 88.** Organizational units

## Resulting Context

The responsibility relationship is not sufficient for modeling all aspects of organizational structures. For example, a concept such as an open position can be modeled as a labor type. Therefore, modeling the organizational structure of a company requires creating an REA model for the company that includes labor, labor type, and labor acquisition contract. This explains why organizational structures differ so much from one organization to another; and why the full model of the organizational structure encompasses several REA concepts.

## 2.10 Custody Pattern

*Warehouse personnel have the custody of the goods in the warehouse*

### Context

Many companies make their employees responsible for specific resources. Such information is useful if something happens to the resources and we need to contact someone able to take care of the situation. This responsibility does not directly imply any exchanges of resources, tasks, or labor the employee performs with the resources he is responsible for; such cases would be modeled as commitments or economic events. We talk about general responsibility for things, such as cashiers in a shop responsible for the cash in the cash register, or warehouse clerks responsible for the goods stored in a warehouse.

### Problem

In the REA framework, how do we model the responsibilities of economic agents for specific economic resources?

### Forces

Application developers may need to address the following forces:

- Some economic agents are responsible for economic resources. If this responsibility is related to exchanges or conversions, it could be modeled as an economic event. However, there are cases in which this responsibility has a longer term, and is not related to individual exchanges or conversions.

- If something happens to specific economic resources, the users of business applications would like to get information about who to contact or hold responsible for the resources.
- The economic agent responsible for the resources can be different from any of the agents involved in conversions or exchanges. For example, a manager of a gas station is responsible for the gas in the underground tanks, although replenishing it is done by supply personnel, and dispensing it is done by customers in self-service gas stations.
- There can be responsibility for a specific resource shared among several economic agents.

## Solution

The responsibility for economic resources is modeled in the REA framework as a *custody relationship* between an economic agent and an economic resource (when an individual agent is responsible for an individual item), between an economic resource group and an economic agent group (when a group of agents has shared responsibility for a group of resources), between an economic resource group and an economic agent (when an individual agent is responsible for a group of resources), or between economic resource and economic agent group (when a group of agents has shared responsibility over an individual resource); see Fig. 89.

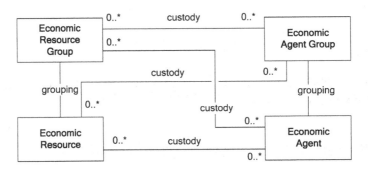

**Fig. 89.** Custody

## Examples

The model in Fig. 90 specifies that warehouse managers should have responsibility for the goods in the warehouse. *Warehouse Managers* is a group of economic agents (even if the group has only one member, as we explained in the chapter on groups and types). The *Items in Warehouse* is the group of items that physically are located in the warehouse.

The custody type implies that there will be a specific custody link from every internal agent instance in the group *Warehouse Managers* to every item instance is in the group *Items in Warehouse*.

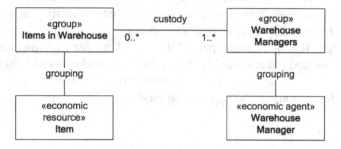

**Fig. 90.** Custody of an economic agent to group of resources.

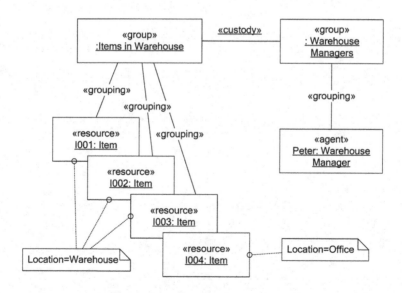

**Fig. 91.** Custody at runtime

The model in Fig. 91 illustrates instances of three *Items*, *I001*, *I002*, and *I003*, that have their location at the warehouse, and a *Warehouse Manager Peter* has custody over these items, because he belongs to the group *Warehouse Managers*. *Peter* does not have custody over the item *I004*, which does not have location in the warehouse, and therefore does not belong to the group *Items in Warehouse*.

## Resulting Context

The concept of custody allows users of business applications to plan, monitor, and control the economic agents that have responsibility for specific economic resources. For example, they can identify the economic agent that has custody over a specific resource.

Custody is not an essential part of the model, as, for example, economic event is. If custody is not used by business logic, and users of business applications are not interested in this information, it is simpler (i.e., better) not to model custody in the application model.

# 3 An REA-Based Example Application

*By Christian Vibe Scheller*

In this chapter I will show you just how easy it is to use REA for developing software applications. I will do so by developing a simple order website, where Joe's customers can order pizzas. The finished webpage will look like this:

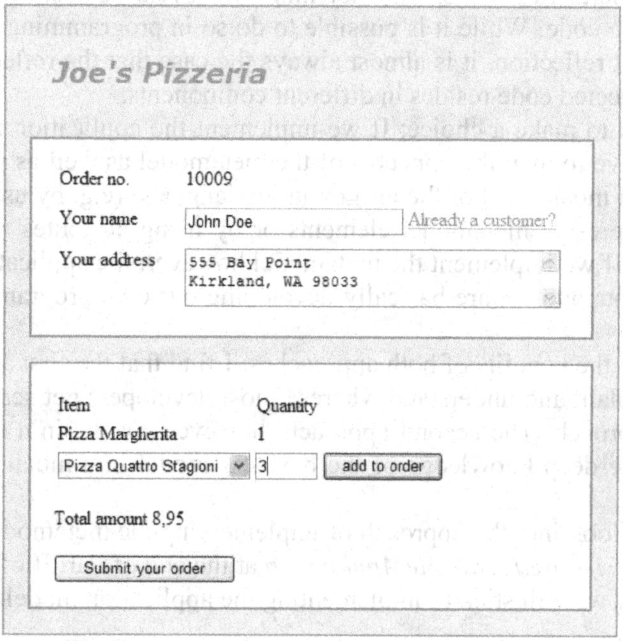

**Fig. 92.** Joe's web shop

The customer enters his order by first entering his name and address. This allows Joe's Pizzeria to know where to deliver the pizzas and to whom. If the customer is already registered in the system, he can press the link labeled "already a customer?" This will cause the web page to display the customer's address without the customer having to type it himself.

The customer proceeds to enter his order by specifying which pizzas he wants to order and how many. The web page responds by calculating the total amount the customer has to pay for the order.

Finally, the customer presses the submit button. Only then will all the order information be stored in the database. In a real web application the customer would then have to specify credit card information, etc., but we will skip this part for the sake of simplicity.

## 3.1    Representing the Metamodel

A special concern when implementing an application based on the REA model is that the REA model exists on two separate levels of abstraction (the application model and the metamodel).

As a general rule we should not mix two levels of abstraction in the same source code. While it is possible to do so in programming languages that support reflection, it is almost always the case that the reflection code and the reflected code resides in different components.

We need to make a choice: If we implement the application model, we will just have to map the concepts of the metamodel as well as possible to the existing metamodel of the programming language (e.g. by using inheritance to represent metamodel elements or by using attributes to describe metadata). If we implement the metamodel however, the application model becomes data and we are basically developing our own programming language.

I can see the benefits of both approaches: I find that the first approach is easy to explain and understand whereas most developers get scared by the second approach. The second approach, however, results in a model that captures the deep knowledge of the business model in a much more profound way.

We will look into the approach of implementing the metamodel in chapter *An Aspect-Based Example Application* at the end of Part II of this book, but for now we will stick to implementing the application model.

## 3.2    Component Model

Let us start out by defining the components that we want to build our application from. The dependencies between the different components are shown in Fig. 93.

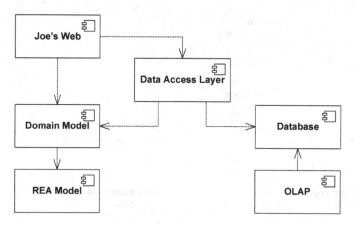

**Fig. 93.** Component model of the REA sample application

*REA model* defines the underlying REA model. Classes such as Order and Customer will inherit from base classes defined in this component. The REA model component will be designed with reusability in mind, so it can be reused in other REA-based applications.

*Domain model* contains all the entities that make up Joe's Pizzeria. In a real-life application the domain model would contain everything including purchase, production, salaries, etc., but in our small sample application we will only model sales orders and customers. We will make the design rule that all classes in the domain model must inherit from one of the base classes in the REA model component.

*Joe's Web* is the actual web site that the customers will be visiting when they want to order pizzas. Joe's web consists of a number of web pages running on a web server. As a design rule we will not put any business logic directly in this component. All the business logic will instead be placed in the domain model and REA model components.

*Data Access Layer* is responsible for retrieving objects from the database as well as storing objects in the database. The process of transforming a domain object to its database equivalent is often referred to as O/R mapping. While O/R mapping tools exist, in the case of this simple web application we will just be writing the code ourselves.

*Database* is where the data (orders, customers, etc.) gets stored. The database is the only persistent component in the application, so if we want our data to be available over time we need to put it in the database.

*OLAP* – In our sample application we would like to provide Joe with all kinds of information about his business: What kinds of pizzas are the most popular? Are sales going up or down? Etc. In my opinion an OLAP cube is the ideal tool for this kind of information.

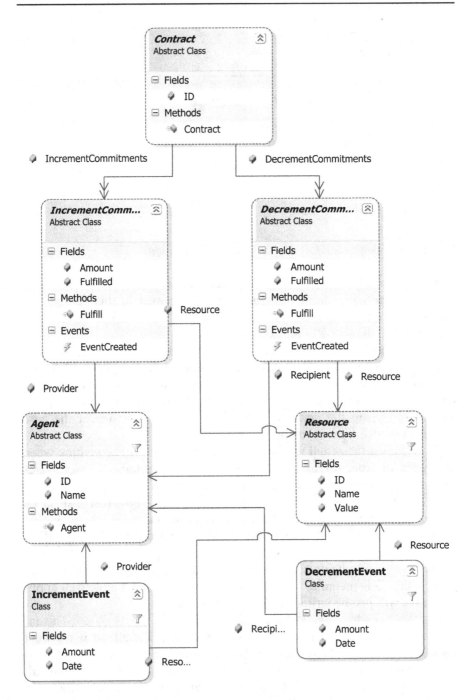

**Fig. 94.** REA Model Component

## 3.3 The REA Model Component

Fig. 93 shows the REA model that we will be basing our application on. As can be seen, the model is not a complete REA model. This is because we don't need concepts such as duality in our sample application. The simplification of the REA model is a pattern in itself called *MODELING COMPROMISE*.

Each object in the REA model is defined as an abstract base class. When we later define our domain model, each of the domain objects is going to inherit from one of these base classes. The exception to this rule is the Event class, which does not have a domain counterpart.

As can be seen from the diagram, the *Agent* class has two fields. The first field is the *ID* which is a unique identifier for the *Agent* class. The main purpose of the *ID* field is to identify the agent record in the database as well as to solve the ambiguity that would otherwise occur if two agents were to have the same name. The *Name* field is also a kind of identifier of the agent but it is less strict than the *ID* in that it is not necessarily unique. On the other hand the *Name* is the identifier that humans use: "Did John Doe receive his pizzas?" Joe might ask. Anyway, here is the code:

```
public abstract class Agent {
    public int ID;
    public string Name;
}
```

Just like agents, *Resources* contain an *ID* and *Name*. In addition a resource has a *Value* which is defined as the value in US dollars of a single unit of the resource, i.e., the price of a single pizza:

```
public abstract class Resource {
    public int ID;
    public string Name;
    public double Value;
}
```

The *Contract* class contains an *ID* field and two collections: A collection of increment commitments and a collection of decrement commitments.

```
public abstract class Contract {
    public int ID;
    public List<IncrementCommitment> IncrementCommitments = ...
    public List<DecrementCommitment> DecrementCommitments = ...
}
```

First of all it is worth noting that the *Increment Commitment* class, unlike the Agent, Resource and Contract classes, does not have an ID. This is because commitments do not have identities – after all what is the difference between receiving ten dollars and receiving five dollars and then another five dollars? Another thing worth noting is that the commitment classes contain a fulfillment mechanism:

Once a certain commitment is fulfilled, the application can call the commitment object's *Fulfill()* method. This will cause the commitment to change its *Fulfilled* field to *true* and will also cause the commitment to generate an economic event based on its own information. Since the commitment itself does not know what to do with this economic event, it will pass it to the calling application using the *EventCreated* delegate.

```
public abstract class IncrementCommitment {
    public Resource Resource;
    public double Amount;
    public Agent Provider;
    public bool Fulfilled = false;
    public event IncrementEventCreatedHandler EventCreated;

    public void Fulfill() {
        Fulfilled = true;
        IncrementEvent e = new IncrementEvent(this);
        EventCreated(e);
    }
}
```

Basically, *decrement commitments* are identical to increment commitments except they have a recipient instead of a provider. While writing this chapter I was debating with Pavel whether decrement and increment commitments should actually be modeled as different classes or if they should rather be merged into a single generic commitment class. In the end we decided that the semantic difference between the two types of commitments is so important to the whole REA model that they should be kept separate.

The *Increment Event* and *Decrement Event* will be generated by the REA model component whenever a commitment is marked as fulfilled by calling its *Fulfill()* method.

```
public class IncrementEvent {
    public DateTime Date;
    public Resource Resource;
    public double Amount;
    public Agent Provider;

    public IncrementEvent(IncrementCommitment commitment) {
        Date = DateTime.Now;
        Resource = commitment.Resource;
```

```
        Amount = commitment.Amount;
        Provider = commitment.Provider;
    }
}
```

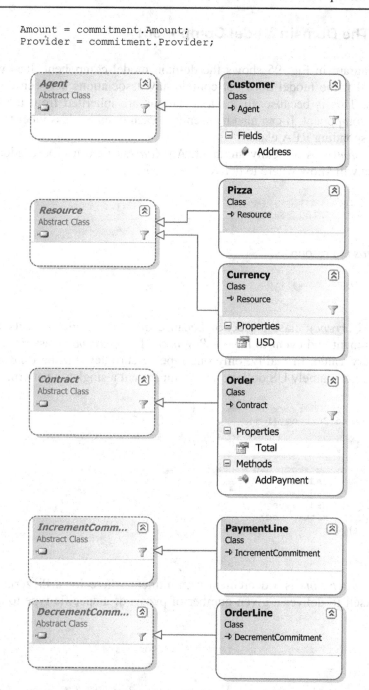

**Fig. 95.** Domain Model Component

## 3.4    The Domain Model Component

The diagram in Fig. 95 shows the domain model component. It is worth noting that the model does not contain any associations between domain classes. This is because all the associations are inherited from the REA model component. It can also be seen that each domain class inherits from a corresponding REA class.

*A Customer* is basically an agent. An *Address* field has been added so that Joe will know where to deliver the *Pizzas*.

```
public class Customer : Agent {
    public string Address;
}
```

*Pizzas* are resources.

```
public class Pizza : Resource {
}
```

The *Currency* class is needed because the REA model expects every commitment and event to have a *Resource*. The *Currency* class represents monetary value. In reality, only one type of currency will be used in the application, namely US dollars, so we implement a singleton pattern.

```
public class Currency : Resource {
    private Currency() {}

    public static Currency USD {
        get {
            Currency usd = new Currency();
            usd.ID = 0;
            usd.Name = "USD";
            usd.Value = 1;
            return usd;
        }
    }
}
```

An *Order Line* is a decrement commitment where Joe's Pizzeria commits itself to deliver a given number of pizzas of a specific type to a customer.

```
public class OrderLine : DecrementCommitment {
}
```

A *Payment* is an increment commitment where the *Customer* commits himself to pay Joe's Pizzeria a certain amount of currency.

```
public class PaymentLine : IncrementCommitment {
}
```

The *Order* class is the only class in the domain model component that adds something that could reasonably be called business logic. The order is able to calculate the total amount (in USD) that the customer should pay for his pizzas. The order can also add a payment line based on this total to its incoming commitments.

```
public class Order : Contract {
    public double Total {
        get {
            double total = 0;
            foreach (OrderLine line in DecrementCommitments) {
                total += line.Amount * line.Resource.Value;
            }
            return total;
        }
    }

    public void AddPayment(Customer customer, Currency currency) {
        IncrementCommitments.Clear();
        PaymentLine line = new PaymentLine();
        line.Amount = Total;
        line.Resource = currency;
        line.Provider = customer;
        IncrementCommitments.Add(line);
    }
}
```

All in all the domain model component consists of only 28 lines of code (not including blank lines and closing brackets).

## 3.5  The Database

The database is designed to mimic the domain model as closely as possible, see Fig. 96. All fields have the same name and are of the same data type as in the domain model. A few exceptions are necessary, however, due to the nature of databases:

- In the domain model order lines and payment lines are part of an order. In the database this is modeled by adding an order ID to each order line and payment line.
- In the domain model resources, providers and recipients are references to resource and agent objects. In the database, resource ID, provider ID or recipient ID are foreign keys to the pizza and customer tables.

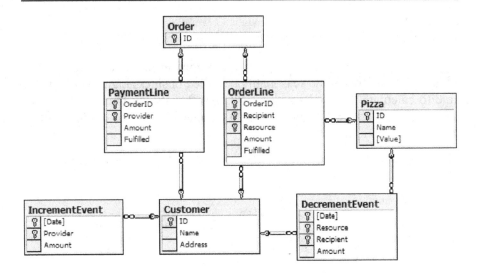

**Fig. 96.** The database

## 3.6   The Data Access Layer

The data access layer contains a single static class with a number of methods for retrieving and saving data to the database, see Fig. 97.

These methods are extremely simple so I will not waste too much space listing all the code. Here is a single example showing the code for the *Get-Pizzas()* method:

```
public static Dictionary<int, Pizza> GetPizzas() {
    Dictionary<int, Pizza> pizzas = new Dictionary<int, Pizza>();
    using (SqlConnection connection = new SqlConnection("…")) {
        connection.Open();
        SqlCommand command = new SqlCommand("select number, name,
                                price from pizza", connection);
        SqlDataReader reader = command.ExecuteReader();
        while (reader.Read()) {
            Pizza pizza = new Pizza();
            pizza.ID = reader.GetInt32(0);
            pizza.Name = reader.GetString(1);
            pizza.Price = (double) reader.GetDecimal(2);
            pizzas.Add(pizza.ID, pizza);
        }
    }
    return pizzas;
}
```

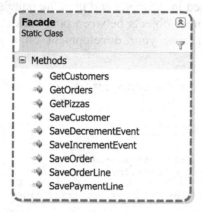

**Fig. 97.** The data access layer

One of the interesting features of the data access layer is that it is responsible for saving the economic events generated by the commitments. It does so by attaching an event handler to the order lines and payment lines in the *GetOrders()* method:

```
public static Dictionary<int, Order> GetOrders() {
...
...
OrderLine line = new OrderLine();
order.DecrementCommitments.Add(line);
line.EventCreated +=
    new DecrementEventCreatedHandler(OrderLine_EventCreated);
...
...
PaymentLine line = new PaymentLine();
order.IncrementCommitments.Add(line);
line.EventCreated +=
    new IncrementEventCreatedHandler(PaymentLine_EventCreated);
...
...
}

static void OrderLine_EventCreated(DecrementEvent e) {
    SaveDecrementEvent(e);
}

static void PaymentLine_EventCreated(IncrementEvent e) {
    SaveIncrementEvent(e);
}
```

## 3.7 Joe's Web

Now that all the underlying components are in place we are ready to develop the user interface.

The order web page is developed in ASP.Net and uses the page's *View-State* to store the order and customer objects between post backs. This is extremely convenient when you base your development on a domain model.

```
public partial class CreateOrder : System.Web.UI.Page {
    Order Order;
    Customer Customer;

    protected void Page_Load(object sender, EventArgs e) {
        if (!IsPostBack) {
            Order = new Order(Facade.GetNextOrderID());
            OrderNumberLabel.Text = Order.ID.ToString();
            Customer = new Customer(Facade.GetNextCustomerID());
            foreach (Pizza pizza in Facade.GetPizzas().Values) {
                ListItem item =
                    new ListItem(pizza.Name, pizza.ID.ToString());
                ResourceList.Items.Add(item);
            }
            ViewState.Add("order", Order);
            ViewState.Add("customer", Customer);
        } else {
            Order = (Order) ViewState["order"];
            Customer = (Customer)ViewState["customer"];
            foreach (OrderLine line in Order.DecrementCommitments) {
                AddOrderLineTableRow(line);
            }
        }
    }
}
```

If the user presses the *Already a customer* link, see Fig. 92, the web page will search the database for a customer with the correct name and then use that customer as the recipient for the order lines. The web page will also display the customer's address information:

```
protected void AlreadyCustomer_Click(object sender, EventArgs e) {
    foreach (Customer customer in Facade.GetCustomers().Values) {
        if (customer.Name == NameTextBox.Text) {
            Customer = customer;
            AddressTextBox.Text = customer.Address;
            ViewState.Add("customer", Customer);
            break;
        }
    }
}
```

When the user presses the *add to order* button, the web page will generate an order line based on the information that the user has entered and then add that order line to the order object:

```
protected void AddToOrder_Click(object sender, EventArgs e) {
    OrderLine line = new OrderLine();
    line.Amount = double.Parse(QuantityTextBox.Text);
    line.Resource = Facade.GetPizzas()[ResourceList.SelectedValue];
    line.Recipient = Customer;
    Order.DecrementCommitments.Add(line);
    AddOrderLineTableRow(line);
    ViewState.Add("order", Order);
    TotalAmountLabel.Text = Order.Total.ToString("#.00");
}
```

The final piece of code that we need for our web page is the code behind the *Submit your order* button:

```
protected void Submit_Click(object sender, EventArgs e) {
    Order.AddPayment(Customer, Currency.USD);
    Customer.Name = NameTextBox.Text;
    Customer.Address = AddressTextBox.Text;
    Facade.SaveCustomer(Customer);
    Facade.SaveOrder(Order);
    Response.Redirect("MainPage.aspx");
}
```

Now everything is in place and Joe is ready to receive orders from his customers.

## 3.8    The Fulfillment Page

Once the customer has submitted the order, Joe needs to keep track of it. He needs to know whether the customer has received his pizzas and whether he has paid for them or not. For this purpose the system contains a fulfillment page, illustrated in Fig. 98.

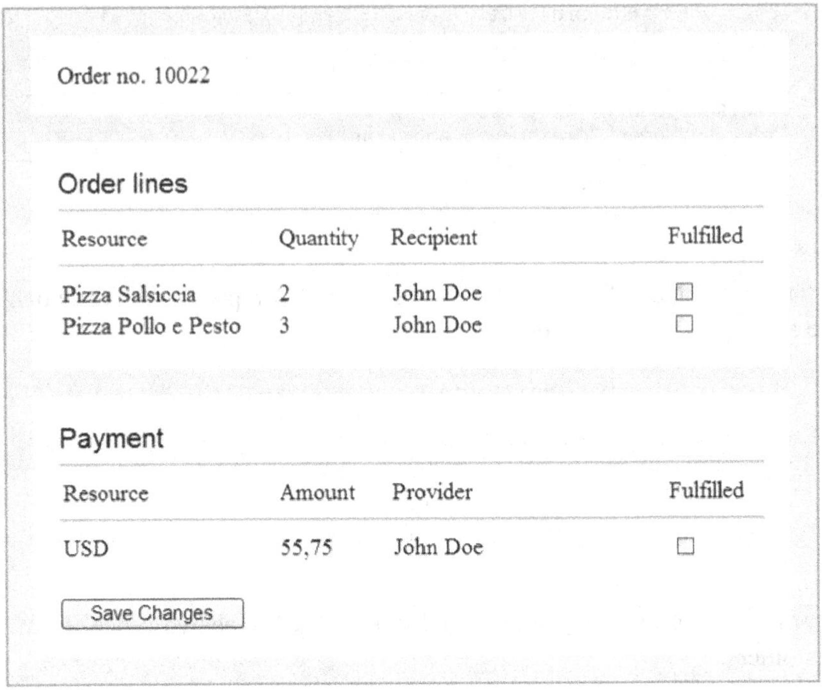

Order no. 10022

## Order lines

| Resource | Quantity | Recipient | Fulfilled |
|---|---|---|---|
| Pizza Salsiccia | 2 | John Doe | ☐ |
| Pizza Pollo e Pesto | 3 | John Doe | ☐ |

## Payment

| Resource | Amount | Provider | Fulfilled |
|---|---|---|---|
| USD | 55,75 | John Doe | ☐ |

[ Save Changes ]

**Fig. 98.** The fulfillment web page

By checking the checkboxes, Joe can mark a specific order line or payment line as *Fulfilled*. The fulfillment page supports scenarios where the customer pays up front for his pizzas as well as scenarios where the customer pays on delivery. At least in the area where I live, both these scenarios occur regularly.

Less realistic is the fact that Joe can partly fulfill an order, but only by providing all the pizzas of a specific type at once. This flaw is caused by the simplified fulfillment mechanism we implemented in the REA model.

Behind the scenes the fulfillment page is using the same domain model, data access layer and database as the order web page. When Joe presses the *Save Changes* button, the web page runs through all checkboxes and calls the associated order line or payment line's fulfill method if necessary:

```
protected void SaveChanges_Click(object sender, EventArgs e) {
    for(int i=0; i < OrderLineTable.Rows.Count; i++) {
        CheckBox checkbox =
            (CheckBox) OrderLineTable.Rows[i].Cells[3].Controls[0];
        if (checkbox.Checked &&
            !Order.DecrementCommitments[i].Fulfilled) {
            Order.DecrementCommitments[i].Fulfill();
        }
    }
    for (int i = 0; i < PaymentLineTable.Rows.Count; i++) {
        CheckBox checkbox =
            (CheckBox) PaymentLineTable.Rows[i].Cells[3].Controls[0];
        if (checkbox.Checked &&
            !Order.IncrementCommitments[i].Fulfilled) {
            Order.IncrementCommitments[i].Fulfill();
        }
    }
    Facade.SaveOrder(Order);
    Response.Redirect("MainPage.aspx");
}
```

This eventually causes decrement events and increment events to be stored in the database, see Fig. 99:

DecrementEvent : Table

| Date | ResourceID | RecipientID | Amount |
|---|---|---|---|
| 2/21/2005 | 15 | 1002 | 1 |
| 8/1/2005 | 13 | 1002 | 1 |
| 6/13/2005 | 10 | 1002 | 3 |
| 10/11/2005 | 11 | 1002 | 2 |
| 4/13/2005 | 12 | 1001 | 1 |
| 10/19/2005 | 12 | 1002 | 1 |
| 9/18/2005 | 10 | 1003 | 5 |
| 6/20/2005 | 15 | 1005 | 2 |
| 3/4/2005 | 10 | 1004 | 2 |
| 7/15/2005 | 11 | 1002 | 2 |
| 8/17/2005 | 13 | 1001 | 3 |
| 9/7/2005 | 12 | 1003 | 1 |
| 11/13/2005 | 10 | 1004 | 1 |
| 9/8/2005 | 11 | 1005 | 1 |

Record: 1

**Fig. 99.** Decrement event table

## 3.9 The OLAP Cube

Now it is time to generate some management reports based on our event data.

To make it really simple let us just add a simple Microsoft Access pivot table on top of each of the event tables. While this is not a real OLAP cube it still provides us with the same basic functionality.

The definition of the cube based on decrement events is in Fig. 100.

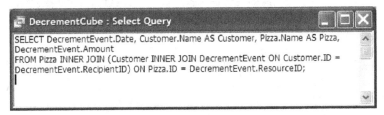

**Fig. 100.** Definition of the decrement event table

We can use this cube to get simple sales statistics based on Joe's pizza sales.

| Pizza | Sum of Amount |
|---|---|
| Pizza Alla Romana | 2109 |
| Pizza Bufalina | 969 |
| Pizza Margherita | 2372 |
| Pizza Pollo e Pesto | 84 |
| Pizza Quattro Stagioni | 740 |
| Pizza Salsiccia | 1444 |
| Pizza Vegetariana | 3366 |
| Grand Total | 11084 |

**Fig. 101.** Pizza sales

It is probably easier to see the results if we present them as a bar chart in Fig. 102.

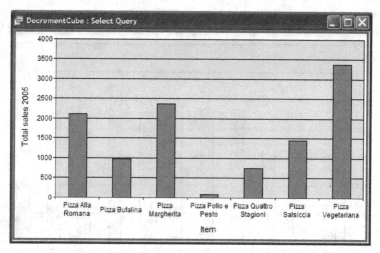

**Fig. 102.** Pizza sales bar chart

Based on these figures Joe should probably remove the *Pizza Pollo e Pesto* from his menu and instead consider adding more vegetarian pizzas. We can also have a look at the increment events in Fig. 103.

| Years | Months | Sum of Amount |
|---|---|---|
| ⊟ 2005 | ⊞ Jan ± | 2404.85 |
| | ⊞ Feb ± | 5114.95 |
| | ⊞ Mar ± | 7177.7 |
| | ⊞ Apr ± | 9402.2 |
| | ⊞ May ± | 9399.85 |
| | ⊞ Jun ± | 10147.15 |
| | ⊞ Jul ± | 10135.35 |
| | ⊞ Aug ± | 11054.8 |
| | ⊞ Sep ± | 9664.8 |
| | ⊞ Oct ± | 10177.2 |
| | ⊞ Nov ± | 12057.25 |
| | ⊞ Dec ± | 12390.95 |
| | Total ± | 109127.05 |
| Grand Total | ± | 109127.05 |

IncrementCube : Select Query

**Fig. 103.** Cash receipts

Again let's look at the data as a bar chart in Fig. 104.

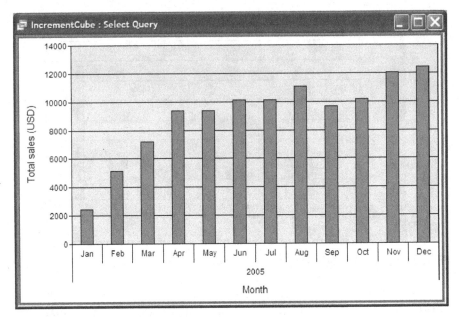

**Fig. 104.** Cash receipts as bar chart

All in all it looks as if things are going well for Joe: sales have been steadily increasing over the year.

## 3.10 Conclusions

Hopefully this example application has shown that it is indeed simple to develop an REA-based business application. The main benefits of doing so are:

- By basing the domain model on a proven and well-understood core model (the REA model) we minimize the risk of design flaws in our application. By demanding that all domain classes inherit from base classes in the REA model we are able to perform a design-time check that the domain model is consistent.
- Due to the fact that we base our domain model on a model that covers a larger set of business cases than the domain model itself, it is relatively easy to extend the domain model at a later time. If for instance Joe decides to track usage of raw materials for making pizza, we know that this will easily fit into the model.

- Because much of the business logic resides in the reusable REA model we can minimize the development effort. In the example application we were able to create a complete domain model for the pizza sales application with only 28 lines of code.

While I strongly recommend that you start using the REA-model there are of course also some caveats that you need to take into consideration:

- If you are developing an application that really is not about resources, events and agents (for instance a document management system), you may end up spending a lot of time trying to "shoehorn" the application into the REA model. It is important to decide early on whether the REA model is applicable.
- While the REA model is very powerful it is also very abstract. If you try to explain your design to a customer or fellow employee, you may find that explaining the underlying REA model is difficult. Trying to hide the fact that you are basing your design on an REA model may also be a bad idea, because major design decisions are based on the decision to use REA (e.g., why should the customer ID be placed on each order line instead of on the order itself).

# Part II  Behavioral Patterns

The previous part, Structural Patterns, discussed the structure of a business application, which conforms to the laws of the business domain, consisting of REA entities and their relationships. To build a useful business application, this structure is only one of the things an application developer has to determine. Users of business applications usually require additional functionality, such as serial numbers, accounts, price calculations, and conversions between units of measure. This functionality is essential in some applications, but it might not be required in others. All depends on the users of a business application, actual configuration of an application, and the common practices in their businesses.

In this part, Behavioral Patterns, we describe how the REA model can be extended to support specific functionality that originates in user requirements.

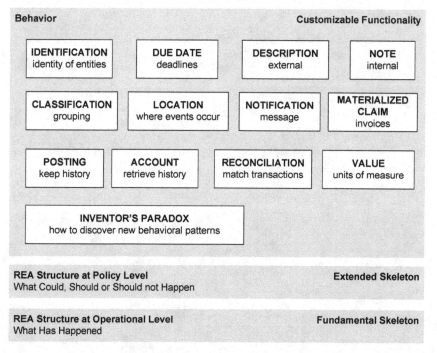

# 4 Cross-Cutting Concerns

## 4.1 Behavior May Not Be Localizable Into REA Entities

Units of functionality that extend the REA model are usually not localizable into a single REA entity. An example is illustrated in Fig. 105. This example shows the economic resource *Vehicle*, which belongs to the *Vehicle Category*, and is used in the economic events *Trip*.

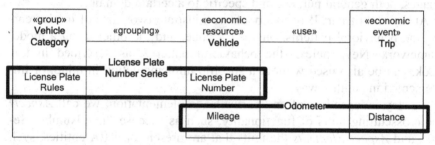

**Fig. 105.** Behavioral patterns often crosscut REA entities

A *License Plate Number* of a vehicle is an attribute of the economic resource *Vehicle*. The *License Plate Number* is usually not a random number. It is constructed using a *License Plate Rules*, which is a property of *Vehicle Category* (for example, numbers of police cars, military cars, and diplomatic cars are constructed using different rules than numbers of other cars). The property *License Plate Rules* contains rules specifying the uniqueness of the *License Plate Number*, its format, its dependency on previous numbers or other attributes, and so on. Therefore, the unit of functionality of a *License Plate Number Series* is present on two REA entities, the resource and the resource group, and the number is constructed by mutual collaboration between the part that resides on the resource and the part that resides on the group.

Likewise, a *Mileage* of a *Vehicle* is calculated as the aggregated number of the trip *Distances* the vehicle traveled. As *Trip* is an economic event, the *Odometer* is a unit of functionality present on two REA entities, the economic resource and the economic event.

It is still useful to think about a *License Plate Number Series,* and about an *Odometer* as single units of functionality, but these units span several REA entities.

We will use aspect-oriented programming as a conceptual framework and a convention of thought for modeling the crosscutting modules of functionality. Aspect-oriented programming is one of the mechanisms for describing the crosscutting features and manipulating them as modular units. Aspect-oriented programming is based on the ideas of Gregor Kiczales, John Lamping, Anurag Mendhekar, Chris Maeda, Cristina Videira Lopes, Jean-Marc Loingtier, and John Irwin, (Kiczales 1996). This group at the Palo Alto Research Center, a subsidiary of Xerox Corporation, developed a general purpose aspect-oriented language called AspectJ, an extension of the Java programming language with aspect-oriented features. Many other research centers have developed other aspect-oriented languages, both general purpose and specific to a certain domain.

At the end of Part II of this book we illustrate two ways of implementing the behavioral patterns, one in C# code, and the other using a model framework. Nevertheless, the behavioral patterns, as described in this book, can be also used without a specific implementation in mind, or implemented in another way.

To stay independent of any particular implementation, we call *Aspects* the crosscutting units of functionality, such as License Plate Number Series, and *Aspect Elements* the units that are present on REA entities, such as License Plate Rule, License Plate Number, Mileage, and Distance.

## 4.2  Framework-Based Approach

Aspect-oriented languages that are not framework-based, such as AspectJ, express the structure of a software application in the form of code in the programming language, and the crosscutting concerns, or aspects, are also expressed as code. During compilation, both the application code and the aspect code are combined together in a process called weaving; see Fig. 106.

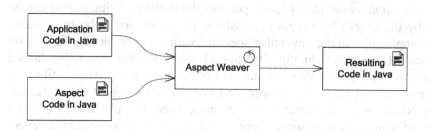

**Fig. 106.** Aspect-oriented programming at the code level (not framework-based)

Keeping in mind requirements such as extensibility and configurability, a disadvantage of such programming languages is that the code has to be weaved (which means recompiled) every time the functionality of an application (expressed as application code or aspect code) changes. The consequence is that upgrading an application is complicated and expensive.

Furthermore, since some or all functionality of an object is provided in the aspect code, it is impossible for the weaver to guarantee a system-wide quality for an application, because the weaver has no way of knowing what the aspect code does.

To satisfy the requirements for extensibility, configurability, and upgradeability, we use the framework approach to model and implement the aspects. Every aspect is represented at two levels of abstraction, the *Aspect type level* and the *Application model level*; see Fig. 107.

We will use a simplified version of the *IDENTIFICATION PATTERN* as an example. The *IDENTIFICATION PATTERN* encapsulates business logic for providing identity to REA entities, such as serial numbers and names. Details about the identification pattern are described in the *IDENTIFICATION PATTERN* chapter.

The *Aspect Type* level specifies the types of the aspects, and metadata that can be applied to the aspects in the application model. This level encapsulates the business logic of the aspect, and specifies the configuration properties, which can be set by application developers. In the example illustrated in Fig. 107, the *Identification Aspect* consists of two element types, *Identifier Type* and *Identifier Setup Type*. The cardinality of the composition indicates that instances of these types (i.e., *Identifier* and *Identifier Setup*) can be configured in the application model several times. These two elements are related by a one-to-many relationship, which indicates that for each configured identification aspect in the application model, for one *Identifier* there can be exactly one *Identifier Setup*, and for one *Identifier Setup* there can be one or more *Identifiers*.

The *Application Model* level specifies the runtime attributes that can be set by the users of business applications or automatically by the system. The application model level also specifies which aspects are configured on which REA entities; in Fig. 107 the REA entities are shown by dashed lines, to indicate that they are not part of the aspect. An REA entity of a type group can contain zero or more *Identifier Setup* aspect elements, and any REA entity can contain zero or more *Identifier* elements. For each *Identifier* instance at runtime, there is exactly one *Identifier Setup* instance; for each *Identifier Setup* instance at runtime, there can be zero or more *Identifier* instances.

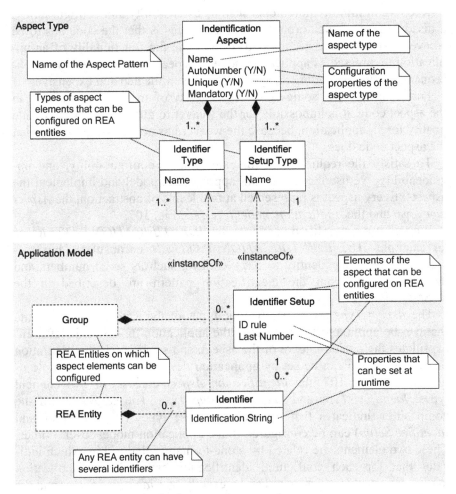

**Fig. 107.** Aspect pattern in the framework approach

In the examples illustrating application models with aspects, we use the notation in Fig. 108. The *Aspect Elements* are shown as rectangles with thick line; their runtime properties are shown similarly, as UML attributes. Properties of the aspect element types (i.e. the properties whose values are set at the aspect type level) are shown in the name compartment of the aspect. Values of the properties of the aspect type are shown as text close to the line connecting the aspect elements, similarly as UML attributes; for example, 'Mandatory = yes'.

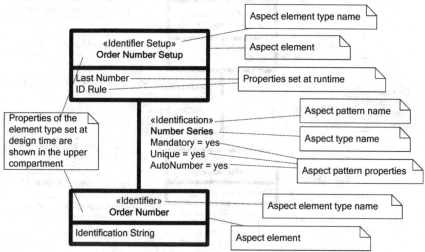

**Fig. 108.** Notation used for aspects in application models

Model in Fig. 109 illustrates a fragment of an REA model with two REA entities, a contract *Sales Order* and a group *Orders*. Application developers would like to implement sales order number on the *Sales Order* entity. They decide to configure the identification aspect on the *Sales Order*. The result is illustrated in Fig. 110.

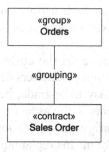

**Fig. 109.** Fragment of an REA model without aspects

The *Identification Aspect Pattern* has the name *Number Series*. The configuration parameters *Mandatory*, *Unique*, and *AutoNumber* are all set to *yes*. The *Identifier Setup* element is called *Order Number Setup*, and the *Identifier* is called *Order Number*.

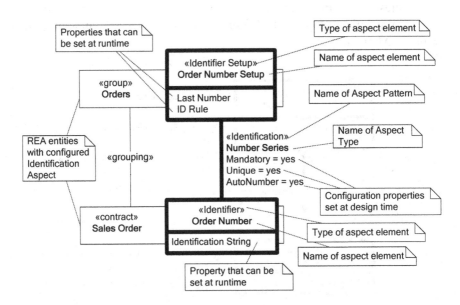

**Fig. 110.** Fragment of an REA model with identification aspect

Advantage of a system with explicitly modeled aspect types is that software business applications are much easier to configure, customize and upgrade than if the aspects were to be represented only as code in a programming language.

Configuration of software business applications using the aspect patterns is basically reduced to creating an REA model, setting the configuration parameters of aspects, and specifying which aspects are present on which objects. This can be done without writing any code in a programming language.

Software applications are easy to customize, as the customization task basically comprises setting up the configuration parameters of the aspects.

Furthermore, software applications are easy to upgrade, because all application logic is encapsulated in the elements at the aspect type level, and it can be extended independently of the configured application model. The upgrade of the software application basically means replacing the elements at the aspect type level with elements with upgraded functionality. The framework developer designs the interface (the configuration properties and the corresponding behavior) that the elements at the aspect type level expose. If the upgraded elements support the old interface, the software applications can be upgraded without reweaving or recompiling the application.

Even if the upgraded elements are not backwards compatible (backward compatibility is considered anti-pattern by some practitioners), it is possible to write an upgrade script that modifies the configured applications to support the upgraded elements.

Quality of the software applications is easier to control, as all functionality of business applications is encapsulated in a framework, and is therefore tested by framework developers. The framework developers, who provide the elements at the aspect type level, have full control over what application developers may do with their aspect elements. In other words, providing application developers a domain-specific modeling language reduces the number of errors the application developers can make, compared to the situation in which the application developers write code in a general programming language.

## 4.3   There Is No Complete List of Behavioral Patterns

While with the structural patterns our aim was to find the minimal, yet complete set of abstractions covering the business domain, this is not possible with behavioral patterns. Users of business applications will always need new features, and behavioral patterns provide a mechanism to add new features to a business application without changing its fundamental structure.

There are behavioral patterns waiting to be discovered. This section describes the patterns we came across in building our business solutions, but it is not a complete list of all patterns that might be needed in any line of business. As the REA structural patterns define more or less a complete set of concepts, if application developers identify user requirements for new functionality, they would likely be either new behavioral patterns which crosscut the REA entities or features in a domain other than the business domain.

# 5 Patterns

## 5.1 Identification Pattern

*Barcode is a machine readable strip for automatic identification of items, by means of printed bars of different widths*

### Context

People refer to real or imaginary things by their names. We name things to identify them, so we can refer to them by their names and not just point to them and say "this!". By naming, we give things identities, but in real life they are not often unique. Many things have more than one name, and sometimes a single name can refer to different things, which is fine as long as everyone who uses that name knows what thing it refers to. In business, people use serial numbers, production numbers, civil registration numbers, and names.

### Problem

How do we specify the identity of things represented by REA entities?

### Forces

The solution needs to balance the following forces:

- An identity is a given feature; it is not an intrinsic part of the objects and things. Therefore, an REA application model must specify whether there is a business reason requiring REA entities to have a distinct identity, and how that identity is modeled. We could omit modeling identity of an entity, but then we could distinguish different instances of this entity only by the values of their attributes.
- Users of business applications do not necessarily require that all REA entities have an explicit identifier. For example, users of business applications might not be interested in managing the identifiers of sales order lines.
- Some identifiers are unique in the universe, such as the GUID (Global Unique Identifier); some are not unique, such as the first name and last name of a person. Some identifiers are unique within a certain group, such as a serial number, which is unique within the group of entities that belong to the same number series.
- There are specific rules on how to construct identifiers. For example, the ISBN (International Standard Book Number) or the numbers of major credit cards are constructed in a way that enables verifying, using a simple calculation algorithm, whether the number is valid.

### Solution

The *Identification Aspect Pattern* can be used in situations in which application developers want to specify the identity of REA entities.

In the REA application model, the *Identification Aspect* consists of two elements. The *Identifier* element represents the name or number of an REA entity. The *Identifier Setup* element specifies the rules for creating the Identifiers.

The *Identifier Setup* is often configured on *group* of REA entities that share the same rules for creating identifiers, for example, on a group that belongs to the same number series. The *Identifier* can be configured on any REA entity that needs to be identifiable, including the groups. As not all REA entities are parts of some group, the *Identifier Setup* is often omitted from the model, or is implicit in a software application, for example, as a system table.

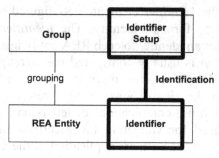

**Fig. 111.** Identification aspect in the application model

## Design of the Identification Pattern

The *aspect type level* encapsulates the business logic of the aspect and configuration parameters, which can be set by application developers. At the aspect type level, the *Identification Type* defines the *Name* of the type of identification, as well as other attributes. *AutoNumber* is a Boolean function that can be set on or off to indicate whether the *Identifier* can be automatically generated by the identification aspect or not; automatically generated number is often referred to as a number series. *Unique* is a Boolean function that can be set on or off to indicate whether or not the *Identifier* is required to be unique at runtime. *Mandatory* is a Boolean function that can be set on or off to indicate if the *Identifier* must be defined at runtime or can be undefined.

The *Identification Type Aspect* has two elements, *Identifier Type* and *Identifier Setup Type*. These elements contain business logic for interpreting the *ID rules*, and logic for creating and validating *Identifiers*. They do not have any configuration parameters; just serve as metadata for the *Identifier* and the *Identifier Type* at the application level.

The rules for creating new *Identifiers* can vary from simple series with linear increments to rules that allow for validity checks of the identification strings, such as credit card numbers. Legislation in some countries requires that numbers of some business documents consecutive, without gaps, which imposes an extra requirement on how the number is constructed. If an REA entity has been created by omission and deleted after another REA entity of the same series has been created, the *ID Rule* must be able to identify the gap in the series and reuse the number of the deleted document.

The *application model level* specifies the runtime attributes that can be set by the users of the business application, or automatically. At the application model level, the *Identifier* element is configured on the REA entity that should have some form of identity. The *Identifier* contains the *ID String*, which provides an identity to each REA entity instance.

The *Identifier Setup* is usually configured on a group of REA entities that share the same ID rule for creating or validating an Identifier. The *ID Rule* determines how the identification strings are created (users of business applications often use combinations of letters and numbers). The *ID Rule* can also be used for validating the identification strings entered manually by the users of the business application. If the *Identification Type* aspect is an *AutoNumber*, the *Identifier Type* also has an attribute *Last ID*, which defines the last used identification string in the series.

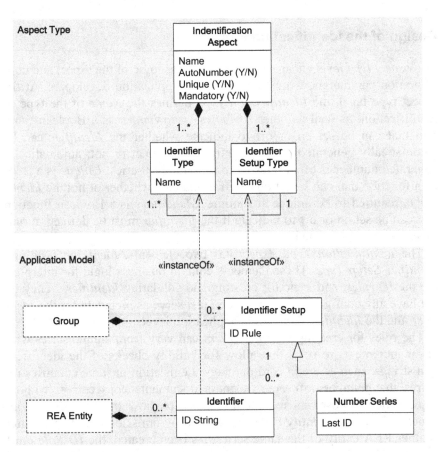

**Fig. 112.** Design of the identification pattern

## Examples

The *Social Security Number (SSN)* of an employee is an identification that is not an *auto-number,* is *unique,* and is *not mandatory.* The *Identifier Setup* has the name *SSN Numbering Scheme,* and contains an *ID Rule* that determines how the social security number is constructed or verified. The *Identifier* has the name *Social Security Number,* and its *ID String* at run-time contains the social security number.

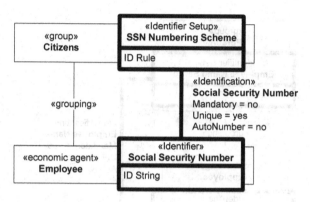

**Fig. 113.** Social Security Number

*Sales Order Number* is an identification that is an auto-number, is unique, and is mandatory. As the *Sales Order Number* is an auto-number, the *Identifier Setup* element contains the attribute *Last ID.*

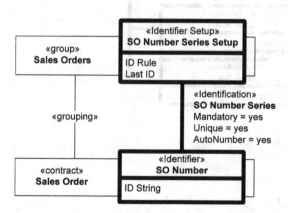

**Fig. 114.** Sales order number

*Product Serial Number* is an identification that is an *auto-number*, is *unique*, and is *mandatory*. The configuration of *Product Serial Number* is similar to that of *Sales Order Number* in Fig. 114; *Identifier* is configured on the economic resource *Product*, and *Identifier Setup* is configured on a group of *Products* that belong to the same series.

*Employee Name* is an identification that is not an *auto-number*, is not *unique*, but is *mandatory*. *First name, middle name, last name* and *nickname* share the same *ID Rule* specified by *Employee Name Setup*.

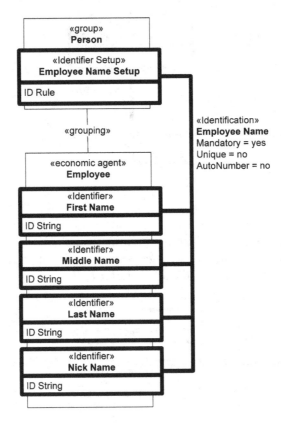

**Fig. 115.** Employee name

## Resulting Context

Sometimes, users of business applications use *phone number, e-mail address*, or *Internet address* as identifiers of their trading partners. These numbers and addresses have multiple and different semantics. Phone number can also be used as a contact address, e-mail address as a contact address and destination location (for sending electronic documents and products), and Internet address as a description of the trading partner. In such cases, different aspects will contain or refer to the same data (both identification and notification will contain or refer to the same phone number).

There are several international standards specifying Identification Strings and ID rules for economic resources and economic agents in various lines of business. Examples are European Article Numbering (EAN) for industrial products, International Standard Book Number (ISBN) for books, International Standard Serial Number (ISSN) for periodicals, and International Standard Music Number (ISMN) for printed music publications. For companies, the Data Universal Numbering System (DUNS) is used. References to these standards can be found, for example, in (Arlow, Neustadt 2003).

## 5.2  Classification Pattern

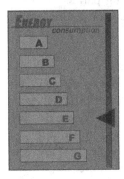

*Classification of a washing machine into an energy consumption class*

### Context

Users of software applications often need to divide REA entities, such as economic resources, into certain categories. The example illustrated above shows a classification of washing machines into categories A-G according to energy consumption.

Such classification is essentially grouping, already described as a part of *GROUP PATTERN* in Part I of this book. The reason we describe classification as a structural pattern is that classification adds specific functionality to the grouping structure. There are other patterns that add different functionality to the grouping structure, for example *BUDGET* and *INVENTORY* (not included in this book).

### Problem

How do we model the hierarchy of classification categories, and classify REA entities into the categories of the classification hierarchy?

### Forces

Application designers have to consider the following forces:

- There is often a hierarchy of categories, and a REA entity can be classified in more than one category simultaneously. For example, if a classification hierarchy for furniture contains category sofas with two sub-categories, leather sofas and sleeping sofas, there can be an economic resource (sofa), which can be both a sleeping sofa and a leather sofa.

- Often, two or more REA entities can use the same classification hierarchy. For example, a software support engineer can be classified according his qualification as a Microsoft Windows supporter, or, more specifically, a Windows 2000 supporter or Windows XP supporter. Thus, the supporter can be classified using the same classification hierarchy as is used to classify the software products.

- Sometimes, it is necessary to match REA entities that are classified in the same categories. For example, the users of a business application need to identify a supporter whose qualification corresponds to a product category.

- In some cases, users of business applications can classify an REA entity themselves, in other cases the category depends on the values of some attributes of the REA entity. In such cases, the REA entity should determine its category automatically, and change it if the values of the attributes change. For example, a customer might be classified as a preferred customer if the volume of sales to him reaches a certain level, or as an ordinary customer if the sales volume drops below that level.

## Solution

The classification aspect in the application model has two elements. The *Member* element on an REA entity classifies the REA entity into a *Category*. The *Category* element defines a node in the classification hierarchy. The *Category* element is usually configured on a *Group* entity, and the *Member* element can be configured on any *REA entity*; see Fig. 116. The *Category* has a reference to a parent *Category*, and thereby describes a hierarchical structure; see Fig. 117.

An REA entity can be a member of several categories simultaneously. These categories can be part of a single hierarchy, but also of different classification hierarchies.

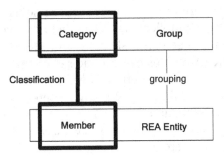

**Fig. 116.** Classification pattern

## Design of the Classification Pattern

The *aspect type level* encapsulates the business logic of the aspect and configuration parameters, which can be set by application developers. At the aspect type level, the *Classification Aspect* defines the *Name* of the classification hierarchy. The *Auto-Classification* is a Boolean parameter that can be set on or off to indicate whether or not the classification aspect will maintain the classification automatically based on the *Membership Rule* of the *Auto-Category*. The classification Aspect has two elements, *Category Type* and *Member Type*. The *Member Type* element has a *Multiple Select* parameter that can be set on and off to indicate whether the REA entities at the application level with an instance of this *Member* can be classified into several categories or only into one. The *Category Type* element defines a *Name* of the node type in the classification hierarchy.

The *application model level* specifies the runtime attributes that can be set by the users of a business application or automatically by the business logic. At the application model level, the *Category* represents a node in the hierarchy of categories. The *Category* is usually contained in the *Group* entity. Each node has a reference to a parent node, and thereby describes a hierarchy of categories. A *Category* has the attribute *Name*, which specifies the name of the category. If the category is an *Auto-Category*, the *Membership Rule* specifies the rule that enables the classification aspect to create links between a *Member* and a *Category* dynamically, based on the values of the *Discriminator* attribute of the *Member*. For example, if the *Discriminator* of a *Member* is Age, the category with 'Name = Minors' has the membership rule "Age is less than 18 years."

A *Member* element can be configured on any REA entity, and has two methods. The *Is (Category)* method allows the business logic to ask at runtime if the REA entity with this member is classified as a specific Category. The method *IsIn (Category)* indicates whether the member is classified in a subcategory of a specific *Category*. If the member is an *AutoCategory* member, the *Discriminator* attribute is used by the *Membership Rule* to automatically determine the *Category* of the member.

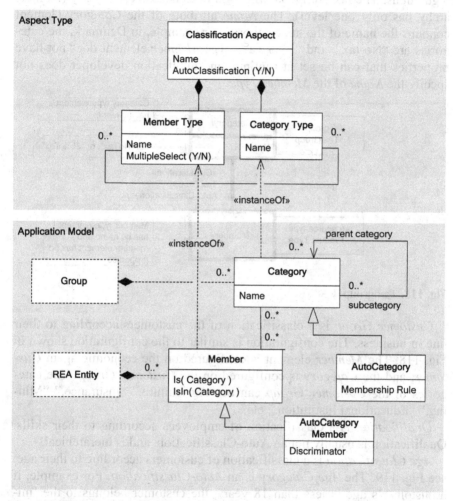

**Fig. 117.** Design of the classification pattern

## Examples

The *Tax Group* of an economic resource is a classification that is not an *Auto-Classification*, because users of business applications explicitly specify a tax group for each product type individually, according to local tax regulations. The tax group classification does not have hierarchy (its hierarchy has only one level). The *Name* attribute of the *Category* element contains the name of the tax category. For example, in Denmark, the categories are "No tax," and "25% Tax." The *Member* element does not have properties that can be set at runtime, and application developer does not specify the *Name* of the *Member Type*.

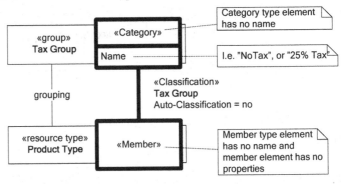

**Fig. 118.** Tax group

*Customer Group* is a classification of the customers according to their line of business. The configuration is similar to the configuration shown in Fig. 118. The *Member* element is configured on the economic agent *Customer*, and the *Category* is configured on the *Customer Group*. The categories of the *Customer Group* can be "Agriculture," "Insurance," "Mining," "Educational Institution," etc.

*Qualification* is a classification of employees according to their skills. Qualification is usually not an Auto-Classification, and is hierarchical.

*Age Classification* is a classification of customers according to their age; see Fig. 119. The *Age Category* is an *Auto-Classification*. For example, if a customer's age is less than 18 years, the customer belongs to the 'minors' category; customers over 18 years belong to the 'adults' category. The *Discriminator* attribute of the *Member* is a reference to the *State* property of the *DUE DATE PATTERN Age*; the membership rule of the 'minors' category is 'Discriminator == Upcoming'; the membership rule of the 'adults' category is 'Discriminator == Expired'. A customer's age changes over time, and if it becomes 18 years, the Due Date *Age* changes its state from *Upcoming* to *Expired*, and consequently, the *Classification* aspect changes the customer's category from the minors category to the adults category.

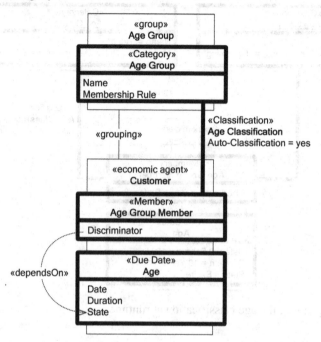

**Fig. 119.** Age classification

Runtime snapshot of the age classification example is shown in Fig. 120. There are two instances of the *Age Group* entity; one has an instance of the *Category* aspect with the name 'minor,' and the other has it with the name 'adult', with corresponding membership rules. The *Customer* has configured two aspects. The *Due Date* aspect determines the age of customer as higher than 18 years. The *Member* element of the *Age Classification* aspect contains a reference to the *State* property of the *Due Date* aspect. The value of *State* determines that a link (an instance of the grouping relationship) exists between customer and the 'Adult' age group.

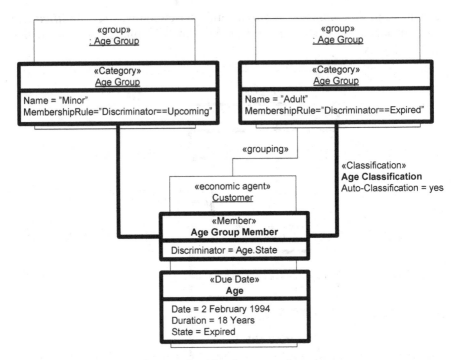

**Fig. 120.** A snapshot of the age classification at runtime

## Resulting Context

The Age Category is often used for specifying policies that originate in legal regulations.

Although the REA entities belong to different categories, they may share the same business logic. In many situations, it is what applications designers intend. However, if the instances of REA entities that belong to different categories should also have very different business logic, a better solution would be to model them as different REA entities, rather than as one entity with a classification aspect.

The design described in Solution in Detail enables users of business applications to create new categories in existing classification hierarchies, and classify REA entities into these categories. However, only application designers (not end users) can create new kinds of classification hierarchies. This is suitable for most applications we came across, because a new classification hierarchy in a sense changes the application design. In the cases where the users of business applications require the creating of new classification hierarchies at runtime, the solution must either be modified by adding the *Classification Type* aspect element at the application model level, or give the users of business applications application development rights.

If a hierarchy of categories is needed in a business application, creating a hierarchy is a nontrivial task, and creating a classification system usually needs the help of a specialist.

Categories are often used to specify policies (see the *POLICY PATTERN*). Categories enable users to introduce more business knowledge into a business application, which has both benefits and drawbacks. The drawback is that the business knowledge in the software system is sometimes hard to create and needs maintenance as the business changes. The benefit is that a software application that is aware of the business knowledge can more efficiently guide and help its users.

## 5.3   Location Pattern

*Location is a point in space*

### Context

Most economic events take place in time and space. For some economic events, the location is an essential attribute characterizing them. Shipment, for example, is an economic event in which an economic resource is moved from one location to another. Users of business application are interested not only in departure and destination, but often also in the actual location of the economic resource during the economic event.

### Problem

How do we specify where the economic events occur?

### Forces

We need to balance the following forces when creating the model:

- Economic resources that are physical in nature are usually located at specific places in the world. Users of business applications would like to know where a resource is.
- Information modeled as an REA economic resource also has location. Information is always stored on a medium that has a location, and information can be transferred from medium to another.
- Economic events contain historical information about changes of features of economic resources or transfers of rights to these resources. These changes and transfers occur both in time and space.

- Economic resources can change their locations as a result of economic events or by forces outside of the scope of the application model. If an economic event changes the location of the resource, users of business applications would like to plan, monitor, and control changes of locations of the resources.

## Solution

In the REA application model, the *Location* is an aspect consisting of two elements, *Position* and *Route*, see Fig. 121. The *Position* element specifies the actual position, and the *Route* element that represents the changes of the *Position*. The *Position* element is usually configured on an economic resource; and the *Route* element can be configured on a commitment, which specifies the indented route, or on an economic event, which specifies the actual route.

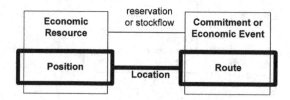

**Fig. 121.** Location pattern

## Design of the Location Pattern

The *aspect type level* encapsulates the business logic of the aspect and configuration parameters, which can be set by application developers. At the aspect type level, the *Location Aspect* defines the *Name* of the location aspect. The location aspect has two element types, the *Position Type* and the *Route Type*, both having properties defining their names. The *Route Type* has a method *DisplayMap()* that displays the actual route and navigation instructions.

The *application model level* specifies the runtime properties of the aspect elements. At the application model level, the *Position* element has an attribute *Actual Position* which contains the actual position of the resource. The *Route* element specifies a route segment that represents a change in the resource location. The *Route* element contains the properties *Origin*, *Destination*, and *Distance*.

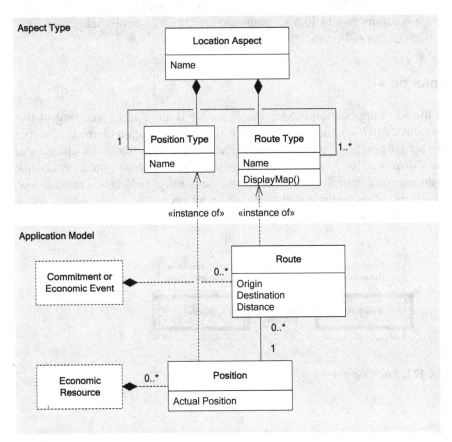

**Fig. 122.** Design of location pattern

## Examples

The example in Fig. 123 illustrates a model of the location pattern configured as *a Shipment Address*. The route segment element is configured on the *Shipment* economic event; the *Destination* property represents the final address. The *Position* element is configured on the Item; the *Location* property represents the actual location of the *Item*.

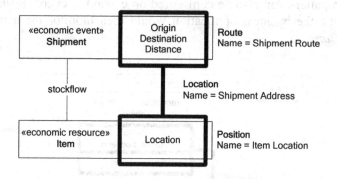

**Fig. 123.** Shipment address

The location pattern can be used to model an itinerary that consists of several route segments. The itinerary is essentially a schedule. There are several ways to construct the REA model for an itinerary, depending on the level of detail of information the users of business application would like to plan, monitor, and control. We will present one possible design. The whole route is represented as an increment commitment, *Transport*, and its *Route* aspect element contains the origin and final destination of the economic resource *Cargo*. The decrement commitment, *Cargo on Carrier*, represents the time interval on which the *Cargo* is loaded onto a specific carrier; it is a decrement commitment because when *Cargo* is on a vehicle, its possible use for other purposes is limited. The commitment *Cargo on Vehicle* has a *Route* aspect element called *Segment*, representing a segment of the scheduled transport. At runtime, there can be several instances of the *Cargo on Carrier* commitment, for example, if cargo is transported using several vehicles or means of transportation.

The other decrement commitment, *Vehicle Use*, has also a *Route* aspect element. The *Origin* and *Destination* of the *Vehicle Use* element and the *Origin* and *Destination* of the *Cargo on Carrier* element can be different, for example, if a vehicle drives unloaded to the loading destination, and then transports *Cargo* and, again, drives back unloaded. The cost of using unloaded vehicle should be reflected in the cost of the transport, which is what the model does.

An itinerary usually also contains information about time, such as when cargo has been loaded, unloaded, and reached the final destination. This can be modeled using the *DUE DATE PATTERN* on commitments and the *POSTING PATTERN* on economic events.

The location pattern can also be configured on economic events instead of commitments; the business application would then monitor the actual movement of *Cargo*.

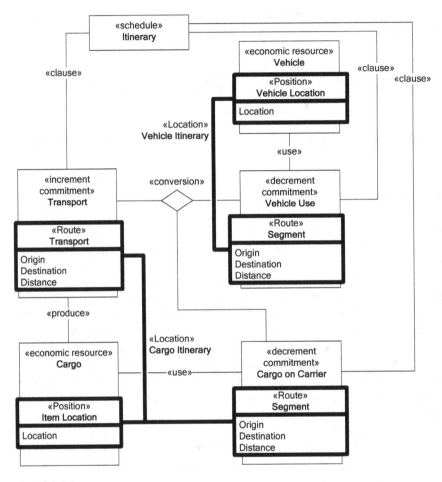

**Fig. 124.** Itinerary

## Resulting Context

How do we determine the shipping address of the customer? Some business applications store a shipping address (as well as the billing address, and many other addresses) as attributes of a customer. These addresses are then used as default addresses for shipments, invoices, etc. Users of business applications have the option to overwrite these addresses in case a customer wishes to use a different address than his default address.

The solution in this pattern does not have a fixed default customer address. Economic events contain all relevant historical information about business relationship between the enterprise and the customer, and commitments that the enterprise gave to the customer. The economic events and commitments also specify the shipping, billing, and other addresses the customer has used in the past. The address for the next shipment can then be determined by browsing the list of economic events. The customer may then choose one of the existing destinations, a new one, or one that the business application can suggest, for example, the destination of the last shipment, as a default address. This solution is more flexible than that of a fixed default address as a property of the customer entity because it develops automatically as the enterprise's information about the customer develops.

## 5.4  Posting Pattern

*The posting behavioral pattern keeps track of transactions and makes their records immutable*

### Context

Registering the history of the realized or intended exchanges of economic resources is an important part of the functionality of most business software solutions. For example, when economic agents agree upon a commitment, the commitment should be registered, and all modifications to the registration should be traceable. Tax authorities often set similar requirements for exchange economic events and for materialized claims; any changes made to the data that influence the economic results of the company should be traceable.

The history of business relationships is typically related to realized or intended exchanges of economic resources, contracts, agreements, and claims, such as the purchase and sale of products and services, invoices, and corresponding payments.

### Problem

How do we keep track of the history of economic events, commitments, contracts, and other entities that represent interactions between economic agents?

### Forces

The solution is influenced by two forces:

- Users of business applications would like to retrieve comprehensive analytical information about economic events, and commitments in their business applications, and to perform data mining on huge amounts of data related to their businesses. This is the purpose of the *ACCOUNT PATTERN*; however, the *ACCOUNT PATTERN* requires that the business application already contains the data describing each transaction.
- There are often legal requirements on traceability of data that affect the financial status of an enterprise. For example, if the users of business applications made an error when entering the financial data into the system, the original (erroneous) information should often not just be deleted or overwritten, but a new record that eliminates the effect of the error should be made.

## Solution

The main purpose of the Posting pattern is to keep a history of the economic events, commitments, contracts, and claims. The posting pattern at the application level consists of two elements; see Fig. 125. The *Entry* element registers the value of the REA entity (for example, it stores it in the database), together with the values specified by the *Dimension* element, which provides additional information about the event. After the entry has been registered, the values of the entry and dimension are immutable; no changes to these values are possible.

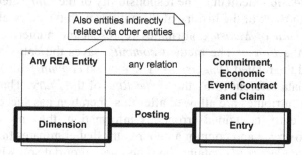

**Fig. 125.** Posting

## Design of the Posting Pattern

The *aspect type level* encapsulates the business logic of the aspect and configuration parameters, which can be set by application developers. At the aspect type level, the *Posting Aspect* defines the possible sets of comparable entries known to the business application. The possible sets are specified by the *Name* property, and can, for example, be inventory posting, finance posting, man-hours posting, or distance posting. The *Posting Aspect* has a property, *Unit of Measure Type*, describing which *Units of Measure* are allowed for the actual entries. A *Unit of Measure Type* can, for example, be *Cash*. This would allow actual entries whose *Unit of Measure* is USD, GBP, or EUR.

The *Entry Type* contains information about actual entries. The *Value Rule* attribute contains information about how the actual entries retrieve the value for the entry. The *Value Rule* is usually a reference to another aspect on the same REA entity.

The *Dimension Type* represents descriptive information that users of a business application register with each entry. Examples of dimensions are data characterizing an economic resource, resource type, economic agent, and agent type related to the REA entity with the *Entry* element. The data stored in the dimension is later used by the *ACCOUNT* pattern to construct comprehensive reports and to retrieve statistical information. The *Value Rule* property contains information about how the actual entries retrieve the value for each dimension. The *Value Rule* is usually a reference to other aspects on the same REA entity as the one on which *Dimension* is configured.

The *application model level* specifies the aspect elements with run-time properties. At the application model level, the aspect consists of one *Entry* and several *Dimension* elements. The responsibility of the *Entry* element is to enable keeping track of the history of the entities with the entry element. The *Value* and *Unit of Measure* attributes represent the numerical value registered with the *Entry*. The method *commit()* saves the data specified by the *Entry* and the related *Dimensions*. The method *commit()* also makes immutable the data referenced by the *Value Rule* of the *Entry*. That is, no changes in these attributes are allowed after this operation has successfully finished. If the entry contained erroneous information, the only way to undo its effect to create and commit another entry that eliminates the effect of the error. *Date Occurred* contains the time interval or date on which the registered event or commitment occurred (it can actually be a start date and an end date), while *When Noticed* contains the date on which the entries were registered.

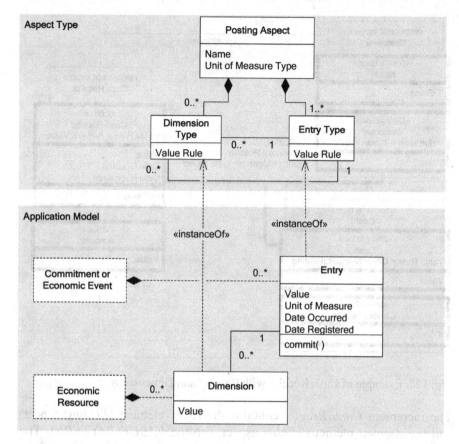

**Fig. 126.** Design of posting pattern

The *Dimension* element describes the information to be registered with each entry. This is typically values of aspects on REA entities related to the entity with the entry element. If the entry is configured on an economic event, the dimensions applicable would be economic agent, economic resource, agent types and groups, and resource types and groups. The *Value* attribute contains the information specified by the *Value Rule* of the *Dimension* at the *Aspect Type* level.

## Example

Fig. 127 illustrates an example of *Financial Posting*. The economic event *Cash Receipt* is related to economic resource *Cash* and economic agent *Customer*.

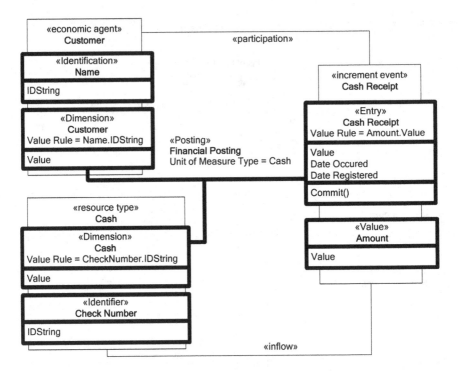

**Fig. 127.** Example of Cash Receipt with Posting and Dimensions

The increment *Cash Receipt* contains the *Entry* element (*Posting* aspect) and the *Amount* element (*Value* aspect, see the *VALUE PATTERN*). The *Value Rule* of the *Entry* element is configured to retrieve data from *Amount*. *Customer* and *Cash* have both a *Dimension* element (Posting aspect) and an *Identification* element. The *Value Rule* of the both *Dimension* elements is configured to retrieve the value of the *ID String* from the identification aspects.

If the method *commit()* on the *Entry* aspect is called, the values of the *Entry* aspect and the *Amount* aspect on *Cash Receipt* are locked, and the data including the values of the dimensions is stored.

## Resulting Context

The solution above allows the application designers to choose which dimensions will be registered with each entry type. By default, it is useful to assume that the dimensions are all data on the REA entities directly related to the entity with the entry aspect, plus groups and types of these entities. However, users of business applications might point exactly to the data in

which they are interested. This level of freedom is useful especially if the
application model is not a full REA model but a modeling compromise.

## 5.5  Account Pattern

*In some cases, keeping track of individual entities is not feasible or even possible. For instance, once wine has been poured into a glass, it is no longer possible to distinguish between the wine that was in the glass before the wine was poured into it and the wine that come from the bottle. The only thing that it is possible to keep track of is the total amount of wine in the glass.*

The total amount of wine in the glass is the difference between the amount of wine added in it and the amount of wine removed from it. However, sometimes it is not precisely this difference. Wine might be poured out of evaporate over time. Wine might also be added to the glass for reasons beyond the scope of the model. There might also be some amount of wine in the glass before we start registering the additions and removals.

It is not feasible to model every possible way in which how wine can be added to or removed from the glass, because many of them are not relevant from the perspective and for the purpose of our model. A model is, by definition, incomplete compared to reality. The only amount we know precisely is that of the wine in the glass at the time we measured it.

### Context

The *POSTING PATTERN* describes how to record the history of economic events, commitments, contracts, and claims. However, merely keeping track of these entities is usually not the main interest of an enterprise's decision makers. Users of business applications are also interested in aggregated information about the state of the enterprise.

## Problem

How do we keep track of the total amount of something being increased or decreased, and eventually compute what constitutes the total amount?

## Forces

To address this problem, the following forces must be resolved:

- Users of business applications would like to retrieve aggregated information about economic events, and commitments in their business applications, and to perform data mining on huge amounts of data related to their businesses.
- Application designers could manually write an algorithm that retrieves the aggregated information from the database; however, they would rather like to anticipate from the application design what information the users of this application will be interested in.
- Business logic should be triggered if certain values reach a certain level. For example, if the inventory goes below a certain limit, a reorder should be planned. If the balance of a bank account goes above a certain threshold, the interest rate should change.
- Users of a business application would like to be informed about what a total amount could be if an economic event occurs. For example, during decrement or increment commitment, users of the business application would like to know the amount of available resources at the promised or expected time.

## Solution

Whenever the value of some REA entity is a sum of the values of related entities, an REA account aspect pattern is applicable.

At the application level, the REA account retrieves the values of all *Addition* and *Subtraction* elements on the related economic events or commitments. The balance of the account is the difference between the sum of the *Additions* on the economic events or commitments and the sum of the *Subtractions* on the economic events or commitments see Fig. 128, unless the balance has changed for reasons outside the scope of the model.

The account pattern usually retrieves the values of the *Addition* and *Subtraction* as well as the supplementary information from the *Entry* element of the *POSTING PATTERN*. Therefore, the *ACCOUNT* and *POSTING* pattern are typically used together. The values of the *Dimensions* registered by the *POSTING* pattern are available to the *ACCOUNT* pattern; therefore, users of business applications can perform an analysis of the aggregated value provided by the *ACCOUNT* pattern.

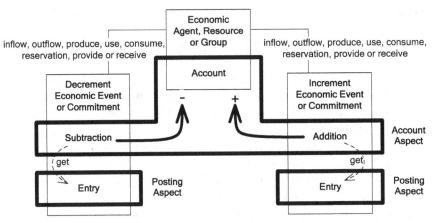

**Fig. 128.** Account in the REA application model

## Design of the Account Pattern

The *aspect type level* encapsulates the business logic of the aspect and configuration parameters, which can be set by application developers. At the aspect type level, the *Account Aspect* defines the possible sets of comparable entries known to the business application. The possible sets are specified in the *Name* attribute and can, for example, be inventory account, finance account, man-hour account, or distance account. The *Account Type* has an attribute, *Unit of Measure Type*, describing which *Units of Measure* are allowed for the accounts. A *Unit of Measure Type* can, for example, be Money. This would allow the *Accounts* to be measured in USD, GBP, or EUR.

The *Addition Type* and *Subtraction Type* contain information about the values that increase and decrease the balance of the account. The *Value Rule* attributes contain information about how the addition and subtraction elements retrieve their values. The *Value Rule* is usually a reference to the *Entry* element of the *Posting* aspect. In this way, the posting dimensions are also available to the *Account*, which are then used in the *Perform Analysis()* method of the *Account*.

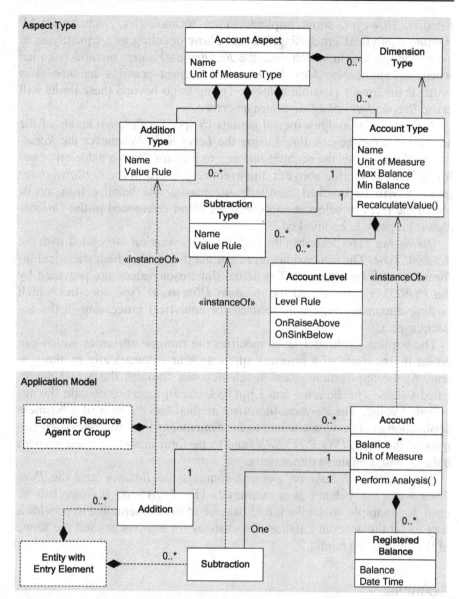

**Fig. 129.** Design of the account pattern

The *RecalculateValue()* method is called whenever the *Balance* of the *Account* should be recalculated. Calling this method will update account *Balance* based on the values of the *Additions* and *Subtractions* and the last *Registered Balance*. The *Balance* can be updated whenever there is a new instance of an economic event or commitment with the *Addition* or *Sub-*

*traction*. However, some implementation technologies, such as OLAP (Online Analytical Processing), do not allow updating as frequently as at every transaction, in which case the *RecalculateValue()* method is called whenever applicable. *Max Value* is the highest possible balance. *Min Value* is the lowest possible balance. Trying to go beyond these limits will cause *RecalculateValue()* to return an error.

*Account Level* assigns special actions to specific *Balance* levels of the account that can be calculated using the *Level Rule*. Whenever the *Recalculate Value* causes the account *Balance* to increase from a value on or below a level to a value above it, the event referenced in the *OnRaiseAbove* property will be invoked. Similarly, decreasing the balance from on or above the level to below it will cause the event referenced in the *OnSinkBelow* property to be invoked.

*Dimension Type* describes the additional information associated with the *Account Type*. The dimensions represent the things for which statistical information can be obtained. The actual dimension values are provided by the *POSTING* pattern, and the *Account Dimension Type* specifies which posting dimension type will be used for analytical processing in the account aspect.

The application model level specifies the runtime attributes which can be set by the users of a business application or automatically by the system. At the application model level, *Account* contains the actual aggregated values. The *Balance* and *UnitOfMeasure* properties contain the aggregated value. The *PerformAnalysis()* method lets the user of a business application drill down according to the dimensions from the associated *Entries* of the *POSTING PATTERN,* and to perform analysis on the account balance based on these dimensions.

The *Registered Balance* element contains the *Balance* and the *Date Time* when the balance was measured. The *Registered Balance* can be used, for example, to set the initial balance of the account, and to provide a way to set the account balance if it changes for reasons beyond the scope of the application model.

## Examples

Fig. 130 illustrates an example of an account on economic resource *Cash*.

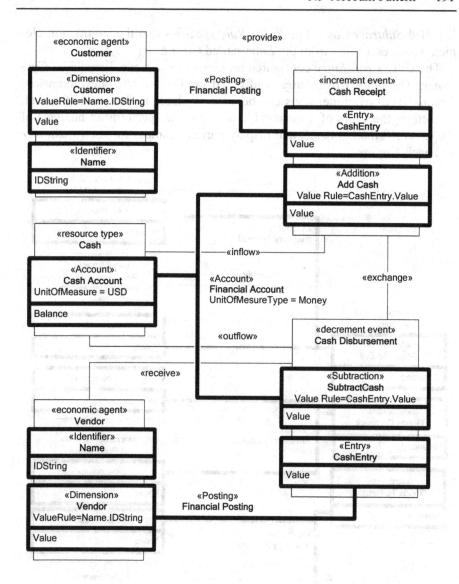

**Fig. 130.** A cash account

This account is part of the aspect called *Financial Account*. The name of the account is *Cash Account*, and its addition element is called *Add Cash*, configured on the *Cash Receipt* economic event. This addition element receives a value from *Entry* called *Cash Entry*. The subtraction element of the account is configured on the *Cash Disbursement* economic event, and is called *Subtract Cash*. The *Value Rule* specifies that the subtraction element receives a value from the *Entry* called *Cash Entry*.

The entry *Cash Entry* configured on *Customer* has one dimension, *Customer*. The entry *Cash Entry* configured on *Vendor* has one dimension, *Vendor*. The two dimensions can become available to the account aspect. Therefore, the users of a business application can perform an analysis of the *Cash Account* balance, and display partial balances for each *Customer* and each *Vendor*.

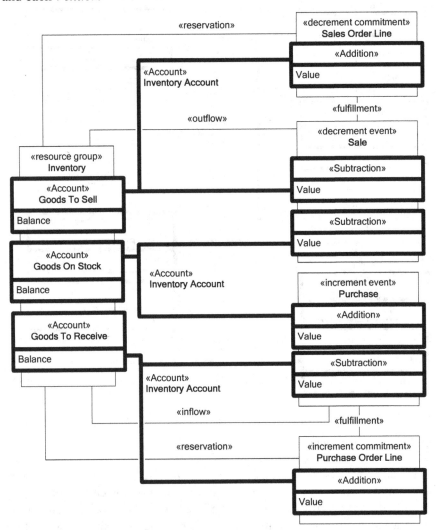

**Fig. 131.** Inventory accounts

Fig. 131 shows an example of three inventory accounts. An inventory is a group of items on hand. The account *Goods to Sell* has increment on commitment *Sales Order Line*, and decrement on economic event *Sale*. The account *Goods on Stock* has increment on economic event *Purchase*, and decrement on economic event *Sale*. The account *Goods to Receive* has increment on commitment *Purchase Order Line*, and decrement on economic event *Purchase*. Observe that there is no rule that the addition aspect element must be on an increment economic event, or vice versa. For example, the *subtraction* element of the *Goods To Sell* account is configured on the *increment* economic event *Purchase*.

## Resulting Context

As described earlier, the REA model differs from double entry accounting because it considers economic transactions (economic events and commitments) as primary data about the enterprise, and aggregated information such as accounts, are information derived from the economic transactions; or, in other words, as reports.

The account in double entry accounting is different than the REA account. In double entry, every account has two sides, the debit or left side, and the credit or right side. Double entry accounting means that every transaction (economic event or commitment) is recorded twice: once on the debit side and once on the credit side. An entry is called balanced if the sum of the debit amounts equals to the sum of the credit amounts.

Double entry accounting is a common practice in many companies for keeping track of financial data, and is required by legislation in some countries.

We can derive all information that is needed for constructing accounts in double entry accounting from the REA model. Therefore, if local legislation or tax authorities require a financial report as it would be in the double entry system, it can be created on demand from the REA model. However, the users of a business application can still keep the richness of the information provided by the REA model for their management decisions.

## 5.6   Materialized Claim Pattern

|  | Invoice |  |
| --- | --- | --- |
| | Hotel: Y    Date: 11 February 2005 | |
| | Guest: X | |
| | Service | Price |
| Materialization | Accomodation | 450,00 |
| Materialization | Accomodation | 450,00 |
| Settlement | Paid | 900,00 |
| Claim | Amount to Pay | 0,00 |

*Outflow and inflow economic events usually do not occur simultaneously, and the exchange duality between the economic events is out of balance for a certain period of time. In this case, it is common practice for one economic agent to send another an invoice to settle the amount owed*

### Context

When a company receives goods or services from its vendor, it often does not pay for them until it receives an invoice. The invoice basically says: "We gave you the goods; give us the money, please."

A contract between the company and its vendor usually specifies the payment terms, so the company could in fact pay for the goods according to the payment terms. If the unbalanced amount is known to both economic agents, the invoice is not necessary; it is just common business practice. However, in some cases, the price is not known when the contract is signed. For example, a service technician who provides maintenance of equipment is paid according to material and time consumption. In this case, the invoice also specifies the value of the economic event, which corresponds to the time and material used to perform the maintenance.

### Problem

How do we keep the economic agents informed about unbalanced economic exchanges?

## Forces

Three forces must be considered when solving this problem:

- If all economic agents involved can keep their models synchronized, the materialized claim would not be necessary. However, this is not always the case.
- Legal reasons might require a document specifying the unbalanced value. For example, value-added tax (VAT) in some countries is calculated as a percentage of the invoiced amount, and the document specifying this amount must be made available to tax authorities.
- The exact unbalanced value between the inflow and outflow events might be unknown to one of the economic agents. For example, a service contract might specify payments according to consumption. When the service is finished, the consumption is known to the service provider and to the customer. Or a vendor sometimes adds a shipping fee to the price of products, whose exact value might not be known to the purchaser at the time of purchase. We want to ensure that economic agents agree upon the unbalanced value.

## Solution

Whenever an economic event occurs without the occurrence of all corresponding dual economic events, there exists a claim between economic agents related to the economic events.

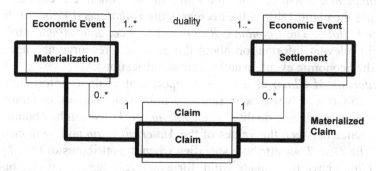

**Fig. 132.** Materialized claim

The *Materialized Claim* is a physical representation of an REA entity *Claim*. A responsibility of a *Claim* is to contain the unbalanced value and business logic determining whether there is an imbalance. The *Materiali-*

*zation* and *Settlement* elements contain information about the unbalanced economic events.

## Design of the Materialized Claim Pattern

The structure of the Materialized Claim pattern is shown in Fig. 133. The *aspect type level* encapsulates the business logic of the aspect and configuration parameters, which can be set by application developers. At the aspect type level, the *Claim Type* contains the *Name* of the materialized claim, such as Invoice or Credit Memo. The *Materialization Type* and *Settlement Type* contain *Value Rule, Resource Rule*, and *Agent Rule* that determine how the *Value, Resource*, and *Agent* properties of *Materialization* are obtained.

The *application model level* specifies the runtime attributes that can be set by the users of business applications or automatically by the system. At the application model level, the *Materialization* element contains the *Value* of an economic event that is used to materialize, i.e., create, the claim. As economic events can contain several value attributes, such as quantity, price, and cost, the materialization element specifies which of these values will be considered as an input for the balance. This *Value* increases the *Unbalanced Value* of the *Materialized Claim*. The *Resource* and *Agent* attributes contain relevant information about the economic resource and agent related to the economic event. What information is considered relevant depends on the requirements of the users of the business application, but it usually is an identification of the resource and agent.

The *Settlement* element contains the *Value* of the economic event that is used to settle the claim. This value decreases the *Unbalanced Value* of the *Materialized Claim*. The *Economic Resource* and *Economic Agent* attributes contain relevant information about the economic resource and agent related to the economic event, usually their identifications.

The *Materialized Claim* element is a report that contains information about the unbalanced value and relevant information about economic events related by exchange duality. The *Unbalanced Value* can be obtained as the difference between the values of the *Materialization* and *Settlement* elements. The *Date Time* attribute specifies when the attributes of the *Materialized Claim* have been made valid, for example, when an invoice has been created.

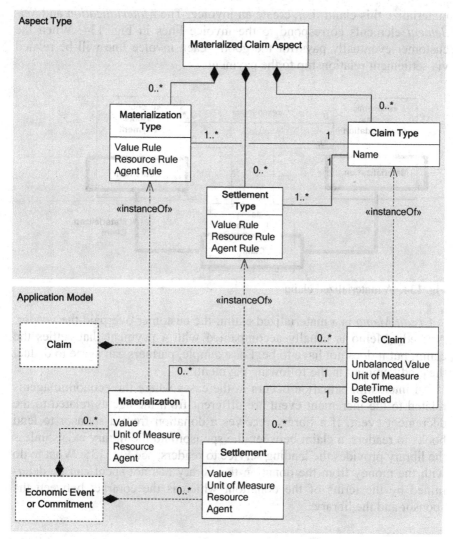

**Fig. 133.** Design of the materialized claim pattern

## Examples

The *Invoice* is a materialized claim: the customer should pay for the goods or services the vendor provided.

When a vendor ships goods to the customer, a claim exists until the customer pays for the goods. At any time after the shipment, the vendor can materialize this claim, i.e., create an invoice. The *Materialization* and *Settlement* elements correspond to the invoice lines in Fig. 134. When the customer eventually pays for the goods, each invoice line will be related via settlement relationship to the payment.

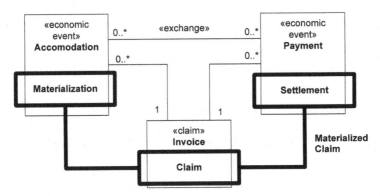

**Fig. 134.** A materialized claim

*Credit Memo* is a materialized claim: the customer overpaid the vendor. A Credit Memo is usually accompanied with a payment that settles the claim, but it does not have to be. For example, partners can agree to deduct the credit amount in the following payment.

An interesting situation occurs in the cases where the economic agents related to the increment event are different from the agents related to the decrement event. If a library receives a donation from a sponsor to lend books to readers, a claim between the sponsor and the library exists unless the library provides the lending service to readers; see Fig. 135. What to do with the money from the donation the library has not spent can be determined by the terms of the donation, which is the contract between the sponsor and the library.

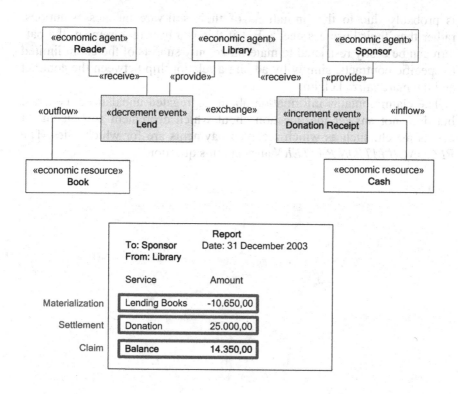

**Fig. 135.** Donations create claims

## Resulting Context

In the REA modeling framework, a materialized claim such as an invoice is a kind of report, containing information derived from economic events. This contrasts with some business software applications, where the invoice is the central part of the business solution. Invoices and other materialized claims are needed when the business management tools are pen and paper, but as the data in business applications of trading partners can be kept synchronized, invoices are not necessary in order to run a business.

A materialized claim can contain information about all unbalanced dualities between participating economic agents. The invoice created according to the model in

Fig. 134 is not limited to a single order, but can contain claims from all shipped but unpaid for orders for a specific economic agent. Many companies have a business practice to create one invoice per sales order, but this is probably due to the limitations of their software business solutions, rather than their business needs. But if this is a user requirement, the pattern can be easily restricted to materialize only subsets of the claim limited to specific contracts, simply by adding a relationship between the contract and the materialized claim.

The claim contains information about aggregated unbalanced amounts, but does not answer the question about which decrement and increment events match, such as which received payments are for which sales. The *RECONCILIATION PATTERN* answers this question.

## 5.7   Reconciliation Pattern

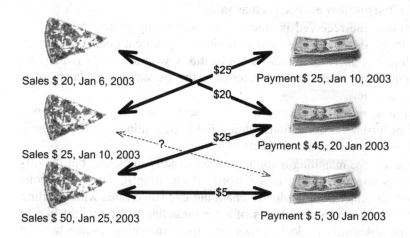

Sales $ 20, Jan 6, 2003     $25     Payment $ 25, Jan 10, 2003

$20

Sales $ 25, Jan 10, 2003    ?    $25    Payment $ 45, 20 Jan 2003

Sales $ 50, Jan 25, 2003    $5    Payment $ 5, 30 Jan 2003

*Have you ever experienced a situation in which a company has received a payment, it was difficult for it to determine what this payment is for?*

### Context

One of the REA domain rules specify that in the REA application model, every increment event must be related to a decrement event, and vice versa. This rule must also be applied at runtime; each actual instance of an increment event must eventually be related to one or more actual instances of a decrement event, and vice versa.

### Problem

How do users of business applications find which occurrences of increment and decrement economic events should match?

### Forces

The following forces must be resolved in the solution:

- Some inflow economic events, such as payments, come with incomplete information about who sent cash, and what the payment was for. Users of business application would like to match this payment with one or more of the outflow events, such as sales.
- Sometimes, the received payment does not exactly match the price of the sold goods or services, and sometimes a payment comes in several installments. Users of business applications would like to match the payments with sales, and to determine the outstanding balance of a given customer.
- Sometimes, economic events do not exactly match the commitments. Users of business applications would like to determine which economic events match which commitments.
- Sometimes, the matching amounts are not exactly the same, but the difference is so small that it is not worth of claiming it. These situations can happen, for example, due to changing exchange rates when dealing with different currencies. Users of a business application might like to have the possibility to declare these events as matching, even when the numbers differ.

## Solution

The *Reconciliation* pattern is essentially a many-to-many relationship between increment and decrement economic events related by the exchange or conversion duality, or between commitments and economic events related by fulfillment, or between commitments related by reciprocity. The *Initiator* and *Terminator* elements hold the values to be reconciled.

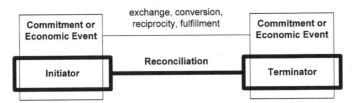

**Fig. 136.** A reconciliation

## Design of the Reconciliation Pattern

The reconciliation pattern at the aspect type level and the application model level is illustrated in Fig. 137.

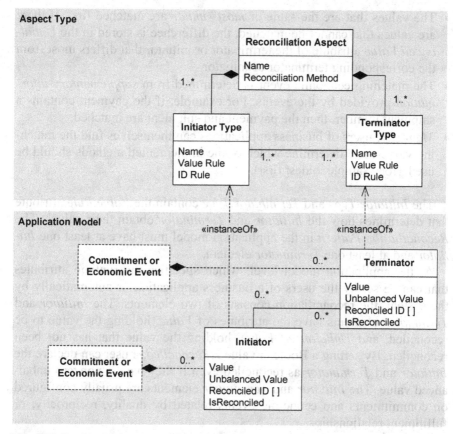

**Fig. 137.** Design of the reconciliation pattern

The aspect type level encapsulates the business logic of the aspect and configuration parameters that can be set by application developers. At the aspect type level, the *Reconciliation Aspect* contains an attribute for its *Name* and a *Reconciliation Method*. The reconciliation method is an enumeration that can be set by the application developer, and determines the strategy of how to match the initiator and terminator values. Some of the reconciliation strategies are:

- The values of *oldest* initiator and terminator are matched first. If these values are not the same, the difference is applied to the next oldest initiator or terminator, and the difference is matched to the next oldest initiator or terminator. The outstanding value is stored in the *Unbalanced Value* attribute of the newest terminator or initiator element.

- The values that are the same or *most similar* are matched first. If there are values that cannot be matched, the difference is stored in the *Unbalanced Value* attribute of the terminator or initiator that differs most from the corresponding terminator or initiator.
- The matching economic event is determined from *supplementary information* provided by the events. For example, if the payment contains a shipment number, then the payment and shipment are matched.
- *Manually*, users of business applications can themselves find the matching values, and determine which of the implemented methods should be used, (for example, oldest first).

The *Initiator Type* and *Terminator Type* contain the *Value Rule* attribute that determines how the *Initiator* and *Terminator* obtain their values. The *Reconciliation Pattern* in the application model must have at least one *Initiator* and at least one *Terminator* element.

At the application model level, which specifies the runtime attributes that can be set by the users of a business application or automatically by the system, the reconciliation consists of two elements. The *Initiator* and *Terminator* elements have the attributes of *Value*, holding the value to be reconciled, and *Unbalanced Value*, holding the value that has not been reconciled. By setting a Boolean value *IsReconciled*, a user can declare the *Initiator* and *Terminator* as reconciled even if they have a nonzero unbalanced value. The *Initiator* and *Terminator* elements are usually configured on commitments and economic events related by duality, reciprocity, or fulfillment relationships.

## Examples

Fig. 138 illustrates how a reconciliation can be applied between a *Sale* and the corresponding *Cash Receipt*.

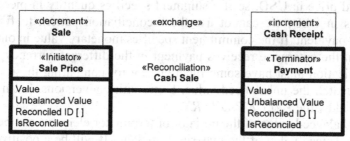

**Fig. 138.** Reconciliation between commitment and economic event

An enterprise made three sales to a customer: S001 for USD20, S002 for USD25, and S003 for USD50; it received three payments from the customer: P001 for USD 25, P002 for USD45, and P003 for 5 USD. The problem is to match sales and payments.

Table 2 below, shows the *Initiator* and *Terminator* in a table format. We decide to match the same or similar values (see also the illustration before the Context section) first. We match *S001* with *P002*, and the payment *P002* will cover the shipments *S001* and *S003*. As the customer has not paid enough to cover the three sales, sale *S003* has an unbalanced value of USD 20.

**Table 2.** Example of reconciliation

| Initiator | | | |
|---|---|---|---|
| Event ID | Value | Unbalanced Value | Reconciled ID |
| S001 | 20 | 0 | P002 |
| S002 | 25 | 0 | P001 |
| S003 | 50 | 20 | P002, P003 |

| Terminator | | | |
|---|---|---|---|
| Event ID | Value | Unbalanced Value | Reconciled ID |
| P001 | 25 | 0 | S002 |
| P002 | 45 | 0 | S001, S003 |
| P003 | 5 | 0 | S003 |

## Resulting Context

In order to use the reconciliation pattern, the values of the initiator and terminator must be comparable; they must have the same or transformable units of measure. For example, we cannot directly compare quantity in pieces and price in USD, so if a shipment specifies quantity in pieces but not prices in USD, we cannot use the reconciliation pattern to find the matching payment. If the commitment specifies monetary value in one currency, but the enterprise receives payment in the different currency, business application must have some functionality for comparing these values in order match the unbalanced value. Some unit conversions, but not all, are handled by the *VALUE PATTERN*.

The unbalanced value of the initiator or terminator elements can be used as an unbalanced value of the materialized claim. It will be a positive or a negative claim, depending on whether the initiator and terminator will be configured on an increment or an decrement economic event, respectively.

## 5.8 Due Date Pattern

*Due date is the time by which something must be finished or completed*

### Context

Deadlines, starting dates, renewal dates, and last payment dates are examples of the dates that are often of high importance to users of business applications. Often certain actions have to be taken, and things have to be done on or before these dates, or within a certain time period after these dates.

### Problem

How to model due dates in the REA model, and how can a business application help users to manage the dates?

### Forces

If you deal with due dates, you many need to address the following forces:

- Due dates specify moments that occur in the future. It usually does not make sense to set a due date for an event that has occurred in the past.
- The due dates are usually properties of commitments, claims, and contracts. Some commitments specify time intervals, such as the commitments in conversion processes; some specify instantaneous events, such as those for change of ownership.
- Some time events are often related to other time events; for example, users of business applications might like to receive a customer's payment within 30 days from the invoice date.

## Solution

We will illustrate a simple version of the pattern that satisfies the forces; it consists of one element, *Due Date*. Due Date is one of the patterns that do not crosscut REA entities. We will discuss a more complex version of the due date pattern in the resulting context section. The *Due Date* pattern can be used whenever the business logic needs to specify the deadlines, milestones, and dates that will or should occur in the future, as well as the dependencies of these dates on other dates.

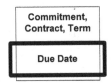

**Fig. 139.** Due date pattern

## Design of the Due Date Pattern

A design of the Due Date pattern is illustrated in Fig. 140. The due date pattern at the *aspect type level* encapsulates the business logic of the due date aspect and configuration parameters, which can be set by application developers. The *Due Date Type* specifies the configuration parameters for the *Due Date* elements. *Editable* is an enumeration indicating whether the user can, cannot, or must edit the *Date* of the *Due Date*. The *Activation Rule* specifies how the *Date* property of the *Due Date* is determined. The *Activation Rule* specifies how the *Date* depends on other dates or other values in a business application. Often, the due date pattern needs to have knowledge of a calendar. The *Activation Rule* can specify, for example, that payment should occur on the fifth day of the month, following a specified date, unless the payment date is Saturday, Sunday, or a public holiday, in which case the date is the preceding week day.

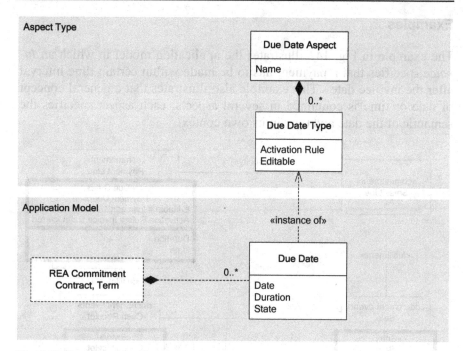

**Fig. 140.** Design of the due date pattern

The *application model level* specifies the runtime attributes of the due dates that can be set by the user of a business application or automatically by the system. The *State* of the *Due Date* can be *Upcoming, Expired,* or *Disabled.* Before the time specified by the *Date*, the *State* of the *Due Date* is *Upcoming.* After the *Date*, the *State* is *Expired.* The *State* of the *Due Date* can also be *Disabled.* The *Date* specifies the date and time the due date expires. The *Date* can be editable by the user of a business application, depending on the configuration property *Editable* on *Due Date Type.* Many *Due Dates* expire after a period of time after the date specified by the *Activation Rule.* The *Duration* specifies the difference between the dates calculated by the *Activation Rule* and the *Date.* The users of business applications may edit the *Duration*; therefore, it is a property of *Due Date* and not *Due Date Type.*

Time intervals, for example, the duration of a task, can be modeled as two due date aspect patterns. One *Due Date* specifies the start of the task. Another *Due Date* specifies the end of the task. The activation rule of the second due date is configured to receive the value of the first due date, and the duration specifies the length of the task. An example is illustrated in Fig. 143.

## Examples

The example in Fig. 141 illustrates the application model in which an *Invoice* specifies that a payment has to be made within certain time interval after the invoice date. This example also illustrates that a general concept of date or time is contained in several aspects; each aspect specifies the semantic of the date and time in its own context.

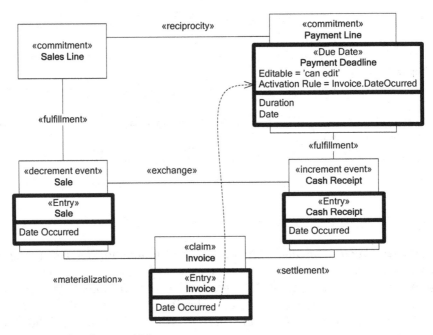

**Fig. 141.** An invoice specifying payment

The moment at which the Invoice is issued is modeled as the *Date Occurred* property of the *Entry* element of the *Posting* aspect on the *Invoice*. The *Activation Rule* of the *Due Date* element is configured to receive the *Date Occurred* value, and the *Duration* specifies the delay.

The model in Fig. 142 shows an example of two due date aspects that specify a time interval. The *Start Task* aspect has a blank activation rule and the *Date* must be set by users of the business application. The *End Task* aspect has an *Activation Rule* set to refer to the *Date* of the *Start Task*; its *Duration* specifies the duration of the task; and users of the business application can edit the date.

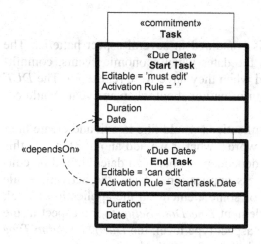

**Fig. 142.** The start and end of a task

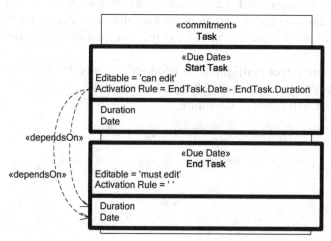

**Fig. 143.** The scheduled end and the duration of a task determines its scheduled start

In the planning of conversion processes, often the scheduled *end date* of an economic event is known, and the planners need to determine the latest start date. The scheduled start and the scheduled end of the economic event, specified by the commitments, are *Due Dates*. The activation rule of the scheduled start due date is set to calculate it from the duration and the scheduled end date, see Fig. 143.

## Resulting Context

The general concept of time is contained in several aspect patterns. The *POSTING PATTERN* contains the dates when economic events, commitments, and claims occurred and when they have were registered. The *DUE DATE PATTERN* captures the information about when an event should occur.

What if users of business applications would like to edit and create their own activation rules? In other words, what if we add another force to this pattern: "The rules specifying dependencies between dates should be editable by the users of the business application." Then, the activation rule must be present as a property of some element on the application model; for example, we must add a element *Due Date Setup* to the aspect at the application model level. At the aspect type level, the *Due Date Setup Type* will specify a language in which the users of the business application express the activation rules. For example, an activation rule '*21D*' in a business software application Navision determines the due date as 21 days from now, '*CM+8D*' means that the due date is at the end of the current month plus eight days. These rules can determine the dependency on the current date, but not a dependency on other dates specified in the business application.

The *Due Dates* are never configured on economic events, because economic events register what has already happened, while the due dates represent moments that will occur in the future.

## 5.9   Description Pattern

### T-shirt with Miami Beach Topics

Relax in this high quality (Hanes-Beefy-T) white T-shirt with Miami Beach Topics silk-screened on the front. The back is plain.

*A description of an item from a product catalogue*

### Context

REA entities, especially economic resources and resource types, contain information about real things. This information is presented to users of business applications in many different ways and formats. Some of the information also comes in unstructured form.

### Problem

How do we store unstructured information about REA entities?

### Forces

The following forces need consideration:

- Products can be described in many different ways. For some entities, simple text is sufficient, but a description can also be graphical. Descriptions can also incorporate sound or other digital multimedia.
- Some forms of description are standardized or regulated by professional bodies, such as various types of specifications and drawings.
- In addition to products, which are economic resources, users of business applications often store unstructured information about other REA entities, such as economic agents and events.

## Solution

Description aspect pattern can be used to store unstructured information about REA entities. The sketch of a solution is illustrated in Fig. 144. Description pattern does not crosscut other entities, and can be configured on any REA entity.

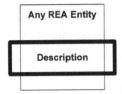

**Fig. 144.** Description pattern

## Design of the Description Pattern

The *aspect type level* encapsulates the business logic of the description aspect and the configuration parameters, which can be set by application developers. At the aspect type level, the *Description Aspect Type* defines the *Name* of the type of description. The *Media* attribute of *Description Type* determines what kind of information can be held by the *Description* element. Examples of *Media* can be text, multiline text, picture, or Web address.

The *application model level* specifies the runtime attributes that can be set by the users of business applications or automatically. At the application model level, *Description* contains an attribute that at runtime contains a description of the instance of the REA entity.

*Textual Description* remains the most flexible means of describing an REA entity. Textual description is always in a specific language; for some business solutions it is necessary to provide the textual information in several languages.

*Graphical Description* is often used in to describe products in product catalogues, but can also be used to store drawings and diagrams.

*Web Page* is a pointer to the description of an REA entity on the Internet. A *Web Page* is often used as a description of economic agents such as companies. The attribute *Internet Address* contains a URL (Universal Resource Locator), a text string pointing to the description of the business object on the Internet. The *Web Page* is often used as a description of the economic agents.

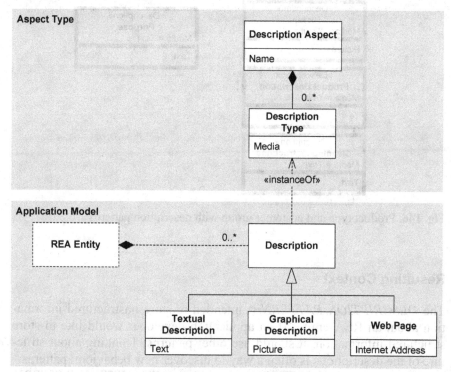

**Fig. 145.** Design of the description pattern

## Examples

An example of a food item *Product Type* is illustrated in Fig. 146. This *Product Type* is an economic resource with configured description patterns *Picture*, *Product Description* (which is supposed to contain textual description of the product, in free text), and *Cleaning Instructions* (a textual description), usually for both before and after opening the product.

The other example illustrated in Fig. 146 is a *Customer VAT Group*. At runtime, users of a business application will classify the customers into several VAT groups, and describe the *Purpose* of each group with free text.

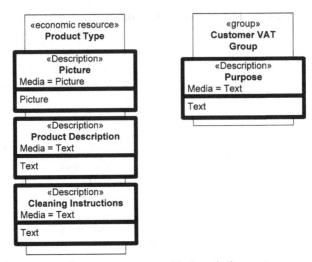

**Fig. 146.** Product type and customer group with description patterns

## Resulting Context

The *DESCRIPTION PATTERN* is intended to store unstructured information about an REA entity. If an application developer would like to store
structured information, it should use other patterns. Thinking about structure of the descriptions is often a way to discover new behavioral patterns.

*IDENTIFICATION PATTERN* is related to *DESCRIPTION PATTERN*.
Although a *Description* can be also used to identify an entity, it is not its
primary purpose. Usually, it is better to have one or more dedicated *Identifiers* using the *IDENTIFICATION PATTERN*.

*NOTE PATTERN* is also related to *DESCRIPTION PATTERN*. Both
*Note* and *Description* store unstructured information. The difference is that
the primary purpose of the *Description* is to store information that describes an REA entity.  The *Note* can be used to store any unstructured information about the REA entity. It is also usual that different users of
business application will have different access rights to the *Description*
then to the *Note*. While a *Description* about the product can be made available to the customers, the *Notes* might contain internal information for
salesmen or warehouse personnel.

## 5.10 Notification Pattern

*SMS (Short Message Service) is a text message to be sent and received to a mobile phone via the network operator*

### Context

Various users of business applications should often be notified when certain events occur, or when certain conditions become true. For example, both customer and bank personnel might be interested in being notified when the customer account has been overdrawn. Business applications can be configured to create and send notifications automatically.

### Problem

How do we notify users of business applications about changes in the REA entities?

### Forces

Several forces arise when designing the solution:

- There are different ways to contact users of business applications. The notification can range from a message box window on a computer screen to sending a letter to a specified address.
- Different users of business applications can be contacted in different ways. Some users can be contacted in multiple ways. The method of notification can vary, depending upon the user and upon the kind of notification.
- Different users are interested in different information resulting from the same change.

## Solution

Notification is a specific unit of functionality that encapsulates the mechanism for notifying users of business applications. A notification pattern consists of two elements. The *Address* element contains the way to contact the economic agent. The *Message* element contains the information forwarded to the agent, as well as the logic determining when the agent is notified.

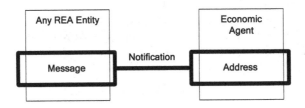

**Fig. 147.** Notification pattern

## Design of Notification Pattern

At the *aspect type level*, *Notification Type* contains the *Name* of the notification, and encapsulates the business logic of forwarding messages to specific addresses. The *Media Rule* defines which *Media* the specific *Address* is allowed to contain, and hence determines which attributes a specific *Address Type* contains (for example, street, city, and zip code for postal address), and consequently also which message types can be delivered to which kinds of addresses; hence, the *Media Rule*. Examples of *Media* are postal address, e-mail address, and SMS address.

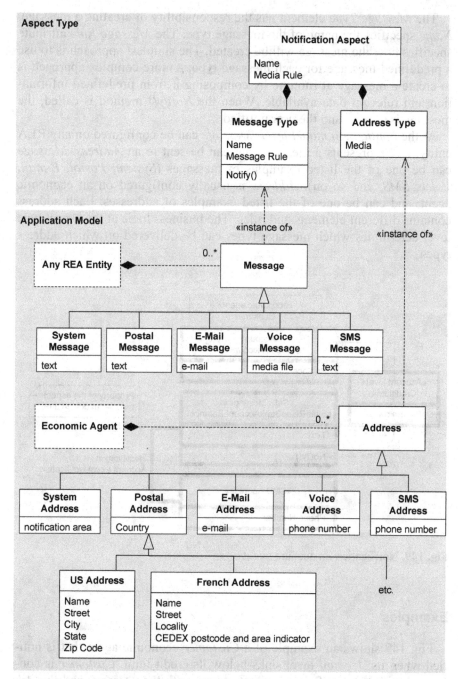

**Fig. 148.** Design of the notification pattern

The *Message Type* element has the responsibility of creating a message. *Name* specifies the name of the message type. The *Message Rule* attribute specifies how the message will be created. The simplest approach is to use a predefined message for each message type; a more complex approach is to create a message at runtime by composing it from predefined information and relevant data available. When the *Notify()* method is called, the message is created and the user notified.

At the *application model level*, *Message* can be configured on any REA entity, and represents a message that can be sent to an *Address*. *Message* can be one of the listed examples of messages (*System, Postal, E-mail, Voice, SMS*, and so on). *Address* is usually configured on an economic agent, and can be one of the listed examples of addresses. Each address contains different elements and rules. The business logic at the aspect type level determines which message types can be delivered on which address types.

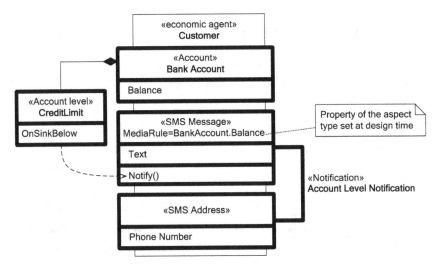

**Fig. 149.** Notification on account event

## Examples

Fig. 149 shows an example of a *Customer* economic agent that is notified when its *Account* level sinks below its credit limit. *Customer* is configured with the *Notification* aspect, where both the *Message* and the *Address* elements are configured at the *Customer* entity. The *OnSinkBelow*

event of the *Account Level* (a part of the *Account Type* element, see the
*ACCOUNT PATTERN*) causes the *Notify()* message of *SMS Message* element to send an SMS message with the *Balance* of the *Bank Account* aspect element as *Text*

A mobile phone operator, T-Mobile, in some countries sends a voice
and an SMS message to its customers every time a customer receives a
message in his voice mail. Fig. 150 shows how this functionality could be
implemented using the notification aspect pattern.

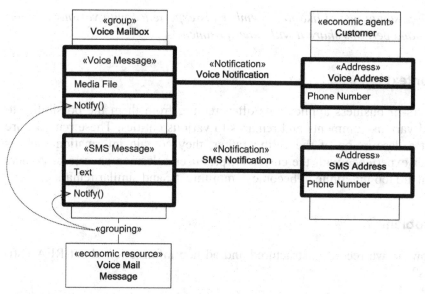

**Fig. 150.** Notification on new voice mail

*Voice Mail Messages* are economic resources that are members of the
group *Voice Mailbox* of a specific customer. Whenever someone records a
new voice mail message, the grouping relationship calls a *Notify()* method
of the *Voice Notification* and *SMS Notification* elements. These elements
create the voice and text messages and send them to the customer *Phone
Number*.

## 5.11 Note Pattern

*The postman would like to remember his experience with various customers, and perhaps share it with other postmen*

### Context

Users of business applications often require from them the possibility to add various comments and remarks to various entities. These remarks are not a description of the entity; rather, they contain information such as their experience with the customer, promises salesmen gave to customers that are too indefinite to become commitments, and similar remarks.

### Problem

How do we record unstructured and ad hoc information about REA entities?

### Forces

The following forces arise:

- The remarks and comments are unstructured and are often written as plain text.
- The stored information is often intended only for internal use in the company.
- An REA entity can have many remarks and comments attached.
- Sometimes it is useful to store the date and author with each remark to keep track of the development of the entity.

## Solution

The note aspect pattern can be used to attach comments, observations, and notes to REA entities. The *Note* aspect pattern is illustrated in Fig. 151. It consists of two elements, the *Note* element, whose responsibility is to record the comment, and the *Author* element, which identifies who wrote the note.

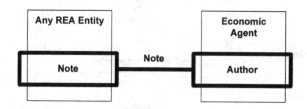

**Fig. 151.** Note aspect pattern

## Design of the Note Pattern

The structure of the Note pattern is illustrated in Fig. 152. At the aspect type level, the *Note Type* specifies its *Name* of the *Note Type*, as users of business applications might want to attach different types of notes to REA entities. *Author Type* specifies the *ID Rule* that determines the information that will identify the author of the *Note*.

At the application model level, *Note* represents one or more comments on an REA entity. *Note* contains the *Text* of the note, and the *Date* when the text was written. The *Author* contains the *Author ID* attribute that identifies the author. There can be multiple instances of the *Note* of the same *Note Type* on a single instance of an REA entity.

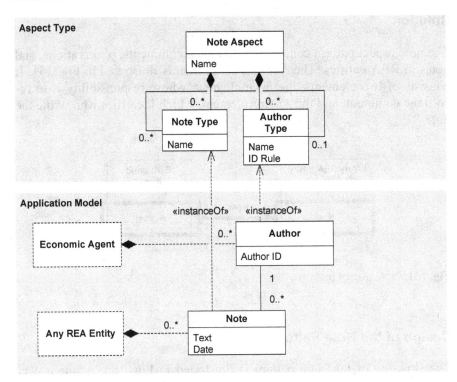

**Fig. 152.** Design of the note pattern

## Examples

The example in Fig. 153 illustrates two note aspects, *Promise* and *Experience*, configured on economic agents *Salesman* and *Customer*. Fig. 154 shows a runtime snapshot of this *Note*; observe that there can be several instances of *Notes* of the same *Note Aspect*, such as several *Promises*.

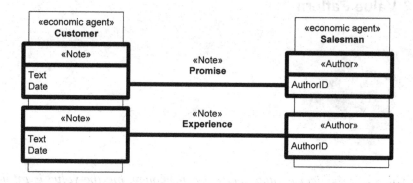

**Fig. 153.** A configured note aspect pattern

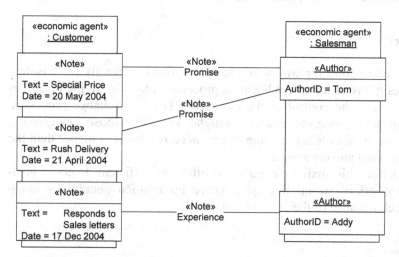

**Fig. 154.** The note aspect pattern at runtime

## Resulting Context

The *NOTE PATTERN* is related to the *DESCRIPTION PATTERN* in the sense that both can store unstructured information. However, the purpose of description and note is different. While the purpose of description is to store the information that actually describes the REA entity, the note can be used to store any unstructured information about an REA entity.

Another difference is that while at runtime there is usually only one *Description* instance per configured *Description Aspect* in an REA entity, there can be multiple instances of *Note*.

## 5.12 Value Pattern

*The value of an object is often measured in money, but the value is influenced by many factors. For example, carat weight, clarity, color, and cut contribute to the value of a diamond*

### Context

A basic assumption for why a rational enterprise has exactly the business processes it has, is that these business processes add value to the resources that are under the control of the enterprise. During exchange processes, economic agents receive resources of higher value than those they give up; in conversion processes the value of produced resources is higher than the resources used and consumed.

In practice, this qualitative answer is often not sufficient. Users of business applications would like quantitative information about how much value each instance of the process adds.

### Problem

How do we represent quantitative information about the value of the REA entities?

### Forces

Resolving this problem effectively requires resolution of the following forces:

- Although rational business processes add value, this is only true on average. Specific instances of value-adding processes can decrease the value of an enterprise' resources[6]. Detailed information about the processes is crucial for process improvement.

- As the value added by business processes is measured through the entrepreneurial purpose of each process, it can be represented in various units; production processes can be measured in terms of quantities and exchange processes can be measured in terms of monetary values.
- Users of business applications might require that value be represented in different units on demand. For example, if an enterprise issues an invoice in one currency and receives payment in another currency, there must be some method how to estimate whether the values of invoice and payment correspond.
- Sometimes, the value must be made immutable; for example, if an enterprise makes an offer to the customer (an offer is a suggested contract), the price must not change, even if the values of the price elements (such as material, tools, and services) change.

## Solution

Value pattern holds information about the value of the REA entities. Values include prices, costs, quantities, taxes, discounts, and bonuses. A value pattern is sketched in Fig. 155. *Value* is calculated from several *Value Components*; for example, the value of tax can be calculated from the sales price and the tax percentage. Both *Value* and *Value Component* are represented as a number and a unit. *Values* and *Value Components* can have different units; it is the responsibility of the *Value Aspect* to perform any conversion.

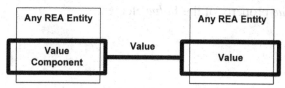

**Fig. 155.** Value pattern

---

[6]  It has been reported that in the film industry, only about 10% of all produced movies are profitable. On average, these 10% must generate enough profit to cover the losses from the 90% of non profitable movies.

## Design of the Value Pattern

The *aspect type level* encapsulates the business logic of the aspect and configuration parameters, which can be set by application developers. At the aspect type level, the *Value Aspect* contains the *Name* of the aspect and *Calculation Rule*, which is an expression of how the *Value* is calculated from the *Value Components*. The *Value Type* holds the *Name*, and the *Unit of Measure*. Further the *Value* has an operation, *LockValue()*, which locks the value in the application model. The *Value Component Type* contains the *Name* of the *Value Component* and the *Unit of Measure*. The *Source Rule* defines how the value of the element is obtained, and usually refers to values of other aspects. The *Multiple* property determines whether there can be multiple elements of the same *Value Component Type* in the application model.

The *Unit of Measure* holds the *Name* and the *Symbol* of the *Unit of Measure* that is used in the *Value Component* and the *Value*. The *Conversion* contains the *Conversion Factor* between various *Units of Measure*. Some conversion factors, such as currency exchange rates, can be obtained dynamically, for example, as Web services.

The *application model level* specifies the runtime attributes that can be set by the users of business applications or automatically by the system. At the application model level, the *Value* element holds the property *Value* together with the *Unit of Measure*. The *Value* element is connected to zero or more *Value Components* from which the *Value* is calculated. The *Value Component* contains the *Value* with the *Unit of Measure*; therefore, it is always possible to determine what *Value Components* the *Value* consists of. The *Value Components* can be given in *Units of Measure* different from that of the *Value* property of the *Value* element.

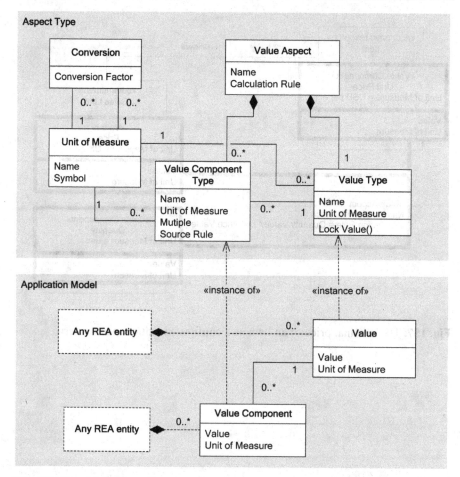

**Fig. 156.** Design of the value pattern

## Examples

The example in Fig. 157 illustrates the value aspect called *Nominal Price*, consisting of one *Value* element and two *Value Component* elements. The element *Price* is configured on the *Sales Line* and is calculated from two elements, *Quantity* and *Unit Price*, simply by multiplying quantity with unit price. When a contract is signed, the *Lock Value()* of the *Price* and *Quantity* is invoked. Then, *Price* and *Quantity* do not change, even if the *Unit Price* changes. Please note that users of business applications can change the *Unit of Measure* of all three elements at runtime; in such a case, the business logic will recalculate the *Value*.

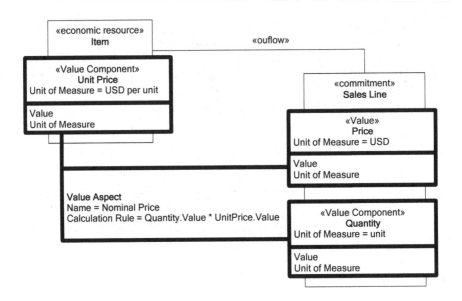

**Fig. 157.** The nominal price of an item as a configured value aspect pattern

## 5.13 Inventor's Paradox Pattern

*How to extend a business application in a consistent manner?*

### Context

Structural patterns describe the REA modeling framework for business systems. The REA concepts have not significantly changed during last ten years; therefore, we do not expect any radical change in it in the near future. The REA modeling framework has survived the test of time and has been successfully implemented in several business standards.

In contrast, behavioral patterns represent the functionality of the business applications that originate in user requirements. It is natural to expect that users of business applications will require richer, more powerful, and generally better software applications in the future. Therefore, it is likely that any limited list of behavioral patterns does not meet all future requirements the users of a business application could possibly have. When application designers implement business applications, they are forced to discover new patterns originating from unexpected user requirements.

### Problem

How do we discover a new behavioral business pattern?

### Forces

A solution is influenced by the following forces:

- Users of your business application require functionality that is not covered by the behavioral patterns we know about.

- Users of business applications sometimes require very specific features that are not always good candidates for behavioral patterns. Behavioral patterns are generalized and reusable units of business logic; therefore, it usually requires substantial work to transform a specific user requirement into a business pattern.
- We would like a general rule or guidelines to help us formulate new business patterns from new user requirements.

## Solution

The solution is known as Inventor's Paradox, described by the mathematician George Polya (Polya 1982):

> "A solution to a general problem is often simpler than a solution to a specific problem."[7]

In summary, the Inventor's Paradox is as follows:

- Solve a specific problem by solving a more general problem.
- The general problem paradoxically has simpler solution.
- But you have to invent an appropriate general problem which covers your specific problem.

To apply the Inventor's Paradox, application designers analyze the users' business problems and try to extract patterns that can be generalized. Then, they solve this generalized problem as one or more behavioral patterns. Finally, they solve each specific problem by configuring the behavioral patterns in a software business application.

The guidelines above are general, and can be applied to solving problems in any domain. In model-driven design for software in a specific domain, the application developers must keep in mind the purpose of the domain, and generalize the specific problems in a way that is consistent with the domain. This sounds easy; but, based on our experience, it is not.

We formulated the following guidelines to help application designers focus on generalizing specific problems in the scope of the business logic domain.

---

[7] Polya's original formulation was "The more ambitious plan may have more chances of success, provided it is not based on a mere pretension, but on some vision of the things beyond those immediately present." We use the formulation by Karl J. Lieberherr (Lieberherr 1997).

The behavioral patterns described in this book

- have business semantics,
- are large units of functionality,
- often crosscut the structural patterns.

These principles are described in more detail below.

### Behavioral Patterns Have Business Semantics

"What business problem does this requirement solve?" is probably the most fundamental question to ask when examining a new user requirement. Users often tend to ask for a low-level or computational functionality, and it is up to the application designer to discover the real business purpose behind this requirement. For example,

– Is a function that computes a sum of numerical values a good candidate for a behavioral pattern in the business domain? Without domain-driven modeling in mind, a designer might think that he can generalize this requirement into an *arithmetic operation* pattern to cover subtraction, multiplication, and division as well. Would it be a good behavioral pattern? We need to discover why the users need to sum values. Do the users need it for making an order total? Do the users need it for calculating the stock value of the product? The arithmetic operation is probably not a good candidate for a behavioral pattern in the business domain, but *contract total* or *account* might be.

– Is a *currency converter* a good candidate for a behavioral pattern in the business domain? We need to discover why the users need a currency converter. If they need it for calculating the value of a payment in another currency, for calculating payment for international customers, and for calculating an offered price of the product, then *monetary value* will be a better candidate for a business pattern than a currency converter.

### Behavioral Patterns Are Large Units of Functionality

If application designers develop a single business application for a specific purpose, they probably do not care about reuse. If user requirements change, the designers just change the application. However, if the application designers are developing a framework that will be used to configure several business applications in a product line, or to configure several very different business applications, then they would like to identify the functionality that is most complex and difficult to implement. Then, they can implement this functionality once in the reusable framework, and configure the actual software applications.

In such an environment, the more the complex and difficult functionality is implemented in the framework, the easier the job becomes for the application designers in configuring the actual business applications, and the less the overall amount of work (framework development plus application development).

Therefore, the more the larger, and most complex and most difficult units of functionality is implemented as behavioral patterns, the easier the job of the application designers becomes. They can then focus on understanding and modeling users' business problems, rather than on implementing them.

### Behavioral Patterns Often Crosscut Structural Patterns

Behavioral patterns often crosscut structural patterns; therefore, if a user requires new functionality or a new data field on an REA entity, this will probably require some collaboration with data on other REA entities.

An example is address. In many business applications customer and vendor entities have addresses, such as shipping address and billing address. However, the addresses are also properties of the purchase order, sales order, and invoice. Therefore, it is useful to think of an address as a module having two elements: the default address on an economic agent, and the actual address on an economic event.

The address pattern presented in this book even has different design, in which the default address is dynamically derived from historical information specified by economic events. Nevertheless, in both cases the address element crosscuts the entities that originate from the domain categories.

# 6 An Aspect-Based Example Application

*By Christian Vibe Scheller*

## 6.1 Setting up the Application Model

In this chapter I will describe how a simple application can be built using aspects. While the example given is very simple, it will hopefully give an idea about the possible complexity of the applications that can be created using the methods described.

The examples described in this chapter are based on a very simple task management system developed in C#. Using the system it should be possible to register tasks. If the task is not completed after a specific time period (e.g., 20 days after the task registration) the system will send a reminder to a specified e-mail address.

For the sake of completeness it should be noted that the tasks managed by this application can actually be thought of as commitments in the REA model. Since this chapter focuses on the use of aspect patterns, however, this knowledge is not used in the examples.

What we want to do is to assemble the task management system from aspects each encapsulating part of the business logic that makes up the system. Using the aspects described in the previous chapters we could end up with something like this:

```
public class Task {
    public Identifier ID =
        new Identifier("TaskIdSequence", 10000, 1000);
    public Description Text = new Description();
    public DueDate Due = new DueDate(20);
    public Notification Notify = new Notification();
}
```

In this example each aspect is defined as a class. The domain class itself is composed of aspects. The metadata used to specify the behavior of each aspect is simply specified as parameters to the aspect's constructor.

What we see is that the *Task* has an *Identifier* which automatically generates a sequence number given a seed of 10000 and a step of 1000. In other words, the first task is called '10000', the next '11000' and so on. The string *TaskIdSequence* specified in the *Identifier's* constructor is necessary for implementation reasons because the *Identifier* class does not know its context and is therefore not able to distinguish the ID of a task from the ID of an employee, sales order, etc. By assigning a unique text string to the identifier, it can use this text string to create different number series for different classes.

An alternative to this solution would be to inform the *Identifier* of its context:

```
ID.Context = this;
```

It is in many ways desirable, however, that the aspects should not know their context. This is primarily due to their nature as cross-cutting concerns. Experience shows that if the context is not known by the aspect the chances of creating a truly "reusable" aspect is greater.

The task also has a description, called *Text*. In the example the description is just a simple text string of arbitrary length. The description does not require any specific metadata.

The *DueDate* describes the date on which the task must be completed or else the system will send a reminder to the responsible person. The implementation of the *DueDate* aspect includes a simple activation rule that calculates the activation date by adding 20 days to the current date.

Finally the *Notification* aspect is responsible for sending the reminder to the responsible person. In this very simple example only the e-mail type of notification is supported and the responsible person's e-mail address is simply assigned explicitly (e.g., through the user interface) to the notification aspect.

A small problem with the way the example is implemented is that some of the metadata is specified directly as parameters to the aspects' constructors. This makes it difficult for other components to gain access to the metadata through reflection. We are in other words "hiding" part of our domain model by hard coding it into the class. A somewhat better solution would be to use .Net attributes to specify the metadata:

```
public class Task {
    [Identifier.Definition(Seed = 10000, Step = 1000)]
    public Identifier ID = new Identifier();
    ...
    ...
}
```

This is a very nice solution because it allows the metadata to be retrieved through reflection. It does however also make the aspect code more complicated because there is no easy way for an aspect class to retrieve the attributes set on a specific property or field. In order to get this to work it would again be necessary for each aspect to know its context. Later in this chapter a solution to this problem will be described.

## 6.2    Creating the Aspect Code

In the task management system described it would probably be overkill to actually write the code for each aspect instead of just including it in the domain class itself. The idea is however that these aspects can be reused over and over again within the same application or even across applications. The aspects can be seen as the business logic equivalents to visual basic controls.

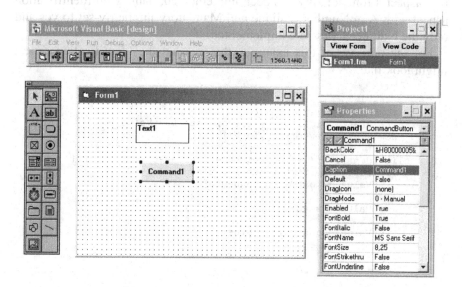

**Fig. 158.** Visual Basic 3.0 development environment with visual basic controls

Visual Basic controls have become popular in the development community because it is extremely simple to create a Windows form by dragging a number of controls onto the form. Often these controls will be very powerful grid controls with spreadsheet functionality, image controls with advanced imaging capabilities and so on. By choosing the right control for the job the developer can minimize the amount of code he needs to write.

Similarly the idea behind aspects is that it should be easy to assemble a domain class from aspects. Each aspect should ideally contain much of the code that the developer would otherwise have to write explicitly on the domain class itself.

Obviously the aspect implementations given in the example are very simple, but they could easily be extended. For instance the Identification aspect could contain code that checked the ID for uniqueness; it could contain different algorithms for generating IDs (GUIDs, Initials, specially formatted IDs such as social security numbers, etc.) and it could contain hashing algorithms for easy retrieval of objects based on their ID.

## 6.3  The Identification Aspect

Let's start with the Identification aspect:

In order to keep the example code simple only a subset of the identification aspect's functionality has been implemented, namely an Identification aspect with AutoNumber, Unique and Mandatory implicitly set to yes and only the NumberSeries rule implemented.

For the purpose of this example, this is what the Identification aspect might look like:

```
public class Identifier  {
    public int Value;
    private static Dictionary<string, int> LastValue =
        new Dictionary<string,int>();

    public Identifier(string sequence, int seed, int step) {
        if (LastValue.ContainsKey(sequence)) {
            Value = LastValue[sequence] + step;
        } else {
            Value = seed;
        }
        LastValue[sequence] = Value;
    }
}
```

## 6.4  The Due Date Aspect

The implementation of the Due Date aspect implements a simple activation rule that adds a number of days to the current date. The implementation does not deal with durations.

With these limitations, the Due Date aspect might look like this:

```
public class DueDate {
    public enum States { Active, Due, Completed, Canceled }
    public DateTime Date;
    public States State = States.Active;
    public event EventHandler Due;
    public event EventHandler Completed;
    public event EventHandler Canceled;
    private static List<DueDate> DueDates = new List<DueDate>();

    public DueDate(int days) {
        Date = DateTime.Now.AddDays(days);
        DueDates.Add(this);
    }

    public static void Check(DateTime date) {
        foreach (DueDate dueDate in DueDates) {
            if (dueDate.Date < date &&
                dueDate.State == States.Active) {
                dueDate.State = States.Due;
                if (dueDate.Due != null) {
                    dueDate.Due(dueDate, null);
                }
            }
        }
    }

    public void Complete(object sender, EventArgs e) {
        State = States.Completed;
        if (Completed != null) {
            Completed(this, null);
        }
    }

    public void Cancel(object sender, EventArgs e) {
        if (State == States.Active) {
            State = States.Canceled;
            if (Canceled != null) {
                Canceled(this, null);
            }
        }
    }
}
```

There are a few things to note about the Due Date aspect: First of all it provides the three event handlers: Due, Complete and Canceled. These event handlers get called by the Due Date aspect when its state changes to Due, Completed and Canceled respectively.

The Due Date aspect also implements the state diagram illustrated in Fig. 159.

The static *Check()* method is meant to be called from time to time to check if any Due Date aspect has reached its due date without being completed or cancelled. The *Check()* method will then raise the *Due* event and change the Due Date aspect's state to *Due*. The *Check()* method uses a static list called *DueDates* to keep track of all the *DueDates* that have been created.

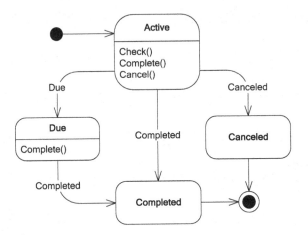

**Fig. 159.** State diagram of the due date aspect

## 6.5   The Notification Aspect

The implementation of the Notification aspect only supports the e-mail type of notification. Furthermore the responsible person's e-mail address is simply assigned explicitly (e.g., through the user interface) to the notification aspect.

This is what the Notification aspect might look like:

```
public delegate string MessageHandler();

    public class Notification {
        public string EMailAddress;
        public event MessageHandler Message;

        public void Notify(object sender, EventArgs e) {
            if (Message == null) {
                MessageBox.Show("Notification caused by " +
                                sender, EMailAddress);
            } else {
                MessageBox.Show(Message(), EMailAddress);
            }
        }
    }
}
```

The Notification aspect consists of a simple text string containing the email address of the recipient and a method called "Notify" that causes the Notification aspect to send a notification to the recipient.

The message handler called *Message* allows the developer to specify the message that the Notification aspect should send to the recipient by providing a delegate to the Notification aspect. The Notification aspect provides a default message in case the developer has not specified a message delegate.

## 6.6   The Description Aspect

The implementation of the Description aspect only supports textual descriptions. The implementation of the Description aspect simply looks like this:

```
public class Description {
    public string Value;
}
```

## 6.7   Interchanging Events Between Aspects

The last thing we need to do in order to get our little task management system to work is to link the Notification aspect to the DueDate aspect so that notifications will be sent out when the due date is reached. This is done by providing a delegate to the Notification aspect's Notify method to the DueDate's Due event.

```
public class Task {
    public Identifier ID =
        new Identifier("TaskSequence", 10000, 1000);
    public Description Text = new Description();
    public DueDate Due = new DueDate(20);
    public Notification Notify = new Notification();

    public Task() {
        Due.Due += new EventHandler(Notify.Notify);
    }
}
```

Now everything is in place. The DueDate aspect will monitor the task and if the task is not completed before the due date it will invoke its "Due" event handler. The Notification aspect in turn will receive the "Due" event and react by sending an e-mail message to the recipient.

The message could either be the default message "Notification caused by DueDate" or it could be a specific message drawing on the task description:

```
public class Task {
    public Identifier ID =
        new Identifier("TaskSequence", 10000, 1000);
    public Description Text = new Description();
    public DueDate Due = new DueDate(20);
    public Notification Notify = new Notification();

    public Task() {
        Due.Due += new EventHandler(Notify.Notify);
        notify.Message += delegate {
            return Text.Value + " is due";
        };
    }
}
```

The use of event handlers as the means of communication creates a publisher/subscriber pattern making sure that the aspects are loosely coupled. This is an important factor in making sure that the aspects are reusable between domain classes.

The type of interaction exemplified by the notification message, where data is sent from one aspect to another, and in the case of the notification message even reformatted, is probably the most complex part of the aspect-based development method. This is where the developer needs to actually write code on the application model-level itself rather than relying on the aspects to do the work.

Again comparing aspects to Visual Basic controls, this is the equivalent of writing Visual Basic code on a button's event handler.

## 6.8  Constructing the User Interface

One of the main benefits of using aspects is that they are truly cross cutting concerns. In our little model of a task management system we have used C# code to describe the definition of a task, but the definition goes further than that. Let us recapitulate: A task is defined by its aspects. In the case of the example application tasks are defined as:

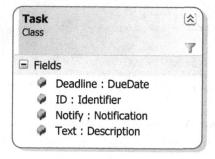

**Fig. 160.** Task class

We can use this definition to derive a number of artifacts: user interface, storage model, documentation, etc. Every one of these artifacts can be seen as a view of the domain model. By using the domain model we can easily construct this rather crude user interface:

**Fig. 161.** User interface of task aspect

The user interface is constructed by iterating through the task's aspects and letting each aspect contribute with its own part of the user interface. This is done in the code below:

```
foreach (FieldInfo fieldInfo in typeof(Task).GetFields()) {
    AspectControl control = null;
    switch (fieldInfo.FieldType.Name) {
        case "Description": {
            control = new DescriptionControl();
            break;
```

```
    }
    case "Identifier": {
        control = new IdentifierControl();
        break;
    }
    case "DueDate": {
        control = new DueDateControl();
        break;
    }
    case "Notification": {
        control = new NotificationControl();
        break;
    }
    default: {
        continue;
    }
}
panel1.Controls.Add(control);
control.Dock = DockStyle.Top;
control.BringToFront();
control.Initialize(fieldInfo.GetValue(obj), fieldInfo.Name);
}
```

Each aspect has a corresponding user interface part (implemented as a user control) that is added to the user interface at runtime.

One importing thing to note is that as the aspects get more elaborate and encapsulate more and more of the business logic, the user interface components will also get more and more elaborate and become small "applications" in themselves rather than just a bunch of textboxes.

The picture below shows a typical screen from Microsoft Navision™. While Microsoft Navision™ does not use aspects explicitly it is obvious that aspect patterns exist per se in the user interface:

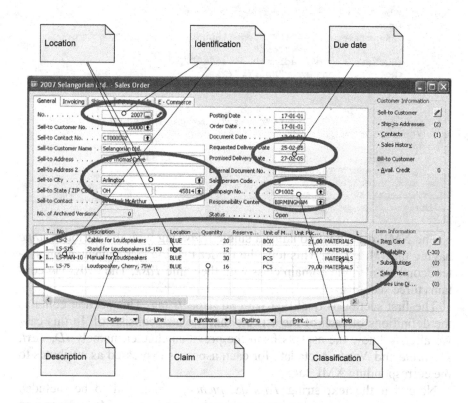

**Fig. 162.** Behavioral patterns in Microsoft Navision

## 6.9  A Model-Based Framework

Until now we have based our task management example on code; in this case written in C#. In the following chapter I will describe an alternative solution: Namely to specify the domain class in an XML document.

In our example we will create an XML document that looks like this:

```xml
<Class name="Task" type="Commitment">
    <Aspects>
        <Identifier name="ID" seed="10000" step="1000"/>
        <Description name="Text" />
        <DueDate name="Deadline" days="20"/>
        <Notification name="Notify"/>
    </Aspects>
    <Subscriptions>
        <Subscription source="Deadline" sourceevent="Due"
                      target="Notify" targetevent="Notify" />
    </Subscriptions>
    <Delegates>
        <Delegate target="Notify" property="Message">
            return Text.Value + " is due";
        </Delegate>
    </Delegates>
</Class>
```

The XML document contains a single *Class* tag with the attribute *name* having the value *Task*. This tells the reader that the task management system contains a single domain class with the name *Task*. The *Class* tag contains three sections.

The first section is qualified with an *Aspects* tag. This section contains the definitions of each of the aspects that the task consists of. In this case we already know the aspects from the previous chapter, namely *ID*, *Text*, *Deadline* and *Notify*. Metadata for each aspect is expressed as attributes to the corresponding XML tag.

Note that the text string *TaskIdSequence*, which had to be included when we used C# is no longer necessary when we use XML. The reason for this is that the context of the aspect's metadata is freely available in the XML document.

The second section is qualified with a *Subscriptions* tag. This section contains all the subscriptions inside the domain class. As we remember, a subscription connects an event raised by one aspect to an event handler on another aspect. In our example only one subscription exists inside the subscription section: The *Due* event of the *Deadline* aspect is connected to the *Notify* event handler of the *Notify* aspect.

The final section is qualified with a *Delegates* tag. This section contains small chunks of code that get called by the aspects on specific occasions. In the example a single delegate is created that returns a text string whenever the *Notify* aspect needs to know its *Message*.

As we can see there is no real difference between the semantics described in the original C# code and in the XML document. The real difference is that XML is much easier to read and manipulate through XPath and XSL stylesheets. It is also easy to validate that the XML document is syntactically correct by using an XML schema.

Let us start by (re)creating the C# code for the domain class using the following XSL stylesheet:

```
<?xml version="1.0" encoding="UTF-8" ?>
<xsl:stylesheet version="1.0"
    xmlns:xsl="http://www.w3.org/1999/XSL/Transform">
    <xsl:output method="text" />

    <!-
    This is the main body of the class
    -->
    <xsl:template match ="/Class">
        public class <xsl:value-of select ="@name"/> {
        <xsl:apply-templates select="Aspects/*" />
        public <xsl:value-of select ="@name"/>() {
        <xsl:apply-templates select="Subscriptions/Subscription"/>
        <xsl:apply-templates select ="Delegates/Delegate"/>
        }
        }
    </xsl:template>

    <!--
    each aspect provides its own code snippet.
    in practice the code only consists of a field declaration.
    the actual code is placed in a separate aspect class
    -->

    <xsl:template match="Identifier">
        public Identifier <xsl:value-of select="@name"/> =
        new Identifier("<xsl:value-of select="../../@name" />" +
        "<xsl:value-of select="@name"/>Sequence",
        <xsl:value-of select="@seed"/>,
        <xsl:value-of select ="@step"/>
        );
    </xsl:template>

    <xsl:template match="Description">
        public Description <xsl:value-of select="@name"/> =
        new Description();
    </xsl:template>

    <xsl:template match="DueDate">
        public DueDate <xsl:value-of select="@name"/> =
        new DueDate(<xsl:value-of select="@days"/>);
    </xsl:template>

    <xsl:template match="Notification">
        public Notification <xsl:value-of select="@name"/> =
        new Notification();
    </xsl:template>
```

```
<!--
the Map section provides the weaving between event sources
and event targets
-->

<xsl:template match ="Subscription">
    <xsl:value-of select ="@source"/>.
    <xsl:value-of select ="@sourceevent"/> +=
    <xsl:value-of select ="@target"/>.
    <xsl:value-of select ="@targetevent"/>;
</xsl:template>

<xsl:template match="Delegate">
    <xsl:value-of select="@target"/>.
    <xsl:value-of select="@property"/> +=
    delegate {
    <xsl:value-of select ="text()"/>;
    };
</xsl:template>
</xsl:stylesheet>
```

By applying the stylesheet to the XML document, the following output is produced (the output has been reformatted for easier reading. It is somewhat difficult to get style sheets to create exactly the indentations and line breaks you want. This is usually no problem however because most compilers disregard indentations and line breaks anyway):

```
public class Task {
    public Identifier ID =
        new Identifier("TaskIDSequence", 10000, 1000);
    public Description Text = new Description();
    public DueDate Deadline = new DueDate(20);
    public Notification Notify = new Notification();

    public Task() {
        Deadline.Due += Notify.Notify;
        Notify.Message += delegate {
            return Text.Value + " is due";
        };
    }
}
```

This is exactly the same code that we created manually in the beginning of the chapter. But now that we have an XML document describing our domain class we may as well create a static user interface instead of relying on reflection. We can achieve this by using the following XSL stylesheet:

```xml
<?xml version="1.0" encoding="UTF-8" ?>
<xsl:stylesheet version="1.0"
    xmlns:xsl="http://www.w3.org/1999/XSL/Transform">
    <xsl:output method="text"/>
    <xsl:template match ="Class" xml:space ="preserve">
        public partial class Form1 : Form {
        public Form1(<xsl:value-of select ="@name" />
        <xsl:value-of select="@name"/>) {
        InitializeComponent();
        Padding = new Padding(5);
        <xsl:for-each select ="Aspects/*">
            <xsl:value-of select ="name()" />Control
            <xsl:value-of select ="@name" /> =
            new <xsl:value-of select ="name()" />Control();
            <xsl:value-of select ="@name" />.Dock = DockStyle.Top;
            <xsl:value-of select ="@name" />.Initialize(
            <xsl:value-of select ="../../@name" />.
            <xsl:value-of select ="@name" />,
            "<xsl:value-of select ="@name" />"
            );
            Controls.Add(<xsl:value-of select ="@name" />);
            <xsl:value-of select ="@name" />.BringToFront();
        </xsl:for-each>
        }
        }
    </xsl:template>
</xsl:stylesheet>
```

Applying this stylesheet to the XML document produces the following output:

```csharp
public partial class Form1 : Form {
    public Form1(Task Task) {
        InitializeComponent();
        Padding = new Padding(5);

        IdentifierControl ID = new IdentifierControl();
        ID.Dock = DockStyle.Top;
        ID.Initialize(Task.ID,"ID");
        Controls.Add(ID);
        ID.BringToFront();

        DescriptionControl Text = new DescriptionControl();
        Text.Dock = DockStyle.Top;
        Text.Initialize(Task.Text, "Text");
        Controls.Add(Text);
        Text.BringToFront();

        DueDateControl Deadline = new DueDateControl();
        Deadline.Dock = DockStyle.Top;
        Deadline.Initialize(Task.Deadline, "Deadline");
        Controls.Add(Deadline);
        Deadline.BringToFront();
```

```
NotificationControl Notify = new NotificationControl();
Notify.Dock = DockStyle.Top;
Notify.Initialize(Task.Notify, "Notify");
Controls.Add(Notify);
Notify.BringToFront();
    }
}
```

This code is different from the user interface code that we created previously. The difference is that we do not use reflection but instead create each aspect control explicitly. Because this code is automatically generated using the XSL stylesheet we still maintain the ability of the user interface to adapt to any domain class without having to rewrite the code manually.

Let me demonstrate this by applying a small change to our task management system: I want the system to send me a reminder five days before the task is due. I can do this by just adding another DueDate aspect to the Task class and providing a few new subscriptions:

```
<Class name="Task">
    <Aspects>
        <Identifier name="ID" seed="10000" step="1000"/>
        <Description name="Text" />
        <DueDate name="Reminder" days="15"/>
        <DueDate name="Deadline" days="20"/>
        <Notification name="Notify"/>
    </Aspects>
    <Subscriptions>
        <Subscription source="Deadline" sourceevent="Due"
                      target="Notify" targetevent="Notify" />
        <Subscription source="Deadline" sourceevent="Completed"
                      target="Reminder" targetevent="Cancel" />
        <Subscription source="Reminder" sourceevent="Due"
                      target="Notify" targetevent="Notify" />
    </Subscriptions>
    <Delegates>
        <Delegate target="Notify" property="Message">
        if (Deadline.State == DueDate.States.Due) {
            return Text.Value + " is due";
        } else {
            return Text.Value + " will be due on " + Deadline.Date;
        }
        </Delegate>
    </Delegates>
</Class>
```

The first new subscription instructs the Reminder to be cancelled if the user marks the Deadline as completed. This is important because otherwise the user would receive a reminder even if she had already completed the task. The other new subscription instructs the Notify aspect to send the user an Email when the Reminder aspect raises its Due event.

A small change has also been made to the notification message delegate. The purpose of this change is to make sure that the user knows whether the task is already due or if the notification is just a reminder.

By reapplying the two XSL stylesheets specified above to recreate the domain class and the user interface respectively we end up with the user interface shown in Fig. 163.

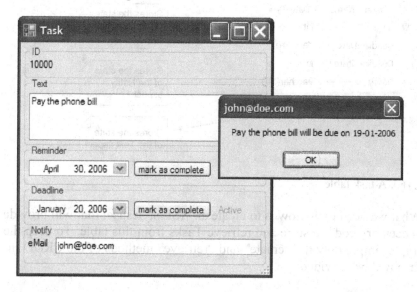

**Fig. 163.** User interface of the task aspect

## 6.10 Storage

The final issue that we need to address in order to have a completely working task management system is how to store and retrieve the tasks from a database.

We could of course use a "traditional" O/R mapper (such as NHibernate or Gentle.Net) for this task, but we could also take advantage of the fact that we already have a domain model of our system to create the storage code ourselves.

The first question that we need to answer is: how should the tasks be stored in the database?

The easiest solution to this question is to create a *Task* table with the columns shown in Fig. 164:

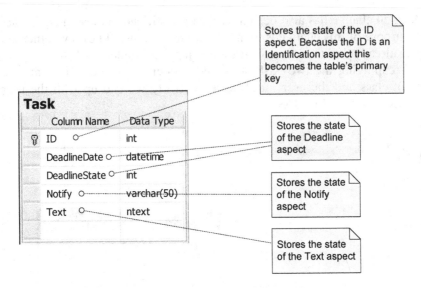

**Fig. 164.** A task table

What we need to do now is to create an XSL stylesheet that will provide the necessary code to store and retrieve Tasks from this table. To keep the example simple only the "create" and "retrieve" methods of the CRUD interface will be provided:

```
<?xml version="1.0" encoding="UTF-8" ?>
<xsl:stylesheet version="1.0"
    xmlns:xsl="http://www.w3.org/1999/XSL/Transform">
    <xsl:output method="text"/>
    <xsl:template match ="Class" xml:space ="preserve">
        public class <xsl:value-of select="@name"/>Facade {
        public static List&lt;<xsl:value-of select="@name"/>&gt;
        GetAll(SqlConnection connection) {
        List&lt;<xsl:value-of select="@name"/>&gt; result =
        New List&lt;<xsl:value-of select="@name"/>&gt;();
        SqlCommand command = connection.CreateCommand();
        command.CommandText = @"select
        <xsl:for-each select="Aspects/*">
            <xsl:choose>
                <xsl:when test ="name() = 'DueDate'">
                    <xsl:value-of select="@name"/>Date,
                    <xsl:value-of select ="@name"/>State
                </xsl:when>
                <xsl:otherwise>
                    <xsl:value-of select ="@name"/>
                </xsl:otherwise>
            </xsl:choose>
            <xsl:if test="position() != last()">,</xsl:if>
        </xsl:for-each>
        from <xsl:value-of select="@name"/>";
        using (SqlDataReader reader = command.ExecuteReader()) {
```

```
    while (reader.Read()) {
    <xsl:value-of select="@name"/> item =
    new <xsl:value-of select="@name"/>();
    <xsl:for-each select="Aspects/*">
        <xsl:choose >
            <xsl:when test="name() = 'DueDate'">
                item.<xsl:value-of select ="@name"/>.Date =
                (DateTime) reader["
                <xsl:value-of select ="@name"/>Date"];
                item.<xsl:value-of select ="@name"/>.State =
                (DueDate.States) reader["
                <xsl:value-of select ="@name"/>State"];
            </xsl:when>
            <xsl:when test="name() = 'Identifier'">
                item.<xsl:value-of select ="@name"/>.Value =
                (int) reader["<xsl:value-of select ="@name"/>"];
            </xsl:when>
            <xsl:when test ="name() = 'Notification'">
                item.<xsl:value-of select ="@name"/>.
                EMailAddress = (string) reader["
                <xsl:value-of select ="@name"/>"];
            </xsl:when>
            <xsl:otherwise>
                item.<xsl:value-of select ="@name"/>.Value =
                (string) reader["
                <xsl:value-of select ="@name"/>"];
            </xsl:otherwise>
        </xsl:choose>
    </xsl:for-each>
    result.Add(item);
    }
    }
    return result;
    }

    public static void Insert(
    <xsl:value-of select ="@name"/> item,
    SqlConnection connection) {
    SqlCommand command = connection.CreateCommand();
    command.CommandText =
    @"insert into <xsl:value-of select ="@name"/> (
    <xsl:for-each select="Aspects/*">
        <xsl:choose >
            <xsl:when test="name() = 'DueDate'">
            <xsl:value-of select ="@name"/>Date,
            <xsl:value-of select ="@name"/>State
        </xsl:when>
        <xsl:otherwise >
            <xsl:value-of select ="@name"/>
        </xsl:otherwise>
    </xsl:choose>
    <xsl:if test ="position() != last()">,</xsl:if>
</xsl:for-each>
) values (
<xsl:for-each select="Aspects/*">
    <xsl:choose >
        <xsl:when test="name() = 'DueDate'">
            @<xsl:value-of select ="@name"/>Date,
```

```
                    @<xsl:value-of select ="@name"/>State
            </xsl:when>
            <xsl:otherwise >
                @<xsl:value-of select ="@name"/>
            </xsl:otherwise>
        </xsl:choose>
        <xsl:if test ="position() != last()">,</xsl:if>
    </xsl:for-each>
    )";
    <xsl:for-each select ="Aspects/*">
        <xsl:choose >
            <xsl:when test="name() = 'DueDate'">
                command.Parameters.AddWithValue(
                "@<xsl:value-of select ="@name"/>date",
                item.<xsl:value-of select ="@name"/>.Date
                );
                command.Parameters.AddWithValue(
                "@<xsl:value-of select ="@name"/>state",
                item.<xsl:value-of select ="@name"/>.State
                );
            </xsl:when>
            <xsl:when test="name() = 'Notification'">
                command.Parameters.AddWithValue(
                "@<xsl:value-of select ="@name"/>",
                item.<xsl:value-of select ="@name"/>.EMailAddress
                );
            </xsl:when>
            <xsl:otherwise>
                command.Parameters.AddWithValue(
                "@<xsl:value-of select ="@name"/>",
                item.<xsl:value-of select ="@name"/>.Value
                );
            </xsl:otherwise>
        </xsl:choose>
    </xsl:for-each>
    command.ExecuteNonQuery();
    }
    }
    </xsl:template>
</xsl:stylesheet>
```

Admittedly this stylesheet is a bit complicated due to its multiple for-each tag, but the output is still very simple (and hopefully readable):

```
public class TaskFacade {
    public static List<Task> GetAll(SqlConnection connection) {
        List<Task> result = new List<Task>();
        SqlCommand command = connection.CreateCommand();
        command.CommandText = @"select ID,
                                       Text,
                                       DeadlineDate,
                                       DeadlineState,
                                       Notify
                                from Task";
        using (SqlDataReader reader = command.ExecuteReader()) {
            while (reader.Read()) {
                Task item = new Task();
```

```
                    item.ID.Value = (int)reader["ID"];
                    item.Text.Value = (string)reader["Text"];
                    item.Deadline.Date =(DateTime)reader["DeadlineDate"];
                    item.Deadline.State =
                        (DueDate.States)reader["DeadlineState"];
                    item.Notify.EMailAddress = (string)reader["Notify"];
                    result.Add(item);
                }
            }
        return result;
    }

    public static void Insert(Task item, SqlConnection connection) {
        SqlCommand command = connection.CreateCommand();
        command.CommandText = @"insert into Task (ID,
                                                 Text,
                                                 DeadlineDate,
                                                 DeadlineState,
                                                 Notify
                              ) values (@ID,
                                        @Text,
                                        @DeadlineDate,
                                        @DeadlineState,
                                        @Notify
                              )";
        command.Parameters.AddWithValue("@ID", item.ID.Value);
        command.Parameters.AddWithValue("@Text", item.Text.Value);
        command.Parameters.AddWithValue("@Deadlinedate",
                                        item.Deadline.Date);
        command.Parameters.AddWithValue("@Deadlinestate",
                                        item.Deadline.State);
        command.Parameters.AddWithValue("@Notify",
                                        item.Notify.EMailAddress);
        command.ExecuteNonQuery();
    }
}
```

The nice thing about this code is that by reapplying the XSL stylesheet to the XML document representing the domain model we can always create storage code that reflects the domain model's actual definition. There is a catch however: While the storage code is automatically updated, this is not the case with the table definition itself. It is of course possible to automatically create the change scripts necessary to update the table definition as well, but often the database is considered such a valuable asset that changes to its definition are required to be done manually.

## 6.11  Storing Aspect Data in Separate Tables

Consider the following situation: In a system we have a large number of DueDate aspects spread out over a number of different domain classes. Employees have DueDates for employee reviews, salary adjustments, bonus payments, etc. Sales orders have DueDates for payment date, shipment date, etc. In order to find out which of these DueDates are due we need to select data from a huge amount of tables in the database.

```
SELECT id FROM employee WHERE employeereviewdate < SYSDATE
AND employeereviewstate = 'Active'

SELECT id FROM employee WHERE salaryadjustmentdate < SYSDATE
AND salaryadjustmentstate = 'Active'

SELECT id FROM salesorders WHERE paymentdate < SYSDATE
AND paymentstate = 'Active'
...
...
...
```

Wouldn't it be nice if all the DueDates were collected in a single table? If this was the case, we could easily retrieve due DueDates using a SQL statement similar to the following:

```
SELECT class, id FROM duedates WHERE date < SYSDATE
AND state = 'Active'
```

By applying this idea in the extreme, we could come up with a database model where each aspect had its own table. Such a database model would look like the model in Fig. 165.

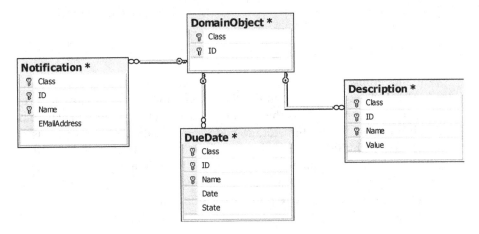

**Fig. 165.** Generic database model

There are some benefits to this way of storing data and some drawbacks. First the benefits:

- Interestingly it often makes sense to look at an aspect across its domain classes: DueDates can be plotted in a calendar so that events coming up can be spotted beforehand, Locations can be plotted on a map as "points of interest", and Notifications can be interesting to the recipient as part of the question "what am I currently subscribing to?". Such requests that crosscut several domain classes will usually perform better if all the aspects' data are stored in a single table.
- The database model does not change even when changes are made to the domain model. This makes it easier to deploy changes to the domain model.

The drawbacks are:

- Selecting a single object from the database requires several select statements. This has a certain impact on performance.
- Creating complex "where"-clauses can become almost impossible. It is also very difficult to write SQL statements that perform well if the "where"-clause spans several aspects (e.g., finding all tasks with a due date in November and with the description containing the text "phone") because the database's execution planner will often resolve this type of query by performing a Cartesian join.
- Often system integration is performed on a database level. Without the domain model to "decrypt" the database it will be very difficult for other applications to make sense of the data in the database.

All in all the best solution will probably be to stick to the conventional way of storing data and perhaps supplement this by creating redundant "aspect" tables where it is deemed necessary.

# Part III  Modeling Handbook

Part I of this book, Structural Patterns described the basic concepts of the REA modeling framework, and how it can be used to create an REA application model of a business system. Part II, Behavioral Patterns, described how the application model can be extended to support specific functionality that originates in user requirements.

Our experience shows that usually the most difficult modeling task is to design an REA application model. Once the application model is created, it is usually straightforward to extend it with existing behavioral patterns. REA leads application designers to the solution that conforms to the laws of the business domain; it is not always straightforward and easy to create application models that follow the domain rules. To make a sound REA model, the application designers must often think deeply before they discover the essence of the customer's business.

In this part, Modeling Handbook, we will illustrate examples of REA application models for elementary exchanges, elementary conversions, value chains with exchange and conversion processes, and REA models with contracts.

The first and second sections illustrate REA models of elementary exchange and conversion processes at the operational level. The third section shows examples of processes at the operational level where the model contains both conversion and exchange processes. The fourth section, Processes with Contracts, illustrates examples of REA models at policy level, which include types, groups, commitments, contracts, and schedules, in addition to economic events, resources, and agents.

# 7 Elementary Exchange Processes

This section illustrates REA models of exchange processes at the operational level. These models contain economic events, economic resources, and economic agents in exchange processes. We describe the REA models for the following exchange processes: *Cash Sale, Product Return, Discounts, Loan and Rent,* and *Financing*.

## 7.1  Cash Sale

The sales process is one of creating revenue; therefore, every company has a process similar to sales. The only exception might be non-profit organizations, but they also have a process of providing services or goods. For organizations receiving donations, the recipient economic agent of these services or goods is different from the economic agent providing cash, but the basic model remains the same.

Cash Sale is the simplest version of the sales process, and is applicable to sales in shops or sales to walk-in customers.

### Problem

How do we create an REA application model for the cash sale process?

### Solution

A sales process is an exchange of products for cash. The value chain model for a cash sale process is illustrated in Fig. 166.

**Fig. 166.** Value chain model for the cash sale process

The REA model in Fig. 167 illustrates a scenario known from retail shops, where a customer buys a product and pays cash. This scenario does not require modeling contracts such as a sales order.

This model contains two economic events: *Sale* and *Cash Receipt*. The economic event *Sale* is related through an exchange duality with economic event *Cash Receipt*. Each instance of *Sale* is related to exactly one *Product*. *Sale* represents change of ownership of *Product* from *enterprise* to *Customer*. Likewise, each instance of *Cash Receipt* is related to exactly one *Cash* instance, which represents, for example, an amount of money in a specific currency.

In general, the relationship between *Sale* and *Cash Receipt* is many-to-many; several instances of *Sale* (a sale of several products) can be related to several instances of *Cash Receipt* (for example, customer pays cash in different currencies).

As *Sale* does not have to happen at exactly the same time as *Cash Receipt* (for example, payment often occurs after entries of all goods go through the cash register), the *Claim* represents the value of the imbalanced exchange duality. This value can be displayed on a cash register, or made in some other way available to the participating economic agents.

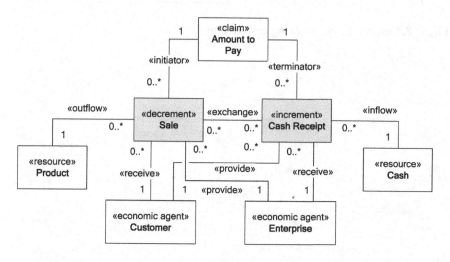

**Fig. 167.** Sales Process

If a customer pays cash, he usually gives the enterprise an amount higher than is claimed. The enterprise then returns the excess payment to the customer to settle the claim. If users of business applications are interested in keeping track of the money returned to customers, the model must be modified by adding a decrement event, *Cash Return*, as shown in Fig. 168. The economic agents are the same as in Fig. 167.

Cash return is possible also in the model illustrated in Fig. 167, but in this model the business application does not keep track of the money returned, while in the model in Fig. 168 it does.

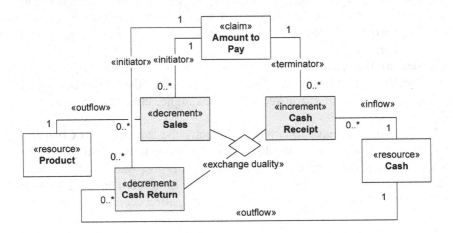

**Fig. 168.** Cash sales with tracking cash returns

## 7.2 Product Return

Many companies allow customers under certain conditions to return Purchased products. Users of business applications would like to track and create reports on economic events related to returns of products.

### Problem

How do we model returns of purchased items?

### Solution

The return of products can occur only if the products have already been sold, and users of business applications might not consider it as a value-adding process. Therefore, we model the return of products as an economic event that is part of the sales process. Its value chain is shown in Fig. 169.

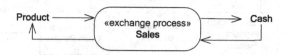

**Fig. 169.** Value chain for the sales process

The REA model for a sales process with the return of products is illustrated in Fig. 170. The *exchange duality* is a 4-ary relationship between economic events *Sale, Cash Receipt, Product Return,* and *Cash Return*. All four events contribute to the claim *Amount to Pay*; *Sale* and *Cash Return* increase the value of the claim and *Product Return* and *Cash Receipt* decrease the value of the claim. The model specifies that the value of the

*Sale* plus *Cash Return* should be equal to the value of the Product Return plus Cash Receipt.

When a customer returns a product (i.e., the enterprise accepts and registers the product return), a positive claim is raised, and business practice determines how the enterprise is going to settle the claim.

- The enterprise can materialize the claim, i.e., issue a credit note to the customer.
- The enterprise can sell to the customer another product, usually of the same or equivalent type, that settles the claim.
- The enterprise can return cash to the customer.

Some companies do not return the full purchase price of the product to the customer in the case of a return. In the model in Fig. 170, this means that the returned product has less value than the sold product. Consequently, the amount of cash returned is less than the amount of cash received.

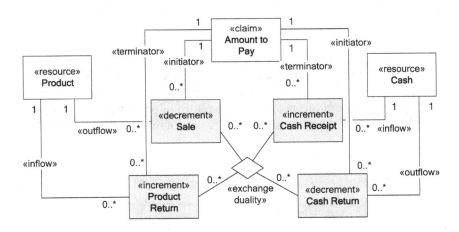

**Fig. 170.** Sales process with return of products

If the product sold and returned is an individually identifiable item (its quantity is measured in pieces as opposed to kilograms or joules), there is a one-to-one relationship between the return event and the sale event. The sale with product return can be considered a kind of sale, and the model can be simplified, as shown in Fig. 171.

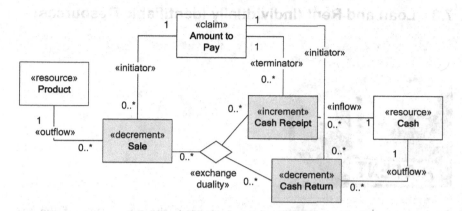

**Fig. 171.** Return of individually identifiable items

The *Sale* event is now a time interval; at the beginning of the sale event, the product's ownership transfer from enterprise to customer, and at the end of the interval, it transfers back from customer to enterprise. The Sale event is still a decrement event, because it decreases the value of the product for the enterprise for several reasons. For example, during the time interval between sale and return, the product cannot be sold to another customer.

## 7.3   Loan and Rent (Individually Identifiable Resources)

To rent an economic resource means to grant the possession of the resource in return for the payment of rent from the tenant, and for the tenant to take and hold the resource (property, machinery, etc.) in return for the payment of rent to the landlord or owner. The grant is always temporary; the tenant must eventually return the rented resource to the owner; however, the length of the rental period can be unspecified.

### Problem

What is loan and rent in the REA terms?

### Solution

The loan or rent process is an exchange of rights to use an economic resource for cash. The value chain model for rental is illustrated in Fig. 172. Note that the arrow means change of value of resources, not physical flow of resources. Renting a property decreases its value for the owner; for example, it cannot be rented during the rental period, or the owner does not keep full rights to the rented resource. The owner receives cash in return.

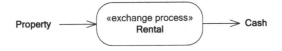

**Fig. 172.** Value chain model for loan and rental

The REA model for rental and loan is illustrated in Fig. 173. The enterprise in this model is renting an economic resource, *Property*, in exchange for *Cash*.

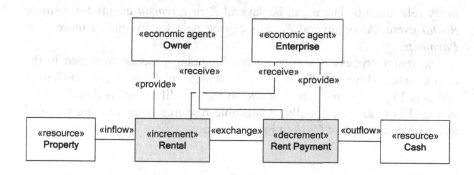

**Fig. 173.** The REA application model for the rental process

A timing diagram with an example of one *Rental* and two *Rent Payments* is illustrated in Fig. 174.

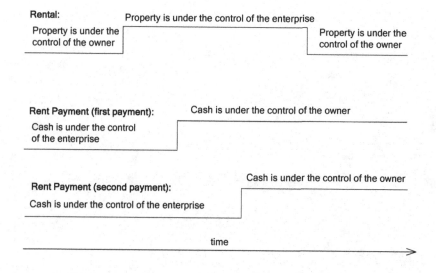

**Fig. 174.** The timing diagram for an example of the rental process

The increment event *Rental* is an economic event with duration equivalent to the rental period. At the beginning of this economic event, the usage rights of the economic resource *Property* are transferred from the *Owner* to the *Enterprise*, and at the end of this event the usage rights are transferred back from the *Enterprise* to the *Owner*. The *Rental* event is paired through an exchange duality with the instantaneous *Rent Payment* event, which causes outflow of economic resource *Cash*. The exchange is a many-to-many relationship. There can be several *Rent Payment* events for a single *Rental* event. Also, several *Rentals* can be paid for by one or more *Rent Payments*.

The rental process is similar to the financing process discussed in the next chapter. However, the models for rental and financing are different; compare Figs. 173 and 176. The reason for this difference is that *Property* in Fig. 173 is an individually identifiable resource (received and returned as a whole unit), while *Cash* in Fig. 176 is not.

## 7.4 Financial Loan (Nonindividually Identifiable Resources)

There are many ways an enterprise can receive the financial resources it needs. We will illustrate a simple form of financing in which the enterprise borrows money from the bank for a specific period. The bank receives interest as a compensation for the loan. For the enterprise, the money it borrows has more value than the interest; for the bank, the interest has more value than the money it lends.

### Problem

What is the financing process in REA terms?

### Solution

The financing process is an exchange of cash for cash. The enterprise receives cash for a limited period of time. Eventually, it returns the cash and also pays interest for the loan. The value chain model is illustrated in Fig. 175.

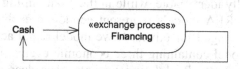

**Fig. 175.** Value chain model for financing

The REA model for a financial loan is illustrated in Fig. 176. The enterprise receives an economic resource, *Cash*, in the *Loan Receipt* event. This event is paired in duality with two economic events, *Loan Return*, in which the *Cash* is returned back, and *Interest Payment*, in which the enterprise pays additional cash to the bank as a compensation for the *Loan*. The whole process can at runtime consist of several *Loan Receipt* events, several *Loan Return* events, and several *Interest Payment* events. The dates for these evens can be specified by commitments, which are part of the contract. The REA model at the operational level does not contain any restrictions on the dates these events occur, or in what order, but commitments that are part of the financing contract usually specify the *Loan Receipt*, *Loan Return*, and *Interest Payment* dates.

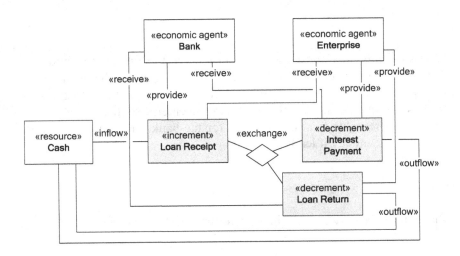

**Fig. 176.** The REA application model for financing

The financial loan is similar to the rental discussed in the previous chapter. However, the models for rental and financing are different; compare Figs. 173 and 176. Can we model rental using the model in Fig. 176?

The reason for the different models is that in the model in Fig. 173 the resources are individually identifiable, while in the model in Fig. 176, they are not. Generally, the REA models represent economic exchanges, i.e., some resources are exchanged for others. If we model rental according to Fig. 176, i.e., with a model containing three economic events, instantaneous increment *Start Property Rental*, and instantaneous decrements *End Property Rental* and *Pay Rent*, the pair *Start Property Rental* and *End Property Rental* is not an exchange; the renter is returning the same property back he rented. Therefore, we prefer to model the rental of a property as one economic event with duration.

On the other hand, in the case of a loan, the economic resource *Cash* is not individually identifiable; there is no way to determine whether the cash received is the same as the cash returned. In fact, banks usually allow renters to return a different *Cash Type* than the one they gave to the renter; for example, a loan can be given as a check and returned by bank transfer. Therefore, as received cash and returned cash might be different, *Loan Receipt* and *Loan Return* are different economic events in the case of *Cash* and other resources that are not individually identifiable. For example, gasoline loaned can be different one is returned (the individual molecules in loaned and returned gasoline will be different), therefore, we would model the loan of gasoline similarly to the model illustrated in Fig. 176. The loan of gasoline would be one economic event, and its return another economic event.

If the enterprise borrows an item (individually identifiable resource) and buys another item of the same type, it is always possible to distinguish which item is borrowed and which is owed. On the other hand, if the enterprise stores borrowed and owed cash in one bank account, it is impossible to distinguish the cash borrowed from the cash owed (the amounts of owed and borrowed cash can be determined only by examining the economic events that changed the amount of cash in this bank account). This difference also indirectly explains why the two models are different.

Another, practical reason why the two models are different is that individually identifiable resources must be returned complete, in one piece, when the rental period ends. However, resources that are not individually identifiable can be returned in different quantities. For example, a renter can pay for the loan in installments. The model in Fig. 176 allows modeling the installments, while the model in Fig. 173 does not.

# 8 Elementary Conversion Processes

This section illustrates REA models of conversion processes at the operational level. *CREATING A NEW PRODUCT* is a fundamental conversion process in which a new instance of an economic resource is created from other resources.

If the conversion process consists of phases, and users of business applications would like to plan, monitor, and control the work in progress and intermediate resources, the process can be split into finer-grain processes in two different ways.

- The *CHAIN OF CONVERSION PROCESSES* is essentially a sequence of processes in which an intermediate product is created and then consumed by the next process in the chain. This process is convenient if the subsequent processes entirely change the identity of the resource.
- The modeling approach *MODIFYING A RESOURCE* is suitable in situations in which the process does not change the identity of the product; for example, only makes some modification of it.

The concept of services in the process *CREATING AND CONSUMING SERVICES* can be used to introduce a level of indirection into a chain of processes, and to represent the results of some processes as a service. This is useful, for example, in outsourcing some conversion processes, and will be described in the section on combined models.

## 8.1  Creating a New Product

Almost every company has a process in which it creates a new service or product. The new product or service is an economic resource, and for its creation the enterprise uses or consumes other economic resources.

When creating an REA model for a conversion process, an application designer must answer the following question.

### Problem

How do we make an REA application model for a conversion process that creates a new product?

### Solution

The output of the conversion process is an economic resource that users of a business application want to monitor and control. One of the outputs is a product, but many conversion processes produce other resources, such as waste. Whether or not to model these resources is a decision of the users of the business application, and is the result of their needs for information about these resources.

We will illustrate the process in a scenario in which the new product is produced, and then inspected for quality. The assembly process encompasses all technological operations of assembling the product, using tools. The assembled product is then inspected for defects.

In this scenario, users of a business application are not interested in planning, monitoring and controlling the work in progress and intermediate resources. Therefore, the assembly and quality inspection are combined into a single conversion process. The value chain model is shown in Fig. 177.

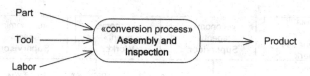

**Fig. 177.** Value chain model for creating a new product

The REA application model for this process is illustrated in Fig. 178. Resources consumed in this process are *Part* and *Labor* (they will not exist after the end of the process), and *Tool* is a resource used (that can be used again). The result of the process is the *Product* resource. In this example, we have decided to model *Part* and *Product* as different entities. However, in many business applications it is not always like this; there is often an entity, usually called *Item*, that represents all economic resources of a physical nature.

The *Material Issue* economic event consumes the *Part* resource. During this economic event, the *Part* is transformed into the *Product*. The provider economic agent *Employee* is responsible for *Part* before it has been issued, and the recipient agent *Supervisor* is responsible for *Part* until it becomes part of the *Product*.

The *Tools Usage* economic event uses the economic resource *Tool* in order to assemble and inspect the *Product*. In this example, we assume that the tools are picked up by the workers and returned after the assembly process is finished; we model the *Enterprise* as a provider agent, responsible for the *Tool* before and after the *Tool Usage* event, and model the *Worker* as a recipient economic agent responsible for the tool during the event.

The *Labor Consumption* economic event consumes the economic resource *Labor* and transforms it into the *Product*. The provider economic agent is *Supervisor*, who is authorized to decide upon labor consumption during the process. The recipient economic agent is *Worker*, who is responsible for his own labor during the Labor Consumption economic event.

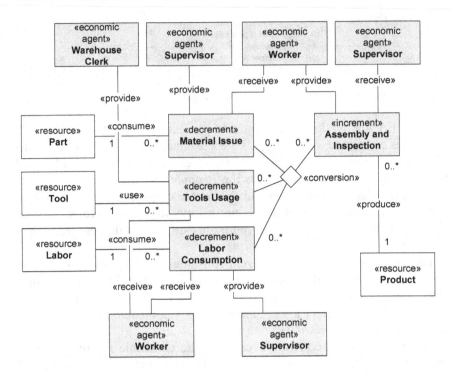

**Fig. 178.** The REA model for creating a new product in a single process

An instance model is illustrated in Fig. 179. The resulting economic re-source is *Product* with a serial number *P3*, assembled of two *Parts* with serial numbers *I22* and *I23*. These parts have been issued at times 7:20 a.m. and 7:25 a.m., respectively, by *Warehouse Clerk Ethel*, and given to *Worker Moe*. *Worker Moe* came to work at 7:00 a.m., but started work at 7:20 a.m., when he got the task and material from his *Supervisor Andy*; the enterprise acquired Andy's *Labor* from 7:00 a.m. to 15:00 a.m., but *Consumed* only 60 minutes, from 7:30 a.m. to 8:30 a.m., on *Producing* the *Product P3*. The rest of Moe's *Labor* was spent on activities beyond the scope of the model in Fig. 179. At 7:40 a.m. *Moe* picked the *Tool T5* and returned it back at 8:15 a.m. *Andy* started assembling and inspecting the product at 7:50 a.m. and finished at 8:30 a.m.

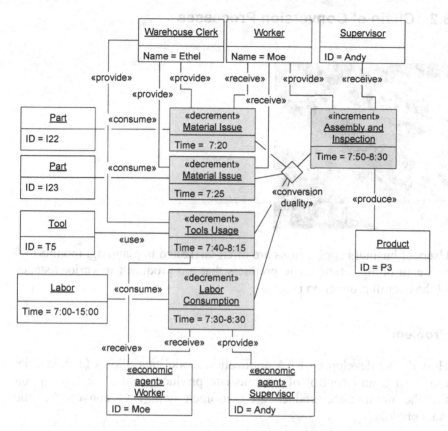

**Fig. 179.** An instance model for creating a product

The creation of a resource is not instantaneous. If users of business applications are interested in modeling various stages of the production, but not interested in the intermediate products, they might use *tasks* to model the production process at a finer level of granularity than that of the level of economic events. We have not illustrated this modeling aspect in this book; we intend to describe it on our web page.

The model in Fig. 178 does not have an entity for intermediate products, work in process inventory and such. If users of business applications are interested in planning, monitoring, and controlling the intermediate products within the production process, application developers must split the production process into a chain of several value-adding processes. This is illustrated in the models in the following pages.

## 8.2   Chain of Conversion Processes

Users of business applications are often interested in planning, monitoring, and controlling intermediate products that are produced in various stages of the overall production process.

### Problem

How do we develop an REA application model that allows for planning, monitoring, and control of intermediate products, under the assumption that the intermediate products are consumed as they are converted to the final product?

### Solution

Split the overall conversion process into a chain of smaller conversion processes. An economic resource produced in the first process is consumed in the second process, and so on. The last process in the chain produces the final product.

We will illustrate this approach on the same example as in the previous chapter, but with the additional requirement that users of the business application would like to keep track of the products that have been assembled but have not been inspected for quality.

The production of a final product consists of two processes: the assembly process creates the assembled product, and the inspection process consumes the assembled product and creates the final product. The value chain model is shown in Fig. 180.

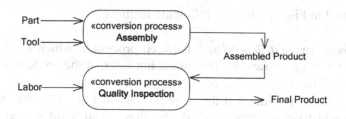

**Fig. 180.** Value chain model for the chain of conversion processes

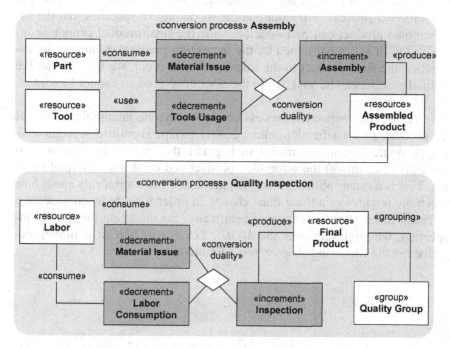

**Fig. 181.** The REA application model for the chain of conversion processes

The REA application model is illustrated in Fig. 181. For simplicity, we assume that the assembly process does not consume labor; it is fully automated. The quality inspection process encompasses all necessary quality inspection activities; for simplicity we assume that this process only consumes labor. The result of the quality inspection is the classification of the product into a quality group, such as first quality, second quality, and waste. We can consider this classification as a feature of the product that is changed by the quality inspection process.

The economic agents are the same as in Fig. 178 and are omitted in Fig. 181.

The model in Fig. 181 has the following features:

- There is an *explicit dependency* between processes, which implies the time order of the processes. The model implies that the product must be first assembled and then inspected.
- The assembled product and the inspected product are *different entities*. They might have different type, description, serial number, and set of features.
- The assembled product and the inspected product can be related each to a *different process*. For example, the model above specifies that the assembled product can be inspected while the final product cannot be inspected (it is not consumed by the inspection process). Similarly, by relating the final product to the sales economic event, we specify that the final product can be sold, while the assembled product cannot be sold.

In reality, the inspection process changes only one intangible feature of the product, its classification, into a quality group. Therefore, it might look inappropriate that in the model in Fig. 181 the inspection process consumes (i.e., destroys) the assembled product and creates a new final product. This is a rather philosophical statement, and not a strict rule about how much the features of a thing must change in order for it to be considered a different thing after the change. Specifically, for modeling the quality inspection, we might consider the *MODIFYING A RESOURCE* model, described in the following chapter, more intuitive.

## 8.3  Modifying a Product

Many conversion processes change only some features of an existing economic resource. Examples are maintenance, transport, and quality inspection processes.

If the conversion changes an economic resource that has been created by another process or received by an exchange process, there are two different approaches to describe the conversion process, depending on how much the resource has changed.

Some experts in the REA modeling framework argue that by changing any feature of an economic resource the process consumes the old resource and creates a new one. For example, by the visual inspection of the quality of a product, the quality inspection process consumes the old product and produces a new one, because it sets the quality group of the resource. If we would like to follow this approach, we should use the model described in the *CHAIN OF CONVERSION PROCESSES* chapter.

In this book, we will follow a more pragmatic approach by allowing *the same instance* of the resource to be both at the input and at the output of the conversion process.

### Problem

How do we make an REA application model for a conversion process that changes only some features of the existing product?

### Solution

Obviously, there must be an economic event related to the resource by the produce relationship, because the process increases the resource value. However, it is important to realize that the conversion process that modifies the economic resource also uses it.

We will use the same example as in the previous chapter, but this time we will model the assembled product and the final product as the same entity. The value chain model is in Fig. 182.

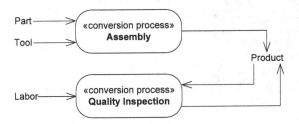

**Fig. 182.** Value chain model for modifying a resource

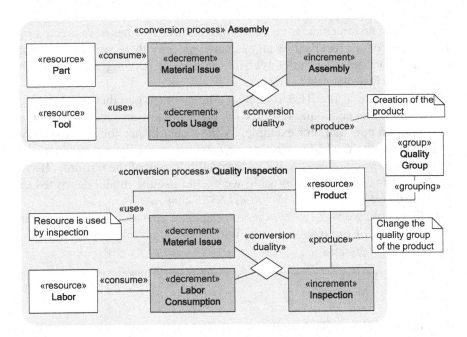

**Fig. 183.** The REA application model for modifying a resource

The REA application model for modifying a product is shown in Fig. 183. The model contains an economic resource, *Product*, created by the increment economic event *Assembly*. The *Product* is used by the decrement economic event *Issue for Inspection* in the Inspection process, and the increment economic event *Inspection* modifies features of the product. The decrement economic event *Issue for Inspection* expresses the fact that, during this event, *Product* might not be available for purposes other than *Quality Inspection.*

Current state of the product, i.e. whether the product is currently assembled or inspected can be determined by examining whether the instances of the relationships to the economic events *Assembly* and *Inspection* exist.

The same structure can be used to model transport, maintenance, and other processes that change some feature of the product, but not its existence.

The model in Fig. 183 has the following features:

- In general, there is *no explicit dependency* between business processes, and the model therefore does not imply the time order of the processes at runtime. We can see that the assembly process must be performed first, because it creates a product. We know it creates a product because it does not contain any decrement event that uses the product. However, if there were several processes modifying a product, such as transport and storage, in addition to inspection, the processes modifying a product (quality inspection, storage, and transport) could happen in any order, and also in parallel.
- The process that modifies the product may occur an *arbitrary number of times*. For example, the model allows for a product that has already been inspected to be inspected again.
- The *product is the same entity* through the whole chain of processes. For example, it has the same type and description, the same identity; it has the same set of features, though production economic events change their values.
- There is *no entity for an intermediate product, but an intermediate product can be identified.* An assembled product is just a state in the lifecycle of the final product, and can at runtime be identified by examining the produce relationships: the actual products linked to an assembly economic event have been assembled; the actual products linked to an inspection economic event have been inspected.

The decision whether to use the model for the *CHAIN OF CONVERSION PROCESSES*, or for *MODIFYING A RESOURCE*, depends on whether the modifying process changes the implementation type of the economic resource.

For example, if instead of quality inspection we had business processes for storage or transport, we would probably consider the resource before the processes the same type and identity as after them. Some features of these products will change during transport and storage (at least their cost attribute will increase), but the *set of features* will remain the same.

On the other hand, in the process of reconstruction of a building, we might consider the building before and after the reconstruction as having different set of features. Therefore, we might consider the reconstruction as consuming the old building and creating a new one. In this case, the *CHAIN OF CONVERSION PROCESSES* model would be more appropriate than the *MODIFYING A RESOURCE* model.

## 8.4  Creating and Consuming Services

Sometimes, modeling the economic resources that are used or consumed in order to increment the value of other resources is not possible or desirable. Instead, we can encapsulate these economic resources in a new economic resource called service. The service resource is created by using or consuming some economic resources, and the service resource is consumed to increment the value of other resources.

The creation of services can be modeled in a similar way as the creation of products, the difference is that an enterprise cannot create a service, store it, and consume it later. Services are economic resources that are created at the same time as they are consumed. This difference has no influence on the REA modeling principles.

Services as transient resources add a level of indirection between business processes, but do not change the operational semantics of the chain of conversion processes. This is useful, for example, if the business process is outsourced, and its result – service – is purchased or sold to other economic agent.

In the following example, we will illustrate this modeling pattern on the inspection process. The *Quality Inspection* process will consume the economic resource *Inspection Service*, instead of *Labor*. *Inspection Service* is produced by business process *Inspection Service Creation*; see Fig. 184.

An REA application model is shown in Fig. 185. The business process *Inspection Service* contains the increment economic event *Inspection Service Creation*, which is paired through *conversion duality* with the decrement economic event *Labor Consumption*. The *Quality Inspection* process consumes the *Inspection Service*, and the result, as in previous cases, is the classification of the *Product* into a *Quality Group*.

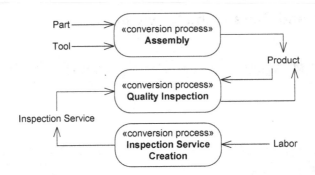

**Fig. 184.** Value chain for creating and consuming services

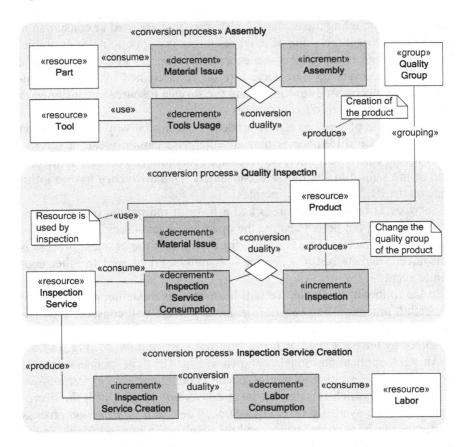

**Fig. 185.** The REA model for creating and consuming services

The REA model with services has the following features:

- Service is a *transient resource*. It is produced at the same time as it is consumed; a company cannot store it. If the service is not exchanged (purchased or sold) with another economic agent, the model can be simplified by omitting the service resource and the production and consumption of the service. For example, in Fig. 185 we can pair the decrement event *Labor Consumption* through a *conversion duality* with the increment event *Inspection*, and omit the events *Inspection Service Creation*, the *Inspection Service Consumption* and the resource *Inspection Service*.
- Service is an economic resource; therefore, it can also be *related through an inflow and outflow* with other events. For example, a company can produce an inspection service and also purchase some of it from a subcontractor.
- The model is especially useful if some or all the *service is obtained by an exchange process*.

# 9 Value Chains with Exchange and Conversion Processes

This section illustrates REA models at the operational level that contain both exchange and conversion processes.

The *SALE AND SHIPMENT* chapter illustrates how the sale and shipment processes are related. The chapters *PEOPLE MANAGEMENT*, and *EDUCATION* illustrate that the REA modeling framework can track the use and consumption of resources that are considered overhead in most business applications. We will also illustrate how the REA models for *TAXES, WASTE, PURCHASING AND SELLING SERVICES*, and *TRANSIENT RESOURCES* look.

## 9.1   Sale and Shipment

The Sale event means transfer of ownership of a product from the enterprise to the customer. The moment of the transfer of ownership must be agreed upon between the economic agents.

Shipment is a conversion process that changes one of the features of the product – its location. The location at which the product changes ownership must be agreed upon between the economic agents. For example, it might be agreed that the product changes ownership when it is delivered to the customer, or when it is accepted by the courier service. It might also be agreed that the product changes ownership when it is picked by the customer at the vendor's premises. For the payment it is usually assumed that money changes ownership when it arrives in the recipient's bank account, or when a check is deposited, but other agreements are also possible.

If the event of the sale is determined by its location of the product being sold, the business application must have some information about the location (the *LOCATION PATTERN* must be configured on the product), or the users of the business application must themselves determine whether the sale has occurred.

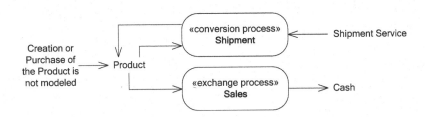

**Fig. 186.** Value chain model for the sales process with shipment

The model in Fig. 187 shows the exchange *Sales Process*, and the conversion *Shipment Process*. The output of the shipment process is *Product*; this process changes one of its features – its location. The *Shipment* process has two inputs, *Shipment Service*, which is an economic resource that the enterprise purchases from a *Courier* (the purchase is not modeled in Fig. 187), and *Product*, which is used during shipment. The *Product Use* decrement event indicates that the value of the product is for the *enterprise* decreased during the shipment process. Indeed, the product, during shipment, cannot usually be used, its amount can become smaller, and it can get damaged. As shipment is a value-adding process, the enterprise expects that the increase in the product value by changing its location is higher than its decrease.

The model in Fig. 187 is not complete in the sense that it does not show how the enterprise uses *Cash*, acquires *Shipment Service* (usually by an exchange purchase process), and obtains *Product* (either by producing it in a conversion process or buying it in an exchange process).

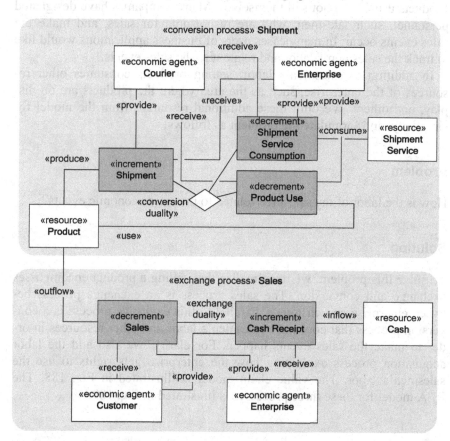

**Fig. 187.** The REA model for the sales process with shipment

## 9.2   Resources Consumed During the Sales Process

Products usually do not sell themselves. Many companies have designated personnel, such salesmen, who are responsible for sales, and make the sales events occur. In many cases users of business applications would like to track the salesmen's labor and relate it to the sales events.

In addition to salesmen's labor, selling products consumes other resources of the enterprise, such as the area where the products are on display, and others. We omit these additional resources from the model for simplicity, and formulate the problem as follows.

### Problem

How is the labor of the salesmen related to the sales economic events?

### Solution

To solve this problem, we must realize that selling a product encompasses exchange and conversion. The sales process is an exchange process between enterprise and customer. Parallel to this exchange process is a conversion process that consumes salesmen's labor and other resources in order to make the sales events happen. For clarity, we also add the labor acquisition process explaining how the enterprise gets rights to use the salesmen's labor. The value chain model is illustrated in Fig. 188. The REA model for these three processes is illustrated in Fig. 189.

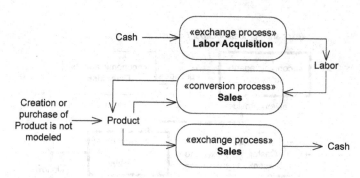

**Fig. 188.** Value chain model for sales process with salesmen labor

The key point to understanding the model in Fig. 189 is to realize that the enterprise acquires *Labor* from *Salesman* by the *Labor Acquisition* event, and consumes this *Labor* to sell the *Product*. These three entities are shown in bold in Fig. 189.

The conversion *Sales Process* consumes salesmen's *Labor*, and changes a feature of the product to "Is Sold"; this is equivalent to creating an instance of the *outflow* relationship between the *Product* and the *Sale* event.

This model enables tracking labor of all human resources that are consumed in the sales process for each individual sale. For example, we can extend the model by including the labor of warehouse personnel, cashiers, etc., and other resources, such as their expenses, during the sales process.

The product is used during the *Sales Process* by the decrement event *Product Use*. This event represents, for example, the time the *Product* is on display on a shelf in a supermarket, or some other event that increases the cost of the product in its relation to *Sale*.

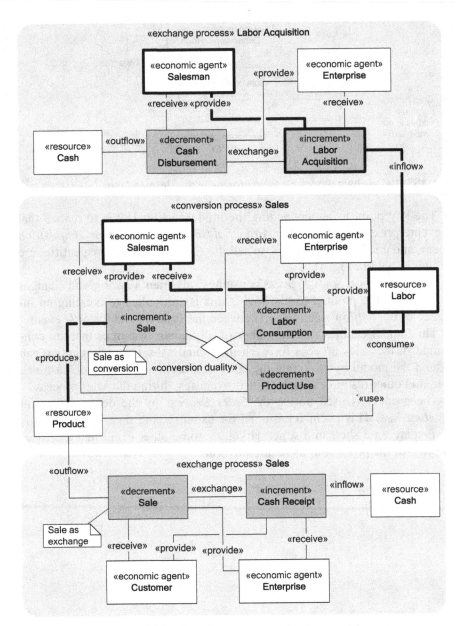

**Fig. 189.** The REA model for the sales process with salesmen labor

## 9.3  People Management

Unless the enterprise is a one person company, the labor of economic agents that work for the enterprise must be coordinated. Companies use designated resources, managers, to be responsible for and to coordinate labor of subordinates. The labor of employees who are not managers is consumed to increase the value of a product. What is managers' labor used for?

### Problem

What does the enterprise receive in return for its consumption of work of managers?

### Solution

The enterprise receives more efficient labor from the manager subordinates. Manager labor is consumed in order to increase value of subordinate labor. Simply, the enterprise perceives the managed labor as having higher value than non-managed labor. The value chain model is illustrated in Fig. 190. The value chain consists of two processes: the labor acquisition process, in which the enterprise acquires both managing and managed labor, and the people management process, in which the enterprise consumes managing labor in order to increase the value of managed labor.

**Fig. 190.** Value chain for people management

The REA model for people management is illustrated in Fig. 191. In the *Labor Acquisition* process the *enterprise* acquires *Labor* in exchange for *Cash*. In the *People Management* process the *enterprise* consumes the managing *Labor* during economic event *Consume Labor*, and the dual economic event *People Management* increases the value of managed *Labor*.

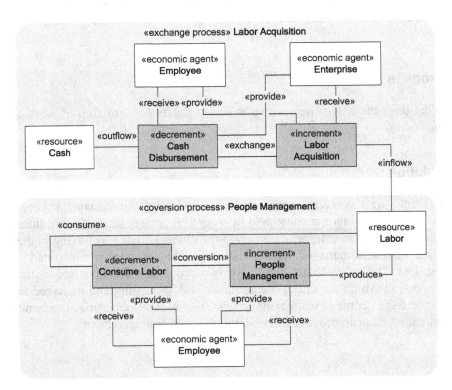

**Fig. 191.** The REA model for people management

What if the users of a business application would like to impose the business rule that only the labor of managers can be used to manage labor? This can be achieved in two ways:

- Application designers can create a new economic resource, *Manager Labor*, and relate it to the *Consume Labor* economic event. This solution has the disadvantage that any change in this policy would require change in the application design.
- Application designers can create a new labor type, for example, *Manager Labor*, and create a policy that specifies that only the labor of *Manager Labor* type is allowed to be consumed by the *Consume Labor* event. This solution is more flexible, as the users of business applications can themselves change this policy, and also decide what to do if the policy is violated.

## 9.4   Education

Many companies provide education to employees. The education process creates costs for the enterprise. When creating an REA model for the education process, an application designer must answer the following question.

### Problem

What does the enterprise receive in return for providing education to employees?

### Solution

Through the education process, the enterprise hopes that it will receive more efficient labor from its employees. *Education* is a resource consumed in order to increase the value of *Labor*. The value chain model is illustrated in Fig. 192. The value chain consists of two processes: the *Education Acquisition* process and the *Learning* process, in which the enterprise uses the *Education* resource in order to increase the value of *Labor*.

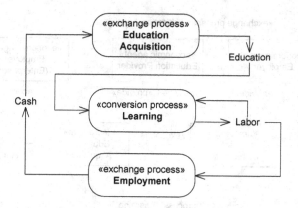

**Fig. 192.** Value chain for education

The REA model for education is illustrated in Fig. 193. This model is from the perspective of a person receiving the education, for example, an employee. Therefore, the agent *Employee* plays the role of the enterprise. First, the *Employee* receives the *Education* in the *Education Acquisition* process. This is an exchange process; note that in this example we make the *Employer* pay for the education. *Education* is an economic resource that the *Employee* uses to increase value of his *Labor*. The *Employee* also uses his *Labor* to improve it, both by using his time for learning, and in "on the job training". In the *Employment* process, the employee sells his labor to the *Employer* for *Cash*.

The economic resource *Education* is a permanent (not transient) resource; it is difficult or nearly impossible to erase the knowledge an employee receives from education. Therefore, the *Education* resource is *used* and not *consumed* during the *Learning* Process.

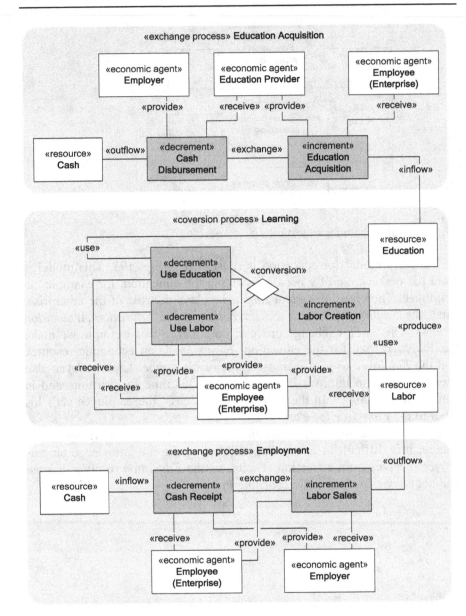

**Fig. 193.** The REA model for education (from the employee perspective)

## 9.5 Taxes

We will illustrate the REA model for taxes on the example for value-added tax (VAT); a similar model can be applied also for other fees to the government. Paying taxes is the outflow of an economic resource, cash. This outflow must be related to some inflow economic event according to the REA domain rules. The usual problem in creating an application REA model for taxes is formulated below.

### Problem

What does an economic agent receive in return for paying taxes?

### Solution

Although it might not be obvious at first, the enterprise often receives certain services from the government in return for paying taxes. Public roads, a legal system, and public security are examples of the benefits that the government provides to the enterprise from collected taxes. We can also consider the government as one of the vendors of the enterprise.

The value chain model for tax payment is illustrated in Fig. 194. The tax payment process is an exchange of cash for government services. The government services are then consumed in some value-adding process whose result is the sales process.

The model in Figs. 194 and 195 represents the theoretical REA model that explains tax. We will simplify the model in Fig. 196, and give an example of a model for VAT. VAT is used in European countries, and is equivalent to the sales tax used in the US.

Is tax payment a value-adding process? As paying taxes is often not a question of voluntary choice, the reason the enterprise pays taxes can be explained by fact that in doing so it avoids a potential penalty, rather than by the fact that it perceives the value of the received services as higher than the value of the cash paid.

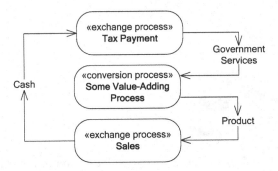

**Fig. 194.** Value chain model for taxes

The REA model illustrating the theoretical solution explaining tax is in Fig. 195. *Government Services* is an economic resource, consumed in *Some Value-Adding Process*, a process adding value to *Product*, which is then sold to customers in the *Sales* process.

The first problem with the theoretical solution in Fig. 195 is that we cannot in practice determine which services from the government the enterprise uses, and the specific amount of these services.

However, we know the exact price for these services. The price is tax. Therefore, the economic resource *Government Services* has an attribute *Owed Tax,* which is the price of the *Government Services* acquired. Governments specify in their legislation a procedure to determine its value; this legislation can be considered as a contract between the *Government* and the *Enterprise*. For example, in Denmark this price is calculated as 25% of the added value.

The second problem in the solution in Fig. 195 is that we do not know how the enterprise consumes the *Government Services* and at what time. Therefore, we simplify the model by omitting the conversion process, and make an assumption that *Government Services* are reflected directly in the price of the sold products, see Fig. 196. This is the same assumption as that in the legal system of most countries.

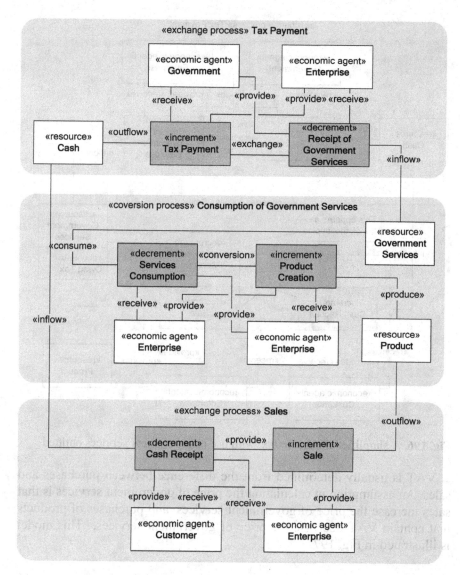

**Fig. 195.** Theoretical REA model explaining what tax is

In the model in Fig. 196, the *Sales Process* contains two decrement economic events, *Sale* and *Government Services*. Both events usually appear on the materialized claim, such as a receipt from a shop or an invoice, which often specifies the price of the product and the tax. If the *Sales Process* occurs before the *Tax Payment* process, the value of the resource *Government Services*, i.e. the property *Owed Tax* is negative.

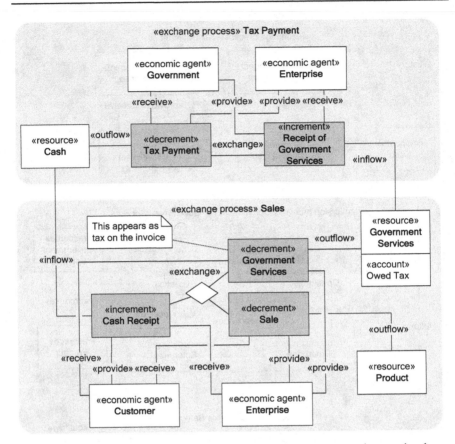

**Fig. 196.** A simplified model for tax, with use of government services omitted

VAT is usually determined from the difference between purchases and sales. An assumption in calculating the price of government services is that sales increase the price of government services, and purchases of products that contain VAT decrease the price of government services. This model is illustrated in Fig. 197.

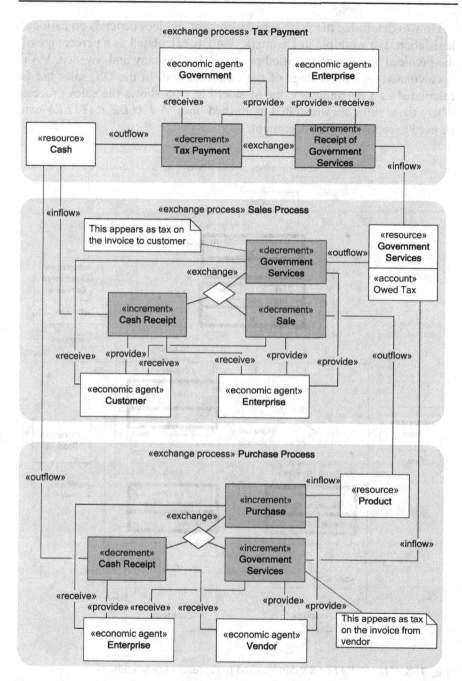

**Fig. 197.** The REA model for tax with purchase and sales

How to determine the price for government services depends on national legislation. For example in Denmark, VAT is calculated as a percentage of the invoiced amount of specified products. In Germany and Sweden, VAT is calculated as a percentage of the cash received. In the US, sales tax is calculated as a percentage value of sale. Fig. 198 shows the sales process where these rules are illustrated by dashed lines. A *VALUE PATTERN* can be used to represent the tax amount.

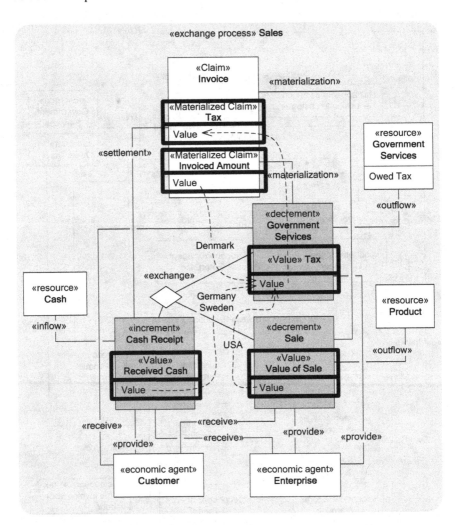

**Fig. 198.** *VALUE PATTERN* can be used to represent tax amount

Fig. 199 illustrates in more detail the *Tax Payment* process. The *enterprise* usually pays VAT periodically, typically several times a year. At the end of each period, the enterprise determines the cost of government services received. It does so by creating an instance of the economic event *Receipt of Government Services* with a value that corresponds to the value of the *Government Services* resource. This economic event creates a claim between the *Government* and the *enterprise*. The *enterprise* often materializes this claim by creating a document called *VAT Settlement*. In this document, the enterprise indicates the amount of *Received Government Services* in a given period. As the materialized claim is essentially a report, it usually also indicates other information that the tax authorities require, such as the amount of sales, and purchases, and the percentage of sales VAT and purchase VAT. The company pays the amount due to the tax authorities; this *Tax Payment* settles the claim.

It can happen that the amount of taxes from purchase processes events is higher than the amount of taxes from sales processes. In this case, the economic event *Receipt of Government Services* has negative value, and the enterprise receives *Cash* from the government.

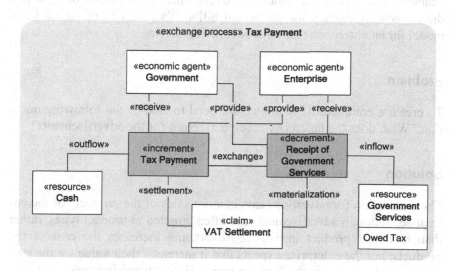

**Fig. 199.** Payment of VAT to tax authorities

In many countries, the amount of tax depends on several factors, for example, on whether a customer is domestic or international, and there can be different percentages of tax for different groups of products. The *POLICY PATTERN* can be used to determine the tax value.

## 9.6   Marketing and Advertising

The purpose of marketing is to increase product awareness. Marketing consists of many activities, including advertising; we will use advertising as an example, that can easily be applied to other marketing activities. For example, a company can place its advertisements on billboards, and pay the advertising agency for the rented billboards. We will create an REA model for an enterprise that buys advertising services.

### Problem

To create a complete REA model, we need to answer the following question: What does the enterprise receive in return for the advertisements?

### Solution

The motivation for advertisements is more sales of the products of the enterprise, although advertisements are often targeted to product types, rather than to actual product instances. Advertising increases the cost of the products; but the enterprise expects that it increases their value for the customers, and, consequently, leads to more sales. Advertising creates an economic resource, *Product Awareness*, which can be used to change one of a product's characteristics, namely, whether the product is commercially known.

The solution consists of three business processes, the *Advertisement Acquisition* exchange process, in which the enterprise acquires an *Advertising Service* from the agency, the *Advertisement Service Consumption* conversion process, in which the enterprise transforms the *Advertising Service* into a *Product Awareness*, which is used to *Make Product Known*. The known product is then sold in the *Sales* process.

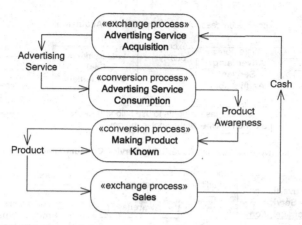

**Fig. 200.** Value chain model for advertising

During the *Advertisement Acquisition* process, the enterprise acquires the *Advertising Service* and gives *Cash* to the advertising company in return. In our example, the *Advertising Service* is the right to use the billboard for a period of time. It could be a column in a newspaper or a slot on TV. The contract with the agency specifies the details about this exchange, such as the advertising media and the payment terms. After the *Advertisement Acquisition* process, the *Advertising Service* resource is under the control of the *enterprise.*

During the *Advertisement Service Consumption* process, the *enterprise* consumes the *Advertising Service*. This event occurs during the time period in which the enterprise had rights to use the billboard, the commercial slot on TV, or in the moment of publishing the column in the newspaper. This event is paired through a *conversion duality* with the economic event *Create Awareness*, which occurs during the time period in which potential customers see the advertisement. The awareness is often related to a product type; the enterprise owns an intangible economic resource *Product Type Awareness*. In the conversion process *Making Product Attractive* the *enterprise* uses the *Product Type Awareness* to increase the value of the actual *Product*. The actual *Product* is then sold in the *Sales* process. The solution is illustrated in Fig. 201.

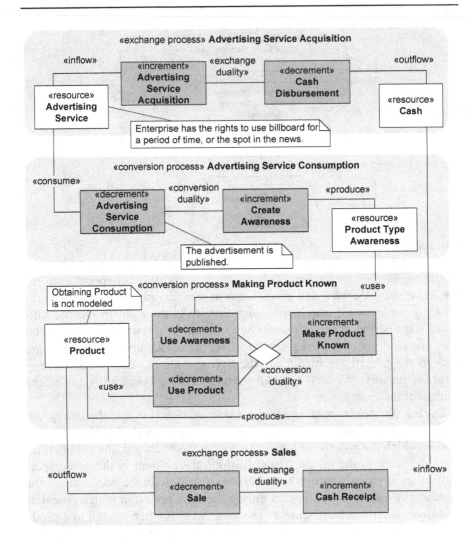

**Fig. 201.** The REA model for advertising

## 9.7  Waste

The use of economic resources means that the resources decrease their value, but still exist after decrement event. After some time the resources can be used up so much that further use is impossible. For example, discharged batteries cannot be used for their original purpose. Such resources can be considered as waste. However, when constructing the REA application model, the application designer must answer the following question.

### Problem

What does the enterprise receive in return for disposed waste?

### Solution

The disposal of waste must be a value-adding process; otherwise, a rational enterprise would not perform it. The disposal of waste consumes an enterprise's resources. For example, for the disposal of dangerous waste, an enterprise usually pays a recycling company. Therefore, the disposal event must be an increment economic event. As the disposal process is a value-adding process, the value of waste must be negative at the disposal.

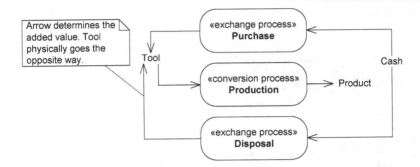

**Fig. 202.** Value chain for tool lifecycle including item disposal

Fig. 202 illustrates a value chain model of the lifecycle of an economic resource *Tool*, including tool disposal. The model contains three processes, *Purchase*, *Production* (in which the *Tool* is used), and *Disposal* (in which the *Tool* is disposed). The *Disposal* process is a value-adding process, which increases value of the *Tool* from some negative value to zero, by giving it to the *Recycling Company*. The corresponding REA application model is shown in Fig. 203.

For the entrepreneurial goals of the enterprise, the value of the *Tool* resource is negative at the time of disposal, and higher in absolute value than the value of *Cash* given to the *Recycling Company* in return. The *Disposal* event increases the value of the *Tool* from a negative value to zero. Therefore, *Disposal* is an increment event. It is paired through an exchange duality to the *Cash Disbursement* event, because the enterprise pays the *Recycling Company* for receiving rights and responsibility of the *Tool*.

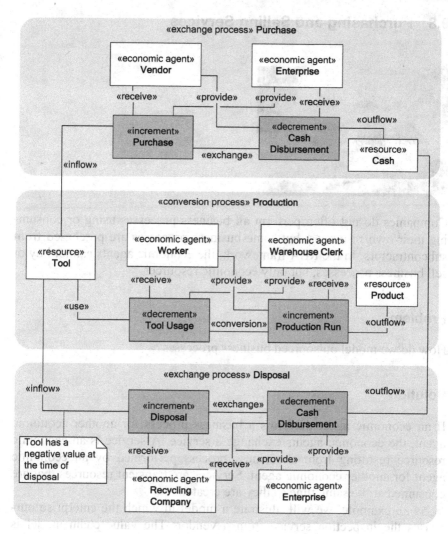

**Fig. 203.** The REA model for tool lifecycle including disposal

## 9.8   Purchasing and Selling Services

Companies do not often perform all business processes using or consuming their own resources; but some business processes are purchased from subcontractors. In the REA framework, the economic agents cannot buy or sell business processes, but only economic resources.

### Problem

How do we model outsourced business processes?

### Solution

If an economic agent performs a business process for another economic agent, the economic agents exchange a service. A service is an economic resource resulting from a business process performed by an economic agent for another economic agent. Services are transient resources that are consumed at the same time as they are created.

As an example, we will illustrate a model in which the enterprise purchases the inspection service from a vendor. The value chain model is shown in Fig. 204.

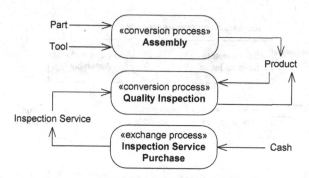

**Fig. 204.** Inspection service exchange

Fig. 205 illustrates the model from the perspective of the provider of the quality inspection service, and Fig. 206 illustrates it from the perspective of the recipient of quality inspection service.

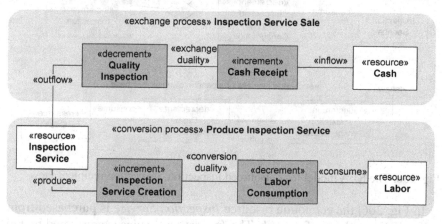

**Fig. 205.** The REA model for outsourced inspection, inspection provider view

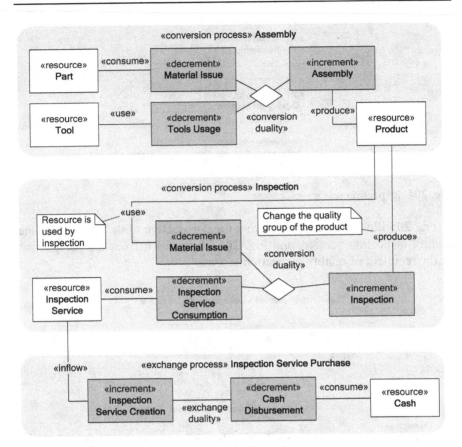

**Fig. 206.** The REA model for outsourced inspection; inspection recipient view

In Fig. 206, the economic resource *Inspection Service* is purchased from a *Vendor* in exchange for *Cash*. The *Inspection Service* is consumed by the decrement event *Inspection Service Consumption*, which is paired through a conversion duality with the increment event *Inspection*.

## 9.9 Transient Resources

Some resources are consumed at the same time they are created. They cannot be stored, and the enterprise cannot put them on stock because of their physical nature. Electricity is an example of a transient resource that we came across earlier. Other examples are services the enterprise receives or provides. The fact that a resource is transient does not change any of the REA modeling principles.

### Electricity

An enterprise receives electricity from an electricity distributor. The enterprise consumes electricity for heating buildings, running machines, supporting its infrastructure, and many other things. Suppose for simplicity that the enterprise consumes electricity only for heating. The model can easily be extended to cover other uses of electricity.

For clarity, we will make a model from two perspectives, that of an electricity provider and of an electricity consumer. A simplified model for an electricity provider is illustrated in Figs. 207 and 208.

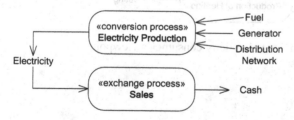

**Fig. 207.** Business processes for an electricity provider

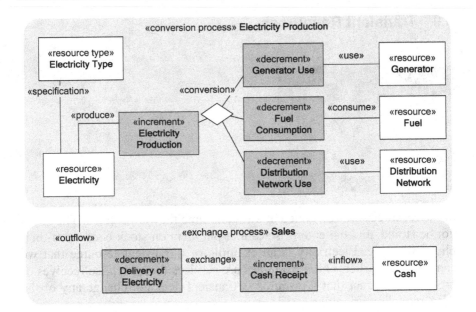

**Fig. 208.** The REA model for an electricity provider

Models for an electricity consumer are illustrated in Figs 209 and 210. The electricity consumer purchases electricity, i.e., the consumer exchanges *Cash* for *Electricity*. The consumer produces heating by using *Radiator* and by consuming *Electricity*.

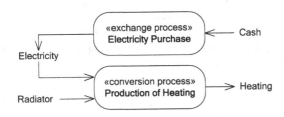

**Fig. 209.** Value chain from electricity consumer's viewpoint

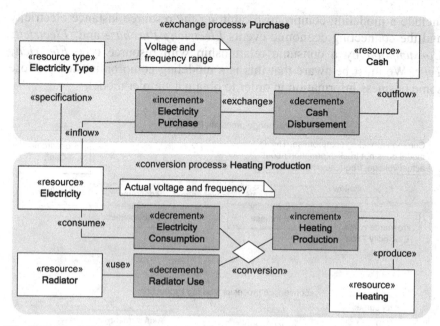

**Fig. 210.** The REA model for an electricity consumer

Electricity is a transient resource. The events *Electricity Receipt* and *Electricity Consumption* occur simultaneously, and the resource *Electricity* is consumed at the same time it is produced. *Heating* is also a transient resource; the event *Consuming Heating* is omitted from the model for simplicity.

## Electricity Instance and Modeling Compromise

Please note that *Electricity* in Fig. 210 is a resource instance. While the resource type *Electricity Type* is at runtime characterized by frequency range of 50 to 60 Hz, voltage from 220 to 230 V, and current from 0 to 20 A at any given time, the resource instance *Electricity* is at runtime characterized by actual values of frequency, voltage, and current. The implementation of such resource instance requires an array or similar data structures to store the values in all moments in time relevant for the users of business application.

The management of many electricity consumers is not interested in data stored in the electricity instance resource. Average electricity consumers are interested only in the total amount of electricity delivered, and this can be obtained from an account (see the *ACCOUNT PATTERN* for details) on *Electricity Type*. Therefore, a simpler and more convenient model would include a modeling compromise omitting the resource instance electricity and the connecting economic events *Electricity Purchase* and *Electricity Consumption* by a consume relationship with resource type *Electricity Type*. We must be aware that this is a modeling compromise and we lose some business information in order to obtain a simpler model.

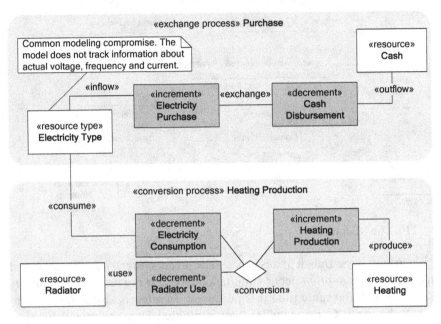

**Fig. 211.** Modeling compromise of the REA model for an electricity consumer

# 10 Processes with Contracts

In this section, we illustrate examples of REA models at the policy level. These models determine what should or could happen, as opposed to what has happened, which is the purpose of the models at the operational level.

The models for *PURCHASE ORDER* and *LABOR ACQUISITION* illustrate typical contracts that are part of most business applications. *GUARANTEE* and *INSURANCE* are contracts might not look like typical exchanges of economic resources; therefore, we will illustrate how their REA models look.

When economic agents sign a contract, they usually expect that both partners will fulfill their commitments. However, this does not happen always, and we will illustrate it in the section *PENALTY FOR NOT FULLFILLED COMMITMENTS*. *PRODUCTION SCHEDULE* is similar to contract, but covers commitments for conversion processes. The REA model for *TRANSPORT* illustrates how the contract and schedule are related.

## 10.1 Purchase Order

In business to business and some business to customer scenarios, a cash sale is rare. Usually, the enterprise places a purchase order for the products, the vendor sells the goods, and the enterprise eventually pays for the goods. The purchase order is a business document that contains names of economic agents, a date, a list of the ordered items, and, often, their prices and other additional information.

### Problem

How are the purchase order and its components represented in the REA model?

### Solution

The REA model does not give an answer to this question.[8] We will present one possible mapping of the REA entities to the components of the Purchase Order, though other mappings might exist as well.

The *Purchase Order*, see Fig. 212, is a contract between economic agents *Vendor* and *Enterprise*. The purchase order lines, *Purchase Lines*, are the commitments of the contract. For the enterprise, the *Purchase Line* is a commitment to receive economic resource *Product*, and the *Payment Line* is a commitment to pay for it. At runtime, the *Purchase Order* can have several *Purchase Lines* – several products can be specified on one *Purchase Order*, and several *Payment Lines* – the products can be paid for in several installments or using different payment methods.

---

[8]  For many people studying REA, this is key information, helping them understand the purpose and scope of the REA ontology.

A *Purchase Line* can be related to a *Product Type* (in the case the *enterprise* orders a product in a catalogue), but, eventually, by the time of the *Purchase*, it must be related to an actual *Product*. A *Payment Line* can be related to a *Cash Type*, specifying the payment method, but, eventually, by the time of *Payment*, it must be related to an actual economic resource *Cash*.

Companies often materialize the claim and create an invoice, which is used to inform the economic agents about the value of the imbalanced duality.

The model in Fig. 212 illustrates the REA model for *Purchase Order*, and also the economic events that fulfill the commitments; so the model contains all REA entities needed to model the expected path of the purchase process. The model in Fig. 212 does not contain invoice, as in a world where information is passed electronically, this document is not actually necessary to successfully conduct business; the economic agents have all the information they need in the contract.

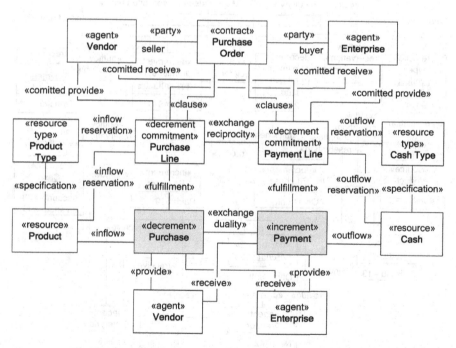

**Fig. 212.** Purchase with purchase order

Model in Fig. 213 is an instance model showing a *Purchase Order*, No. S567, between *Vendor C42* and the *enterprise*. The *Purchase Order* has two commitments, the *Purchase Line* on two *Product Types No. 123* and the price agreed upon for these two products (the *Payment Line*), $10. The *Payment Line* commitment is fulfilled by two economic events, *Purchase*, each on an actual *Product*. The *Payment Line* commitment is fulfilled by an event *Payment* of $10.

The purchase order number, the product type number and the product serial number can be implemented using the *IDENTIFICATION PATTERN*. The commitment *Purchase Line* contains information about quantities of the resources and their prices. These properties can be implemented using the *VALUE PATTERN*. The economic event *Purchase* does not contain information about the quantities of the products, as at run-time every *Purchase* event represents the purchase of one unit of the *Product*.

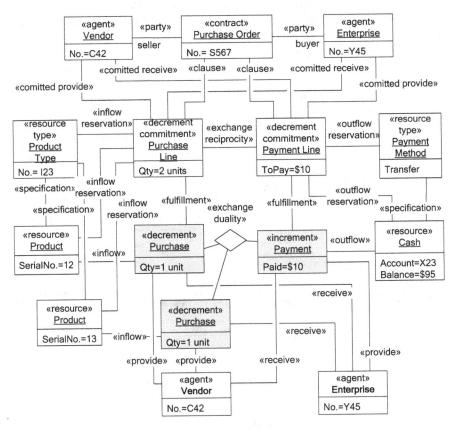

**Fig. 213.** An instance model of a purchase order

The model in Fig. 213 is in some sense a minimal model that illustrates one possible implementation of the REA application model. Users of business applications usually require much more functionality on the REA entities, most of can be implemented using the behavioral patterns illustrated in Part II of this book. Users usually tolerate many modeling compromises; for example, many current business applications do not use the *Payment Line*, but place its information on the *Purchase Order*. This compromise does not allow, for example, for payments in several installments.

## 10.2 Labor Acquisition

Labor is one of the resources of an enterprise; in many businesses, such as in information technology, labor is probably the most important resource.

### Problem

How does the enterprise acquire labor?

### Solution

The enterprise usually acquires labor in exchange for cash. At the operational level, the labor acquisition process is similar to the purchase process. The different forms of labor acquisition, such as employment, consultancy services, etc., are modeled by different kinds of contracts, but the models are similar at the operational level.

Cash ⟶ «exchange process» **Labor Acquisition**

**Fig. 214.** Labor acquisition

Labor acquisition with employment contract is illustrated in Fig. 215. The economic resource *Labor* is a transient resource (it is consumed at the same time it is created). The increment event *Labor Acquisition* specifies the time interval in which the *Enterprise* acquires *Labor* from the *Employee*.

The *Employment* commitment specifies the time interval in which the *Employee* agrees to provide his *Labor* to the *Enterprise*. If the employment is for unspecified time, the end of the *Employment* commitment is also unspecified. In such a case, the terms of the *Employment Contract* usually specify a procedure or condition for the end of the *Employment* commitment. The *Employment* commitment reserves *Labor Type*, which specifies the kind of *Labor* the *Employee* is committed to providing, and often also qualifies types of tasks. The commitment *Salary* specifies the amount of *Cash* to be paid in exchange for the *Labor*.

Users of business applications usually decide to materialize the claim between *Labor Acquisition* and *Salary Payment*, and print a report, sometimes called *Deposit Notification*, with the details of the acquired *Labor* and *Cash* paid, and send it to the *Employee* with the payment.

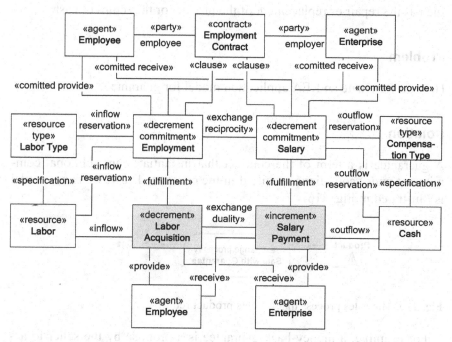

**Fig. 215.** Employment

An employment contract might specify multiple kinds of compensation for the labor, such as salary and bonus. In these cases, the model will contain several decrement commitments, such as Salary commitment and Bonus commitment; they can be fulfilled by single or multiple salary payment economic events.

## 10.3 Guarantee

The guarantee is a promise by the provider that the economic resource provided will either perform satisfactorily for a given length of time under certain conditions, or the recipient will receive a specified compensation, such as the repair or replacement of the product or the return of cash.

### Problem

How do we create an REA application model for guarantee?

### Solution

A guarantee is a term of the contract that instantiates an additional commitment under conditions specified in the contract. The value chain model is illustrated in Fig. 216.

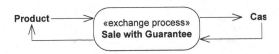

**Fig. 216.** The sales process that accepts product return

For example, a money-back guarantee is a promise by the seller to accept the return of the product under certain conditions (such as the product not having been used), within a limited period of time (for example, 30 days).

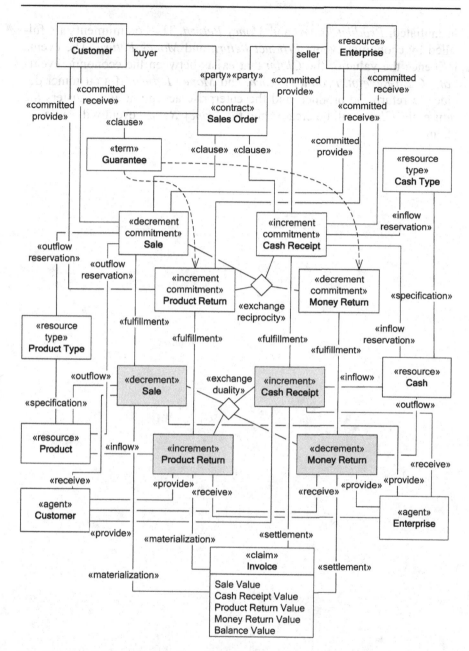

**Fig. 217.** The REA model for the sales process that accepts product return

An REA application model for money-back guarantee is specified in Fig. 217. If the conditions of the guarantee are met, two commitments are instantiated; *Product Return* and *Money Return*. The commitments are fulfilled by economic events *Product Return* and *Money Return*. The events influence the value of the *Claim* that exists between the economic events *Sale*, *Cash Receipt*, *Product Return*, and *Money Return*. If a customer decides to return the product, and the enterprise accepts it and registers the return, the *Claim* will be created and the *Money Return* event will settle the claim.

## 10.4 Insurance

An insurance contract is a contract between two economic agents, in which one agent (the insurer) agrees to reimburse another agent (the insured) in the case of loss or harm of an insured economic resource, such as property or life, in specified contingencies, such as fire, accident, and death, that occur under the terms of the contract. The insured agent agrees to provide a payment proportionate to the risk involved.

When making an REA model for an insurance contract, application developers have to answer the following question.

### Problem

What does the insured economic agent receive in return for his payment?

### Solution

In a sense, the insured economic agent receives security, but this is not the correct answer. The insured economic agent receives reimbursement in cash in the cases specified in the terms of the insurance contract. Therefore, the REA model at the operational level is a simple exchange of cash for cash; see Fig. 218.

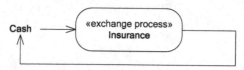

**Fig. 218.** Insurance

The insurance contract from the perspective of the insured enterprise, is illustrated in Fig. 219. The contract contains the *Cash Disbursement* commitment, specifying the premium the *enterprise* pays the *Insurer*. The reciprocal *Cash Receipt* commitment is not instantiated when the contract is signed, because the *Insurer* does not have to pay anything to the insured enterprise unless there is loss of or harm to the insured resource. These conditions are specified by the *Insurance Policy*, a term of the contract, which can instantiate the *Cash Receipt* commitment.

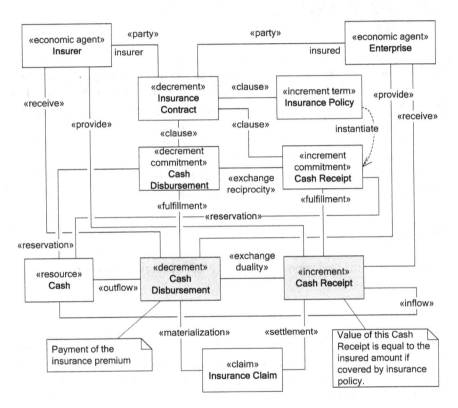

**Fig. 219.** Insurance contract

## 10.5 Penalty for Violated Commitment

A sales order contains commitments that represent promises of future economic events that both contracting parties promise to fulfill. Contracts
usually also specify terms for what should happen if some of the commitments are not fulfilled as promised. For example, it can be specified that an
economic agent that cannot fulfill a commitment has to pay a specified
penalty to the other economic agent. The promise to pay a penalty is not a
commitment when the contract is signed; it may become a commitment
under the conditions specified by the terms of the contract.

The payment of the penalty is an outflow of resources. To make a full
REA model that includes penalties for violated commitments, an application designer must answer the following question

### Problem

According to the REA rules, every resource outflow must be paired
through an exchange duality with some inflow. What does an economic
agent receive in return for a paid penalty?

### Solution

The short answer is nothing, for the penalty as such, because a commitment to pay a penalty for a violated commitment makes sense only when
considering the original commitment that has been violated. However, a
penalty reduces the value of the claim of the original exchange.

**Fig. 220.** Sale with possible penalty payment

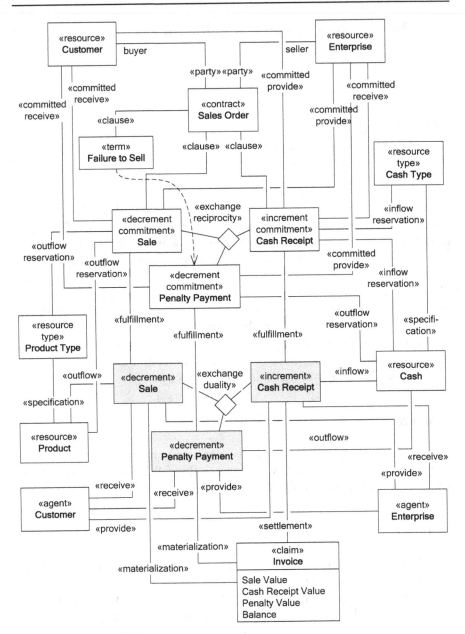

**Fig. 221.** Contract with penalty for failure to sell

An REA model for a *Sales Order* with a penalty for failure to sell is illustrated in Fig. 221. The contract term *Failure to Sell* specifies that the *Enterprise* pays *Cash* as a penalty in the case where it fails to deliver (and consequently to sell) products in a specified time. If the condition in a contract term becomes true, the *Penalty Payment* decrement commitment is created, which can be fulfilled by the decrement event *Penalty Payment*. The consequence of this economic event is that the difference in the *Claim* between *Sale* and *Cash Receipt* is reduced by the value of the *Penalty*, so this *Claim* can be settled by a *Cash Receipt* of less value; the original value of the Claim is decreased by the value of the *Penalty*.

Note that, at runtime, the decrement commitment *Penalty Payment* is instantiated by the *Sales Order* contract only if the conditions specified in the *Failure to Sell* term are met. The *Penalty Payment* commitment is not instantiated when the *Sales Order* is registered. An analogous model can be made for a penalty for late payment.

The economic resource transferred as a penalty can be different from *Cash*; it can, for example, be a product or a service.

## 10.6 Schedule

Creating a product is seldom a spontaneous thing. Companies usually plan and schedule the usage and consumption of their resources. The aim is to optimize the usage and to fulfill the exchange commitments to other economic agents.

### Problem

How do we create an REA application model for a production schedule?

### Solution

A production schedule consists of commitments to use, consume, and produce economic resources. A value chain model for the product creation process is illustrated in Fig. 222, and an REA application model for a production schedule is illustrated in Fig. 223.

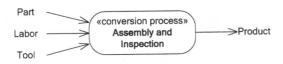

**Fig. 222.** Value chain model for creating a new product

In Fig. 223, the *Production Schedule* consists of four commitments; *Material Requisition*, *Tools Requisition*, and *Labor Requisition* are the decrement commitments paired through a *conversion reciprocity* with the increment commitment *Production Order*.

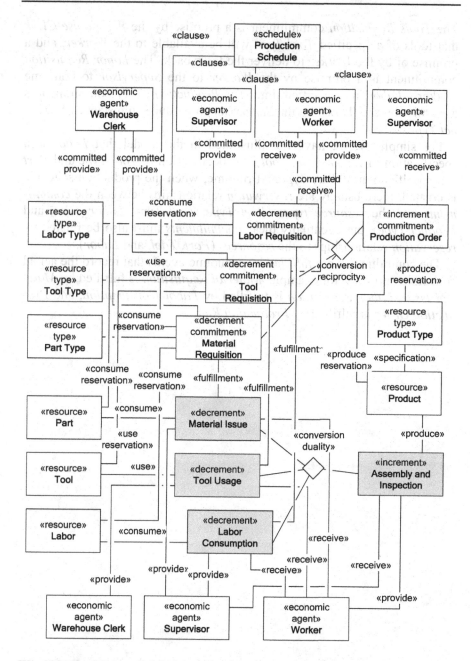

**Fig. 223.** The REA model for a production schedule and a production run

The *Material Requisition* commitment is a promise by a *Warehouse Clerk* to make a specified amount of *Part Types* available to the *Worker*.

The *Tools Requisition* commitment is a promise by the *Warehouse Clerk* that tools of a specified *Tool Type* will be available to the *Worker*, and a promise of by the *Worker* to deliver the tools back. The *Labor Requisition* commitment is a promise by the *Worker* to the *Supervisor* to consume worker's *Labor* in a specified time. The *Production Order* commitment is a promise by the *Worker* to the *Supervisor* to produce an instance of *Product Type*.

For simplicity, we have not illustrated in the model that *Labor* is a specification of *Labor Type*, *Tool* is a specification of *Tool Type* and *Part* is a specification of *Part Type*. At runtime, when the production schedule is created, there usually are *reservation* relationships between the *commitments* and the *resource types* (*Part Type*, *Tool Type*, *Labor Type*, and *Product Type*), but eventually these *commitments* must also be related by *reservation* relationships to the *resources* (*Part*, *Tool*, and *Labor*).

The commitments are *fulfilled* by economic events that record the actual conversion process; for example, *Material Requisition* is fulfilled by *Material Issue*, *Labor Requisition* is fulfilled by *Labor Consumption*, and *Production Order* is fulfilled by *Production Run*.

## 10.7 Transport

The following example illustrates an REA application model of a company transporting its employee on a business trip. The employee is represented as labor; the transport changes value of the labor for the enterprise, which believes that the employee's labor will be more worth at his destination location than at his original location. The transport is a service purchased from a transportation provider. The enterprise consumes the transportation service (in this example manifested as a seat on an airplane) in order to move labor from one location to another. The value chain model for this example is illustrated in Fig. 224.

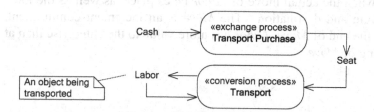

**Fig. 224.** Value chain model for transport

The solution consists of two processes. During the *Transport Purchase* process, the *enterprise* receives the economic resource *Seat* in exchange for *Cash*. In the *Transport* process, the enterprise consumes the resource *Seat* to modify the value of *Labor*. The basic idea is that the employee's labor at the destination location has more value for the enterprise than at his location of origin.

The REA model is illustrated in Fig. 225. The resource *Seat* represents an actual place in the transport vehicle. The resource *Seat Type* specifies some features of the seat, such as business or economy class, and window or aisle. Please note that the specification of class, a window or aisle can be modeled as a *Seat Type* attribute, or as a relationship to the *Seat Category* group.

Sometimes, a *Seat Reservation* is for an actual seat in the transport vehicle. In this case, the reservation relationship to *Seat Type* is omitted and the reservation relationship is directed to the actual *Seat* instead of to *Seat Type*.

The exchange process *Seat Transport* is governed by a *Transport Contract*, consisting of clauses *Seat Reservation* and *Cash Disbursement*. The commitment *Seat Reservation* specifies when the reservation took place and the reservation terms (such as in what time interval the place can be occupied). The commitment *Cash Disbursement* specifies the price for the *Seat Type*, and, usually, also when the payment should occur. The economic event *Rights to the Seat* specifies when, i.e., in what time period, an actual seat has been sold.

The conversion process *Transport* is governed by *Transport Schedule*, consisting of the clauses *Seat Occupation* and *Move* commitments. The commitment *Seat Occupation* specifies when the employee is supposed to use the *Seat*. *Seat Occupation* is a decrement commitment because during transport *Labor* usage of *Labor* for its original purpose might be limited. The economic event *Seat Occupation* might be different from *Seat Reservation*; for example, there can be scheduled a one-way trip, but a reserved return ticket, because the return flight is cheaper. The *Move* commitment represents when the actual move of *Labor* takes place, as well as the locations of origin and destination. The *Move* is an increment commitment, because, at the end of *Move*, *Labor* has more value to the enterprise than at the beginning of *Move*.

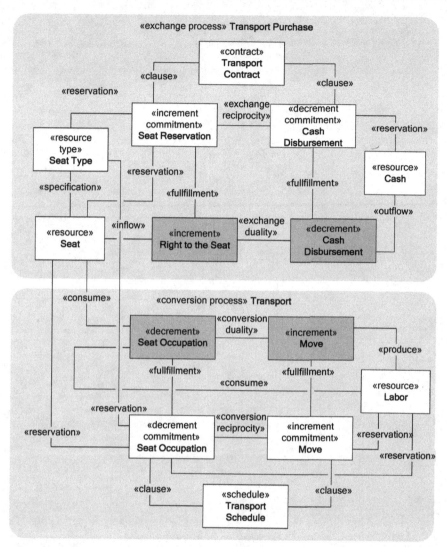

**Fig. 225.** The REA model for transport

# Appendices

# A. REA Ontology

"An ontology is a study of the categories of things that exist or may exist in some domain" (Sowa 1999). Ontological categories define the concepts that exist in the domain, as well as relationships between these concepts. Geerts and McCarthy (Geerts, McCarthy 2000, 2002) formulated REA as an ontology for business systems. The REA ontological categories are illustrated in Fig. 226.

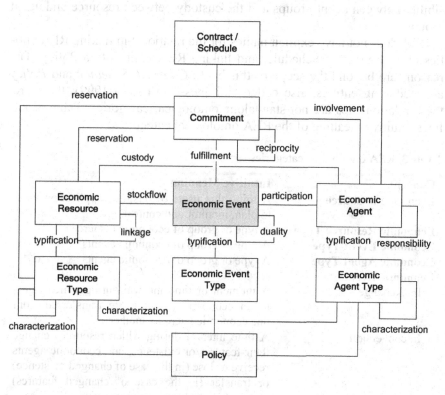

**Fig. 226.** REA ontology

The purpose of this appendix is to outline the difference between the model illustrated in Fig. 226 and the model we described in Part I of this book. We described in this book exchanges and conversions as separate patterns, because the semantics of the modeling elements in exchanges and conversions are different, although the models are structurally similar and can be mapped to common concepts. Only the economic resource and policy have the same semantics both in exchange and conversion, because economic resources link the exchange and conversion processes, and a single policy may be applied to some entities in an exchange process and some entities in a conversion process.

The ontological categories not described in this book are stockflow, participation, and characterization. *Stockflow* is a common concept for the inflow, outflow, use, consume and produce relationships. *Duality* is a common concept for the exchange duality and conversion duality. *Participation* is a common concept for the provide and receive relationships. *Characterization* is a common concept for the linkage type, responsibility between agent groups and the custody between resource and agent groups.

REA does not have explicit names for the relationship linking REA entities to a Contract or Schedule; and linking REA entities to a Policy. The reasons are beyond the scope of this book: *Contract*, *Schedule* and *Policy* are mediating entities, also called "thirdness" in (Sowa 1999); therefore, these relationships are not standalone ontological categories. Table 3 outlines intuitive meaning of the REA ontological categories.

**Table 3.** REA ontological categories

| Concept | Intuitive Meaning |
|---|---|
| **Economic Resource** | A thing that users of business application want to plan, monitor and control |
| **Economic Resource Type** | A type or group of economic resources |
| **Economic Event Type** | A type or group of economic events |
| **Economic Agent Type** | A type or group of economic agents |
| **Economic Event** | |
| In exchange | A moment or time interval during which rights to an economic resource are transferred from one economic agent to another |
| In conversion | A time interval during which resources change their features or existence, and economic agents receive or lose (in the case of changed existence) or transfer (in the case of changed features) physical control over the resource |
| **Economic Agent** | |
| In exchange | A legal entity possessing rights to an economic resource |
| In conversion | A person having physical control over an eco- |

| | |
|---|---|
| | nomic resources |
| **Characterization** | A relationship between economic resource type, economic event type and economic agent type. |
| **Responsibility** | |
| In exchange | A relationship specifying hierarchical structure of legal entities |
| In conversion | A relationship specifying responsibility of a person for another person. |
| **Duality** | |
| In exchange | A relationship between one or more economic events linked to inflow, and one or more economic events linked to outflow |
| In conversion | A relationship between one or more economic events linked to produce, and one or more economic events linked to use or consume |
| **Participation** | |
| In exchange | A relationship between an economic event and an agent receiving and losing rights to economic resources, i.e. common concept for provide and receive |
| In conversion | A relationship between an economic event and an agent receiving and losing physical control over economic resources, i.e. common concept for provide and receive |
| **Stockflow** | |
| In exchange | A relationship between an economic event and a resource specifying inflow and outflow of the rights to the resource |
| In conversion | A relationship between an economic event and a resource specifying produce, use and consume of the resource |
| **Commitment** | |
| In exchange | Promise of an economic event representing inflow or outflow of resources |
| In conversion | Promise of an economic event representing produce, use or consume of resources |
| **Contract/Schedule** | |
| In exchange | A collection of commitments and terms, which are components of a contract |
| In conversion | A collection of commitments and terms which are components of a schedule |

# B. Notes on Modeling

This book contains many examples of business models. All of them have something in common. We have tried to formulate the fundamental principles that the models in this book try to follow. We started to compile these principles in order to capture the essence of the way we model business processes and, consequently, design business applications. The ultimate goal is to design a scalable business process model of the enterprise that is open to extensions over time.

This section describes the driving force behind such models. The principles can be used to evaluate various business process modeling approaches, as well as your own models if you want them to have the same essence as the models in this book.

## B.1 There Is No Top-Level Business Process

We consider a business system as a value chain of independent processes. The approach with the top-level process, which is decomposed into lower-level processes, is suitable only for very simple systems. The top-level processes often tend to change as the business application evolves. What has been originally perceived as the top process might become less important over time as the business conditions change. The top-down approach is useful for describing existing systems, and for developing systems that are static, but not as a method for developing systems that can evolve during time.

## B.2 Premature Sequential Ordering Is Not Advisable

Many approaches to business modeling describe business processes as scenarios or sequences of tasks: "First I receive a customer order. Next, I fulfill the order. Then, I receive the payment from the customer."

This approach has both advantages and disadvantages. Its advantage is that the description it is easy to understand. It gives users a time axis, and well-defined points on where to start and where to end. It is often useful to offer such a view of business processes, simply because describing business processes in this way is intuitive for the users.

However, when we design a software solution that should support the a process specified as a sequence of steps, we quickly realize that the goal of the process can be reached in more than one specific sequence: "For some orders, we require that customer pay before we fulfill the orders." Moreover, there are exceptions: "The customer might return the goods"; "The customer might not pay for the goods in due time and must pay a penalty"; "Sometimes, we cannot fulfill the order." The *precise* and *complete* description of a business process in the form of a scenario, necessary for the executable software model, then becomes overly complex.

A better approach is to focus on the essence of the business processes by describing the purpose of the processes and the list of the applicable activities, but defer as long as possible specifying their order of execution. If there are constraints that restrict the order of the activities, they can be expressed as logical constraints rather than temporal constraints. Often the ordering can be postponed to as late as runtime, and business processes emerge over time from specified logical constraints.

## B.3  Bottom-Up Approach for Designing the System, and Top-Down Approach for Explaining It Are Advisable

The top-down approach, also called functional decomposition, means starting with the system as a single function, decomposing it into a small number of subsystems, and repeating this process for each subsystem until your reach the level granularity that allows implementation.

The top-down approach is useful in analysis and in developing an understanding of the business system, but leads to monolithic design when this approach is applied as a method for developing software.

In the bottom-up approach, we identify the atomic business processes, create the components corresponding to the business processes as generally as possible, and combine them into a business system. This approach allows us to develop business components applicable in contexts other than our specific system, and to adapt to changes over time.

## B.4   Trading Partner View and Independent View

The models in this book are created from the perspective of a company; we call this company *enterprise*. If a model of the same phenomenon is seen from the perspective of another company, we receive a "mirror image" of this model. For example, a purchase order for the enterprise is a sales order for the enterprise's customer; and the enterprise's sales order is a purchase order for its vendor.

Models in the trading partner view (i.e. the views of the *Customer* and the *Vendor*) are illustrated in Fig. 227. For example, the *Sales* process of the *Vendor* specifies an outflow of *Goods* and inflow of *Cash* to the *Vendor*. The model of the same process from the perspective of the *Customer* is a mirror image of the vendor's *Sales* process in Fig. 227. The *Purchase* process of the *Customer* specifies the inflow of *Goods* and outflow of *Cash* from the *Customer*.

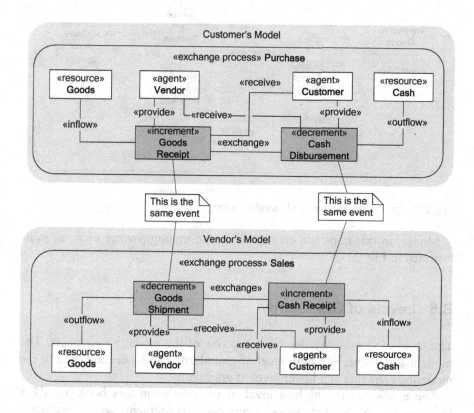

**Fig. 227.** Exchange process, trading partner view

In contrast to the trading partner models created from the perspective of the enterprise, we can create the models from the perspective of an independent observer. This independent view is useful in modeling the supply chain collaboration. An independent view is illustrated in Fig. 228.

Note that in the independent view the concepts of increment and decrement do not exists, economic events represent *transfer*. Likewise, inflow and outflow do not exist, and are represented by *stockflow*.

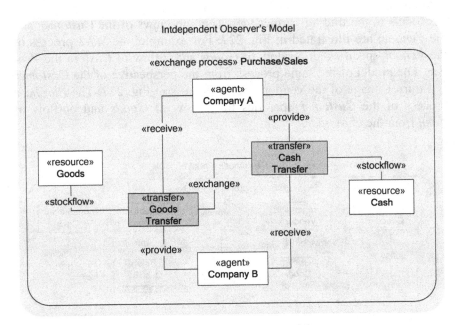

**Fig. 228.** Exchange process, independent view

Models in this book are created using the trading partner view, as is illustrated in Fig. 227.

## B.5  Levels of Granularity

The level of granularity describes the size of the modeling elements. The modeling elements at a high level of granularity can be decomposed to the modeling elements at a lower level of granularity.

The entities at the highest level of granularity in this book are REA business processes, such as sales process, procurement, warehouse management, and human resources. Each business process can be implemented as an independent business application, but there are business applications that cover several business processes.

Each REA business process can be decomposed into REA entities, such as economic resources, events, agents, contracts, and claims.

The lowest level of granularity is the task level, describing details about how to perform each economic event. We have not discussed the task modeling in this book, as this is well known from techniques such as flow-charts and workflows.

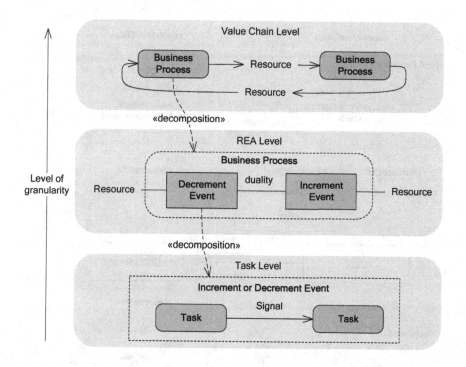

**Fig. 229.** Levels of granularity

## B.6  Models, Metamodels and UML

We use UML (UML Superstructure Specification 2005) for the notation in the models and diagrams in this book. When we refer in a text to a concept shown in a diagram, we write it in *italics*.

The diagram in Fig. 230 illustrates models of the real world at three levels of abstraction: the runtime model, the REA application model and the REA metamodel.

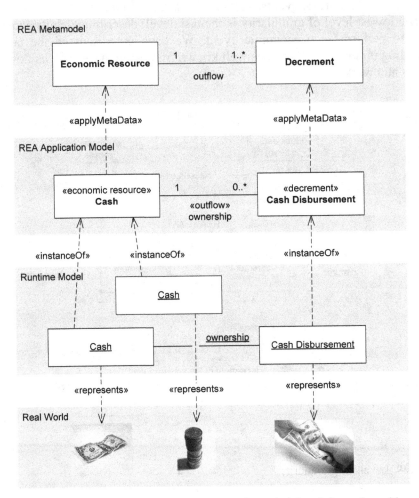

**Fig. 230.** Metamodel, application model, runtime model and the real world

The *real world* contains the actual real world entities that users of business applications want to monitor using the application.

The *runtime model* contains software representations of the real world entities, for example, in a computer memory or in a database. We call the entities in this model *runtime instances*. In UML, the names of the entities in the runtime model are written with an underlined font, such as <u>Cash</u>.

The *REA application model* is an actual configuration of a business software application. This model specifies the behavior and structure of the instances in the runtime model. For example, the application model in Fig. 230 specifies that every *Cash* instance must be related to zero or more *Cash Disbursement* instances. The runtime model conforms to this rule: there are two *Cash* objects, one is related to *Cash Disbursement* and the other is not. *Cash* may even be related to several *Cash Disbursements*, for example, if the same bill is received and given away several times. In the UML, the names of entities in the application model are shown in bold font, such as **Cash**. The text in guillemets, such as «outflow», represents the names of metamodel elements shown in the application model. This naming convention is not strictly UML (where text in guillemets means stereotypes), but we use it for convenience.

The *REA metamodel* level specifies constraints and rules for constructing application models. For example, the metamodel in Fig. 230 specifies that every *economic resource* must be related to one or more *decrements*, and the application model conforms to this rule: the *Cash* resource is related to the *Cash Disbursement* decrement. However, we can construct other application models in which the *Cash* would be related to several *decrements*, such as *Cash Disbursement* and *Penalty Payment*.

# C. Patterns and Pattern Form

Patterns are elements of reusable design. Patterns specify abstractions and models above the implementation level; thus, a pattern can be implemented in many different ways depending on the technical and implementation platform. Patterns have usually carefully selected names, therefore, patterns also create a common vocabulary for expressing designing concepts. The patterns in this book are written in a modified Coplien form (Coplien 1996); each pattern consists of the following sections:

- *Name* is a name of the pattern. References to a pattern are written in capital italics, e.g., *REA EXCHANGE PROCESS.*
- *Context* describes the situation in which the pattern may be applied.
- *Problem* formulates a problem that repeatedly arises in the given context.
- *Forces* are constraints that restrict the solution of the problem, requirements, and properties that the solution must have.
- *Solution,* in this book, is a model that solves the problem and satisfies the forces.
- *Design* shows how the solution can be implemented in a software application.
- *Examples* illustrate how the pattern can be applied.
- *Resulting Context* outlines consequences of the solution that the user should be aware of.

When reading a pattern, we recommend focusing on the *Problem* and the *Solution* sections first. The problem and solution usually capture the essence of the pattern, and other sections are needed to understand the details.

However, to fully understand what patterns are all about, we recommend the readers to write one or two. Pattern writers can get expert help in writing (and, consequently, understanding) patterns if they submit them to one of the pattern conferences, such as PLoP (Pattern Languages of Programs). More information on pattern conferences, and patterns in general, can be found at http://www.hillside.net.

# References

Appleton B (2000) Patterns and Software: Essential Concepts and Terminology, http://www.cmcrossroads.com/bradapp/docs/patterns-intro.html

Arlow J, Neustadt I (2003) Enterprise Patterns and MDA: Building Better Software with Archetype Patterns and UML, Addison-Wesley Professional

Arnold TRJ (1991) Introduction to Materials Management, 3$^{rd}$ edition, Prentice-Hall Inc.

Borch SE (2004) Typification in REA, First International REA Technology Workshop, Copenhagen 2004

Carroll L (1996) The Complete Illustrated Lewis Carroll, Wordsworth Editions, Ltd. Herfordshire

Coad P, Lefebvre E, DeLuca J (1999) Java Modeling in Color with UML, Enterprise Components and Process, Prentice Hall PTR, New York

Cockburn A (2000) Writing Effective Use Cases, Addison-Wesley Professional

Coplien J (1996): Software Patterns, SIGS Publications, New York,

Czarnecki K. Eisenecker UW (2000): Generative Programming - Methods, Tools, and Applications, Addison-Wesley

David JS (1997) Three events that define an REA Methodology for Systems Analysis, Design and Implementation. Proceedings of the Annual Meeting of the American Accounting Association, 1997

Dunn CL, Cherrington OJ, Hollander AS (2004) Enterprise Information Systems: A Pattern Based Approach, McGraw-Hill/Irwin, New York

Evans E (2003) Domain-Driven Design: Tackling Complexity in the Heart of Software, Addison-Wesley Professional

Eriksson HE, Penker M (2000) Business Modeling with UML, John Wiley & Sons, Inc.

Fowler M (1996) Analysis Patterns: Reusable Object Models, Addison-Wesley Professional

Graham I (1998) Requirements Engineering and Rapid Development, Addison Wesley

Geerts GL, McCarthy WE (1997) Using Object Templates from the REA Accounting Model to Engineer Business Processes and Tasks. Paper presented at European Accounting Congress, Graz, Austria.

Geerts GL, McCarthy WE (2000a) The Ontological Foundations of REA Enterprise Information Systems. Paper presented at the Annual Meeting of the American Accounting Association, Philadelphia, PA.

Geerts GL, McCarthy WE (2000b) Augmented Intensional Reasoning in Knowledge-Based Accounting Systems. Journal of Information Systems, Volume 14, No. 2, 2000, pp. 127-150.

Geerts GL, McCarthy WE (2002) An Ontological Analysis of the Primitives of the Extended REA Enterprise Information Architecture" at http://www.msu.edu/user/mccarth4/

Greenfield J, Short K (2004) Software Factories: Assembling Applications with Patterns, Models, Frameworks, and Tools, Wiley and Sons

Gruber TR (1996) A Translation Approach to Portable Ontologies. Knowledge Acquisition, 5(2):199-220

Forman IR, Danforth SH (1998) Putting Metaclasses to Work, A New Dimension in Object-Oriented Programming, Addison-Wesley Longmann, Inc.

Haugen, B (2005) Resources and Rights, Discussion in REA Technology Mailing List, http://groups.yahoo.com/group/REATechnology

Hay DC (1996) Data Model Patterns, Conventions of Thought Dorset House Publishing, New York

Hay DC, Healy KA (2000) Business Rules, What Are They Really? The Business Rules Group

Hessellund A, Balthazar S, Chohan A (2005) REA-VMI Model, A General Framework for Vendor Managed Inventory (In Danish). MSc. Thesis, IT University Copenhagen

Henglein F et al (2006): Formal Specification of Commercial Contracts, Journal on Software Tools for Technology Transfer

Hollander AS, Denna E, Cherrington OJ (1999) Accounting Information Technology and Business Solutions, Irwin/McGraw-Hill

IDEF0, Integration Definition for Function Modeling (1993) National Institute of Standards and Technology, FIPS publication 183, http://www.idef.com/idef0.html

Jaquet M (2003) Realistic – A REA Model without Perspectives (In Danish). MSc. Thesis, IT University Copenhagen

Kiczales G et al (1996) Aspect-Oriented Programming, ECOOP 1996, Jyväskylä, Finland

Lampe JC (2002) Discussion of an Ontological Analysis of the Economic Primitives of the Extended-REA Enterprise Information Architecture. International Journal of Accounting Information Systems, March 2002 pp.17-34.

Lieberherr K J (1997) Inventor's Paradox, http://www.ccs.neu.edu/research/demeter/adaptive-patterns/AOP/IP.html

Marshall C (2000) Enterprise Modeling with UML: Designing Successful Software Through Business Patterns, Addison Wesley Longman, Inc.

McCarthy WE (1982) The REA Accounting Model: A Generalized Framework for Accounting Systems in a Shared Data Environment. The Accounting Review (July 1982) pp. 554-78

Mellor SJ, Balcer MJ (2002) Executable UML, A Foundation for Model-Driven Architecture, Addison-Wesley

Meyer B (1997) Object-Oriented Software Construction, second edition, Prentice Hall, Inc.

MDA Guide Version 1.0.1 (2003) OMG document omg/03-06-01.

Peyton-Jones S, Eber JM (2003): How to write a financial contract. In Jeremy Gibbons and Oege de Moor, editors, The Fun of Programming. Palgrave Macmillan

Polya G (1982) How to Solve It: A New Aspect of Mathematical Method, Princeton University Press

Porter M (1980) Competitive Strategy: Techniques for Analyzing Industries and Competitors, Free Press, New York

Rising L, Manns ML (2004) Fearless Change: Patterns for Introducing New Ideas, Addison-Wesley Professional

Rothbard MN (1978) For a New Liberty, Libertarian Manifesto, Collier Macmillan Publishers, London

Samuelson PA, Nordhaus WD (1989) 13 edition, Economics, McGraw-Hill, Inc.

Sowa JF (1999) Knowledge Representation: Logical, Philosophical, and Computational Foundations, Course Technology

Silverston L, Inmon WH, Graziano K (1997) Data Model Resource Book, A Library of Logical data Models and Data Warehouse Designs, John Wiley & Sons, New York, Chichester, Weinheim, Brisbane, Singapore, Toronto

UML 2.0 Superstructure Specification (2005), OMG document formal/05-07-04

# Index